LUCKY PEACH

A QUARTERLY JOURNAL OF FOOD AND WRITING

Chris Ying
EDITOR-IN-CHIEF

Peter Meehan &
David Chang
EDITORS

Rachel Khong
MANAGING EDITOR

Walter Green
ART DIRECTOR

Helen Tseng
ASSOCIATE DESIGNER

Mark Ibold
**SE PENNSYLVANIA
CORRESPONDENT**

Anthony Bourdain
FILM CRITIC EMERITUS

COVER ART BY
Jordan Speer

NEON SIGN BY
Kamran Sheikh

Adam Krefman
PUBLISHER

Sue Chan, Marguerite Mariscal
& Rebecca Palkovics
PUBLICITY & MARKETING

Priya Krishna
OUTREACH & CUSTOMER SERVICE

GENERAL ASSISTANCE: Amanda Arnold, Aralyn
Beaumont, Jen Gann, Ryan Healey, Eli Horowitz,
Becca Levenson, Lauren Ro, Jill Schepmann, Pat Sims

THANKS TO: Mark Bittman, Laurel Braitman,
Richie Brown, Wendy Carlson, C.B. Cebulski,
Ed Chase, Hannah Clark, Brian Close, Naomi Duguid,
Renata Follmann, Kate Greene, Jesse Harris, Michael
Hurley, Jim Johnson, Kathryn Johnson, Thomas
Kemeny, Anastasia Kozak, Amy Krefman, Harry
Leeds, Mimi Lok, Fred Lucena, Laura McCartney,
Tim McCartney, Will McCartney, Tessa Mozdzyn, Raj
Patel, Lauren Peinado, Kate Petersen, Bridie Picot,
Sian Proctor, Russell Quinn, Amy Rossetti, Julia
Rothman, Andrew Rowat, Gabriele Stabile, Aaron
Thier, Justin Tripp, Miranda Tsang, Angelo Vermeulen,
Jim Walker, Jessica Wang, Matt Werth, Stephen
Winkler, Jami Witek, Vic Wong, and 1MSQFT for
hosting our all–ewe–can–eat party at Art Basel

ADVERTISING INQUIRIES: ads@lky.ph
PRESS INQUIRIES: press@lky.ph
CUSTOMER SERVICE: helpme@lky.ph

Lucky Peach is published quarterly
in February, May, August, and
November by Lucky Peach LLC, 853
Broadway, Suite 1211, New York,
NY, 10003. Periodicals postage
pending New York, NY and additional
mailing offices. POSTMASTER: send
address changes to Lucky Peach,
853 Broadway, Suite 1211, New York,
NY, 10003.
CanadaPost customer number
42740020.
Printed in St. Cloud, MN,
by Quad/Graphics.

The spot illustrations sprinkled throughout
this issue are by **Domitille Collardey**, and
depict the crowning achievement of a man
named **Michel Lotito** (1950-2007). Lotito
suffered from Pica, a disorder that compels
people to ingest large quantities of not-at-
all-nutritious materials (chalk, dirt, sand,
ice, etc). Over the course of his life, Lotito
consumed an estimated nine tons of
metal—plus a good deal of rubber and
glass—and his feats of intestinal fortitude
became the stuff of legend. Most famously,
he ate an entire airplane: a Cessna 150 that
was broken down into pieces small enough
to consume with the help of mineral oil and
lots of water. It took him two years
to accomplish, but hey, if eating a plane
were easy, everybody would do it.

ALL YOU CAN EAT

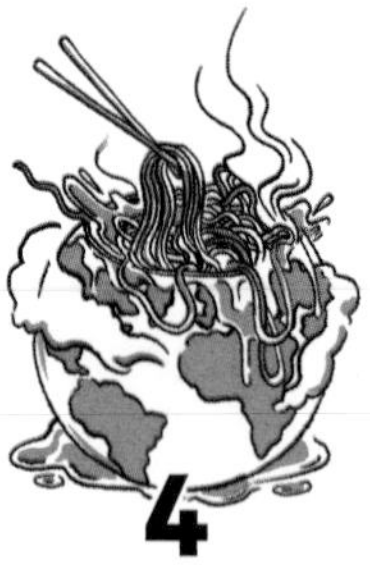

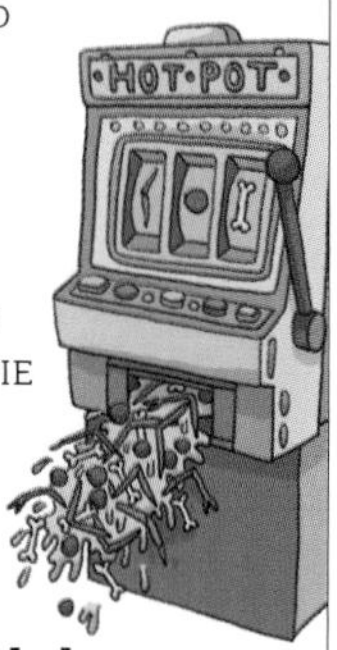
HOT·POT

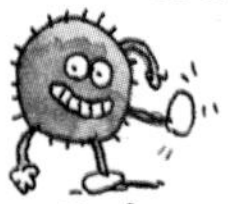

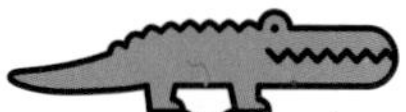

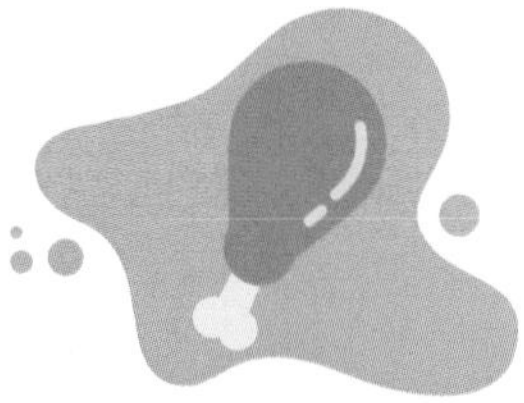

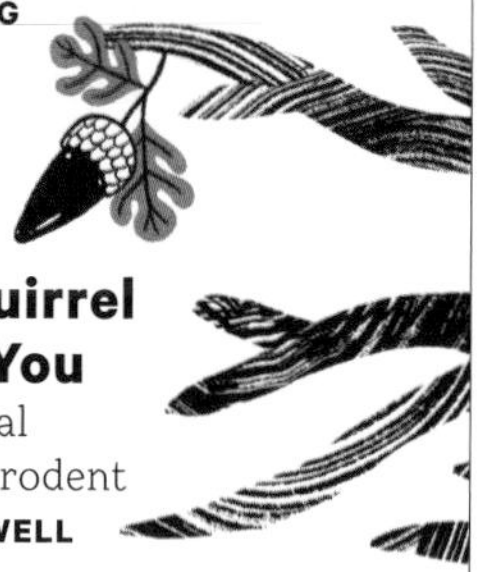

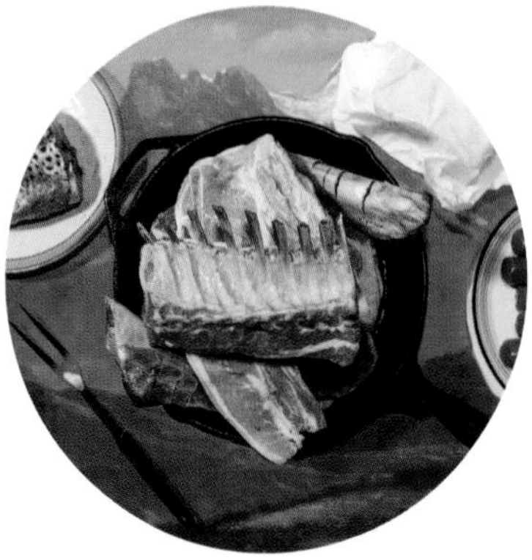

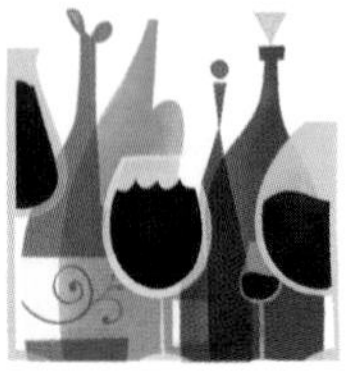

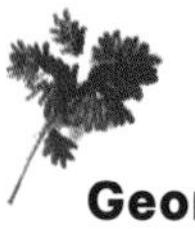

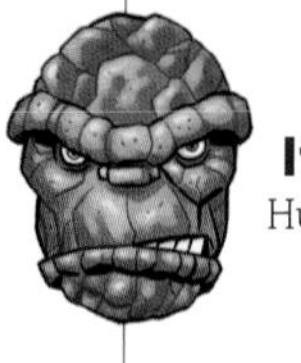

EDITOR'S NOTE

A baby pool full of guacamole made by high school cheerleaders.

The whole story is pretty much in that sentence. The tableau renders immediately; the implications spool out to infinity.

The cheerleaders were mean. They doled out guac and collected singles with clinical detachment. I imagined that their presence was compulsory.

They wore red and white uniforms fringed in the kind of pleated skirt that flips up without the slightest hesitation. A blocky serif, stepped on a diagonal from shoulder to waist, spelled out their affiliation. They stood sentinel around a blue plastic baby pool half-full of greenish-brown guacamole that sat right on the pavement. It did not appear as if they had stomped avocados into guacamole in the pool, which would be one of the only reasons I could imagine serving it from one. My guess is that they'd slaved away the night before in some dour commissary kitchen, slicing and scooping, incrementally depleting their cheer supply with every dull thwack of knife into pit.

The sell was that this was some kind of record-breaking bowl of guacamole, and that the girls were doing it to support their school. I bought in because I was at an avocado festival. I bought in because I had never before eaten food made expressly for the sake of the size of the end result.

My girlfriend was dubious of my interest and their enterprise. She watched me order with my eyes fixed on the ground, so as not to indulge in the promise of cheerleader flesh, and then sit on a curb—this was a street fair—and eat about half of the too-big, too-bland basket of guacamole I'd charitably overpaid for.

I had special, extra time to contemplate the experience as I spent the following days in and out of bed, feverish and food-poisoned. My girlfriend was unaffected; there was only one thing I'd eaten that she hadn't. And since then I've vowed never again to go to a single-ingredient-themed food event, never to indulge in that kind of carnival gluttony.

Scarring experiences like this are among the reasons why our All You Can Eat issue sometimes strays from portraits of joyous excess, opting instead to examine issues of access and availability that hang on the implications of the word "can."

But don't worry, there's also plenty of drinking from horns, historical French-Canadian gorging, chicken wings, and Falstaffian misbehavior. More than you can stomach, probably.

—PETER MEEHAN

THE LUCKY PEACH ATLAS

THIS MONTH: Chang reports from Hong Kong; Meehan on a comedian's egg moat in Los Angeles and sour soup in Toronto; and Alex Raij—chef (with her husband Eder Montero) of Basque spots Txikito, El Quinto Pino, and La Vara in New York—gives us the low-down on eating in Bilbao.

Bilbao, Spain

Arbolagaña

*Museo de Bellas Artes Bilbao, Alda,
48011 Bilbao, Spain*

Everybody's obsessed with the Guggenheim in Bilbao, but there's lots to recommend about the Museo de Bellas Artes, too. First on that list is Arbolagaña, Aitor Basabe's restaurant on top of the museum. Aitor's a little bit famous, mostly in Spain and within Euzkadi (Basque country), but to me he's nowhere as well known as he should be. He's an idea guy: his food is current and gorgeous and even though his technique is completely up to date, he never lets it get out in front of the flavors of his food.

He is a forager since forever and a fisherman, too, and his wife runs the wine list, where there is always something to discover at every price point. For me, Aitor is a cook's cook like few others. His food is consistently good—it changes, but the pleasure it delivers doesn't. He exhibits a true joy for cooking and the food has an intimacy that is missing for me in some restaurants that cook in that modern Spanish style. —ALEX RAIJ

Category: CHEF'S SPOT
What to Order: Anything with mushrooms; the tasting menu.

Gure Toki

Nueva Plaza, 12, 48005 Bilbao, Spain

Gure Toki is my favorite place for *pintxos*—aka Basque tapas—in Bilbao, which is an excellent city for pintxos. I try to hit it up on Sunday afternoon, when there are *rabas* (fried squid, like the best calamari you'll ever have. And while my go to pintxo is their oxtail *croqueta*, there's always something new to discover in the spread they put out. Gure Toki's pintxos balance creativity and beauty with excellent flavors that actually go together, minus the excess of sweetness that I find pervasive and fashionable of late in Bilbao. Despite the crowds—and there is usually a crowd—the service is super friendly and the beer, wine, and particularly the gin and tonics are proudly and professionally poured. —ALEX RAIJ

Category: SIMPLE PLEASURES
What to Order: Fried squid on Sundays, oxtail croquetas every day, and whatever else is new as often as possible.

Los Angeles, California

Kang Hodong Baekjeong

3465 W 6th Street, Los Angeles, CA

Why is it that Kang Hodong Baekjeong, a Korean BBQ joint in a city jammed with them, is a place I eat every time I'm in Los Angeles? I know beefeaters are partial to Park's and I've beheld the majesty of Eight Flavor's pork belly spread, but pound for pound the flesh that gets grilled at KHB always does it best for me.

And the periphery at KHB is better looked-after than it needs to be. For example, take the invigorating gochujang-spiked bean sprout salad that's on the table when you sit down, or how the dipping sauce for grilled meats is enlivened with a welcome blast of wasabi.

The tabletop grill is ringed by a sectioned moat that I find utterly transfixing. In one chamber, melty cheese and raw corn meld into cheese-corn, a compulsively edible drinking snack; in another, beaten eggs slowly coalesce into a custardy omelet. And then there's the "lunch box": a waiter presents a neatly organized metal box of all the things you'd find in bibimbap, then he closes that box and shakes the bejesus out of it, rendering it a delicious mess.

Is it the best BBQ in LA? Who knows? As we were going to print, Mr. Chang told me that the real way to judge a Korean BBQ place is by its naeng myun, a dish I've never tried at KHB. But there's no doubt in my mind that as a stop for guaranteed good times and good food, it deserves a place on your map.

Tips: go during the odd hours—afternoons and late at night—and go with big groups. Since the restaurant's name is just about impossible to master, find it by Googling "Korean comedian BBQ LA"—the owner, Kang Ho-dong is a super ginormous comedy star in Korea. You'll see life-size-ish paper cut outs of him outside the restaurant—and note that the entrance is in an interior courtyard, not the streetside address on 6th that the internet will send you to. —PETER MEEHAN

Category: LATE NIGHT
What to Order: Your usual Korean BBQ order, which will come with happy tidings of corn cheese and custardy omelet. Plus, the "lunch box" (a shaken-not-stirred bibimbap).

Pho Hung
350 Spadina Avenue, Toronto

I have envied *Lucky Peach* contributor and very inspiring cookbook author Naomi Duguid's life for a long time, but I'd never had the chance to toddle after her on her home turf until this winter. The morning we met, there was a driving snowstorm, but that didn't stop her from walking me this way and that, into and out of Chinatown haunts and Kensington Market yielded a choice discovery: the pickle shop called Thomas Street, brews what I'd call the world's finest ginger beer.) After lugging around a bag of rice for an hour, we landed at Pho Hung, an older Vietnamese spot with a nice corner dining room that was empty-ish at eleven thirty on a weekday and packed, with a line, by noon. shops. (These errands Lavers, at 193 Baldwin

Since we'd been grazing all morning, we ordered modestly: pho, *canh chua*, and *banh xeo*. And as each dish hit the table, Naomi made me a better eater. With the pho, she taught me to mix salt and pepper in the little dipping bowl (where I'd always previously squirted hoisin or Sriracha) and to dredge the unseasoned beef from the soup in that. She taught me that the right way to eat canh chua—a sour soup seasoned with tamarind, and filled with tomatoes, mushrooms, and pineapple, among other things—was with rice. Pho is for noodles, canh is for rice, she said. I filled my soupspoon with rice, then dunked it in the broth to fill will sour broth. Perfect: I'd always liked the soup, but now I feel like I really know how to eat it.

And then there was the banh xeo, a crepe stuffed with sautéed bean curds and shrimp. This one was crisp like I'd always wanted banh xeo to be, flavorful and formidable, and Naomi explained why: because this was the real-deal traditional style, made with no egg (because eggs would have been too valuable and not necessary), but with a rice flour mixture more closely related to a dosa than an omelet. It was a revelation and a new fixation: I've got to get back here soon. —PETER MEEHAN

Category: SIMPLE PLEASURES

What to Order: Pho (mix salt and pepper as a dip), canh chua with rice, banh xeo.

Lung King Heen
8 Finance Street, Hong Kong

You don't have to stay at the Four Seasons Hotel to eat at Lung King Heen—the first Chinese restaurant to get three stars from Michelin and still the only dim sum place to do so. But the Four Seasons connection might help you secure a reservation at lunch, which is definitely the time to eat there.

Lung King Heen has no dim sum carts, because all the dumplings are made to order, from scratch. As delicious as they are, don't kill yourself with dumplings, though—you have to save room for their roast chicken. It is a deep and dark mystery to me how the skin can be so crispy and light—like a great Peking duck—while the meat remains juicy. You are advised to dip everything in their trio of sauces: chili, classic xo, and vegetarian xo. All are exemplary.

If you think you can find better dim sum, let me know. But I just don't think there is a better spot anywhere—as much as I love Tim Ho Wan, it's just not the same.

If you order all the dim sum and no booze, lunch at LKH should set you back about $70 a person, which is stupid pricey for dim sum but super cheap for one of the best meals in your life. —DAVE CHANG

Category: PINNACLES
What to Order: Dim sum, in moderation; you must have the roast chicken.

Kau Kee
21 Gough Street, Hong Kong

One of the building blocks of Cantonese cuisine is beef brisket noodle soup. The brisket is braised until tender; the broth is the braising liquid. Garnishes are sparse—maybe just a little scallion.

And while there are many places to get a worthy bowl of beef noodle soup, my favorite is Kau Kee. This is problematic only in that it's like rooting for the Yankees. Kau Kee is so popular that it's not at all cool to say that it's awesome, but I've been on several brisket-noodle-eating excursions and I still think Kau Kee reigns supreme. There is far more beef fat in their soup, which is why it's both better and a little bit gnarlier-looking than others around town.

The move is to order two bowls of soup per person; you will be hungry because there is always, always a queue. Order the clear beef brisket soup with flat noodles, eat it first, then chase it with a bowl of beef tendon curry soup with e-fu noodles. The e-fu noodles are perfect for the curry soup, absorbing the liquid like a sponge. —DAVE CHANG

Category: SPECIALISTS
What to Order: First a bowl of clear beef brisket soup with flat noodles; then, because you will definitely still be hungry, a bowl of beef tendon curry soup.

PENNSYLVANiA POT PIE

Makes 4 to 6 servings

Chicken Pot Pie is a staple of Pennsylvanian Dutch cooking and a fixture at Amish Country buffets. What we call chicken pot pie in central PA is more like a thick chicken noodle stew, a relative of what they call chicken and dumplings in Edna Lewis's part of the country.

1 **Cut the chicken into pieces, nestle them into a cozy pot,** and cover with broth by about an inch. Sprinkle in the saffron, cover with a lid, and bring to a simmer over high heat. Once it has simmered, turn the heat down as low as it'll go and let the chicken poach for 25 minutes. Then turn the heat off, leave the lid on, and let the pot sit until the chicken is cool enough to handle.

2 **While the chicken is cooling, make the noodles:** Sift together the flour, baking powder, and salt. Cut in the butter, then work in the eggs and water. As soon as the dough comes together, roll it thin and cut it into 2" by 2" noodles. (I like to make rippled noodles; if you've got a wavy-edged rolling cutter, do so.)

3 **Move the chicken from the pot to a bowl** and bring the broth to a boil over high heat. Add noodles, a handful at a time, stirring well after each addition. The noodles will puff up in a minute or two (and eventually disintegrate to a degree, which is perfectly fine). Add the onion and potato, stir, and once the broth returns to a boil, reduce the heat to a simmer. Cook until the potatoes are soft and almost breaking up.

4 **While the potatoes are simmering, shred the chicken by hand,** and season the meat amply with salt and lots of black pepper. Add it to the pot and let it heat through before serving.

INGREDIENTS

- **1** chicken, 3 to 4 pounds
- **2 to 3 Q** chicken broth (store-bought is fine)
- **1** large pinch saffron (like 20 strands)
- **1 C** flour
- **2 t** baking powder
- **1 t** salt (more as needed to season)
- **1 T** butter
- **1** egg
- **½** eggshell full of cold water
- **1** small white onion, halved and thinly sliced
- **1** largish Russet potato, peeled, halved lengthwise, and thinly sliced
- **+** freshly ground black pepper

Hundreds of thousands of tourists visit central PA each year, hoping to glimpse an Amish buggy, snag a deal at the outlet malls, or be entertained at the Christian Broadway–style shows staged there. These activities are located outside of downtown Lancaster, smack in the middle of Amish Country, just east of the city. The area is full of contradictions: along the major roads leading to Philadelphia there are huge shopping centers catering to busloads of New Yorkers, but at every turn off there are quiet country lanes of time-warp Amish farms with outhouses and zero electrical power.

All-you-can-eat buffets—or *smorgasbords*, as the PA Dutch call them—are a fixture of Amish Country. Some cater almost exclusively to tourists arriving in buses; others serve a more local crowd. The quality of the buffets varies quite a bit, but all offer the same types of diner-style food with an emphasis on the PA Dutch classics like chicken corn soup, pork and sauerkraut, chicken pot pie, fried chicken, ham, and meatloaf.

When I'm going to hit a smorgasbord, Dienner's out on Lincoln Highway East is where I head. Firstly, it's scenically located: while Dienner's itself is fairly unremarkable, it is right next to a gigantic fake revolving windmill, and there's a very pretty farm right behind it. The people who work at Dienner's are friendly and very efficient. And the dining room is populated with a higher ratio of locals than other buffets, though it rarely tops 50 percent of the crowd (and is often lower in the summer, when the lines to get in are longer and tourist season is really in full swing).

You are seated, then asked if you want the buffet. I imagine most people say yes. The buffet is $10.65 at dinner, $9.65 at lunch, and $6.50 at breakfast, and kids are charged just 45 cents per year of age (my son's breakfast set me back $1.35 the last time we went). After the waitperson takes your order, you are given a card that you place on your table to indicate whether you're going to eat more from the buffet or if you're finished—this way your drinks aren't cleared while you're at the buffet.

Dienner's has three buffet counters to navigate. One holds the salads and cold appetizers (red beet eggs, pepper slaw, cottage cheese). Another hosts main courses (pork and kraut, rotisserie chicken, ham loaf), hot sides (mac and cheese, beets, string beans, mashed potatoes, cabbage), and sauces.

In keeping with PA tradition, a huge number of desserts line the third buffet counter. If that seems insufficient, there is also a help-yourself soft-serve ice cream machine and a diner-style vertical refrigerator full of slices of what I counted to be eight kinds of pie.

Overwhelmed by the choices? Keep in mind the old Amish saying: "Them that works hard, eats hearty!" **LP**

—Mark Ibold, Southeastern Pennsylvania Correspondent

Photograph by Colin Lane

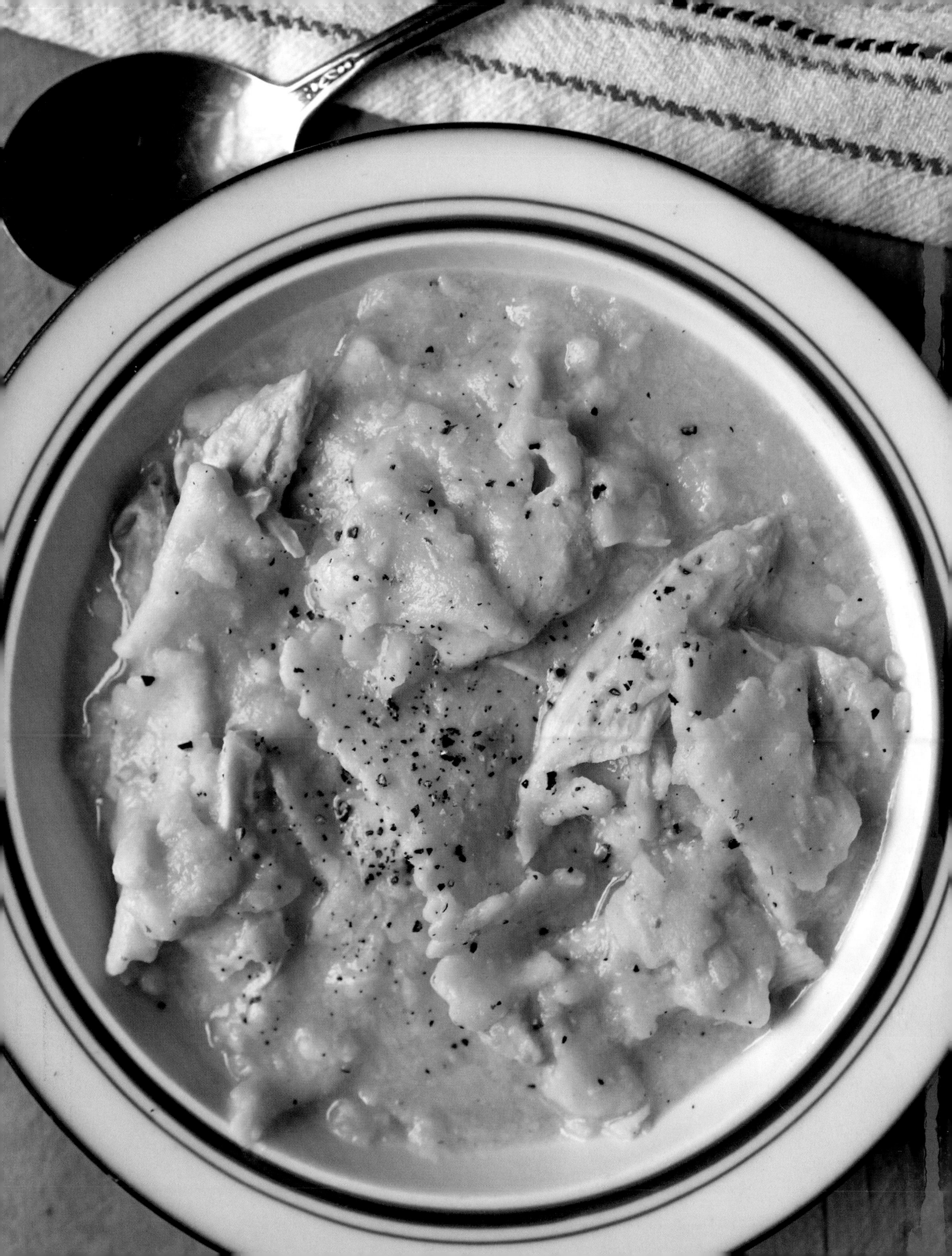

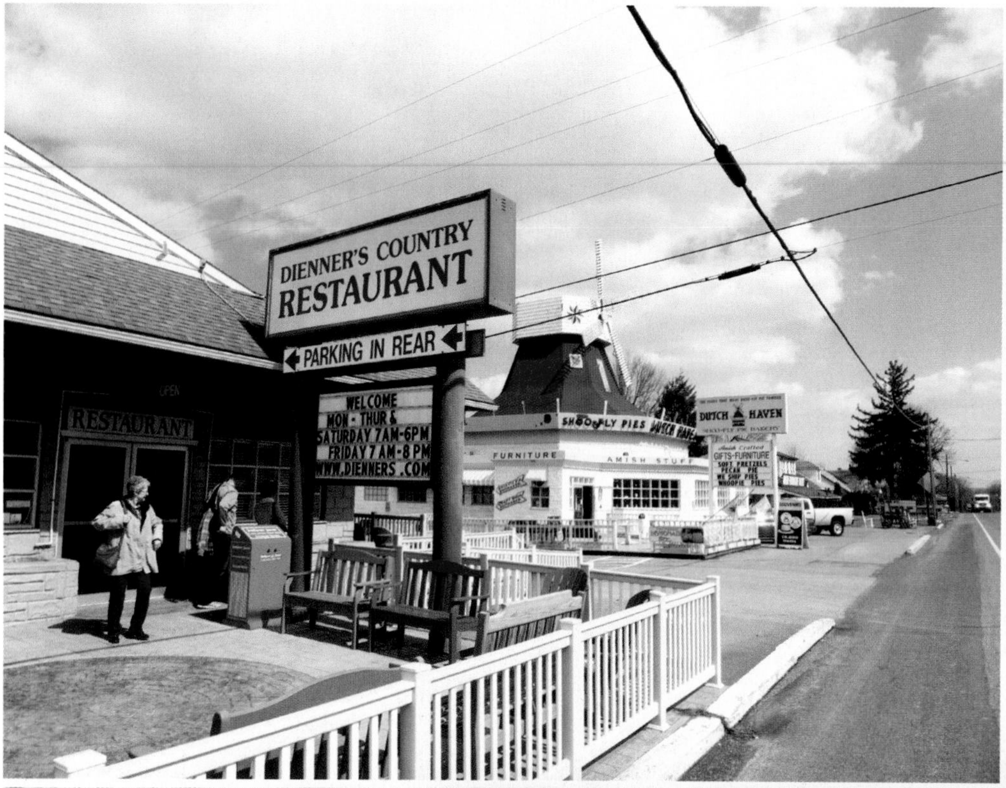
DIENNER'S COUNTRY
RESTAURANT
PARKING IN REAR
WELCOME
MON - THUR &
SATURDAY 7AM-6PM
FRIDAY 7 AM-8 PM
WWW.DIENNERS.COM
RESTAURANT
DUTCH HAVEN
FURNITURE
AMISH STUFF

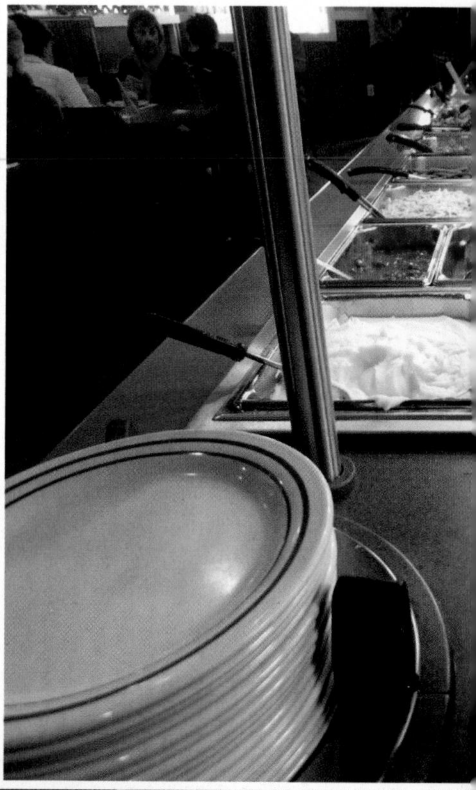

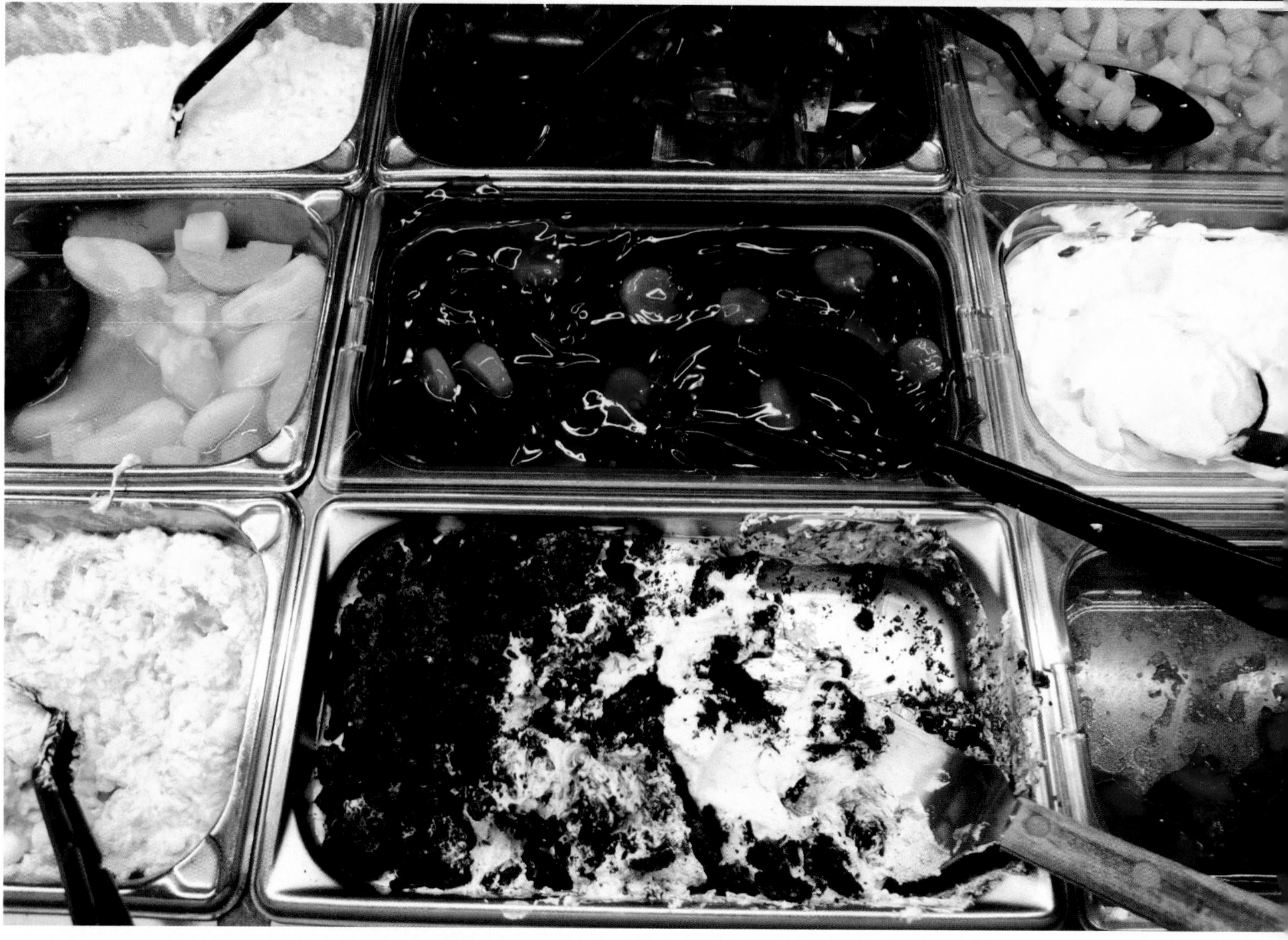

Tapioca
Pudding

Fruit
Salad

orange
creamsicle

Photographs by Mark Ibold

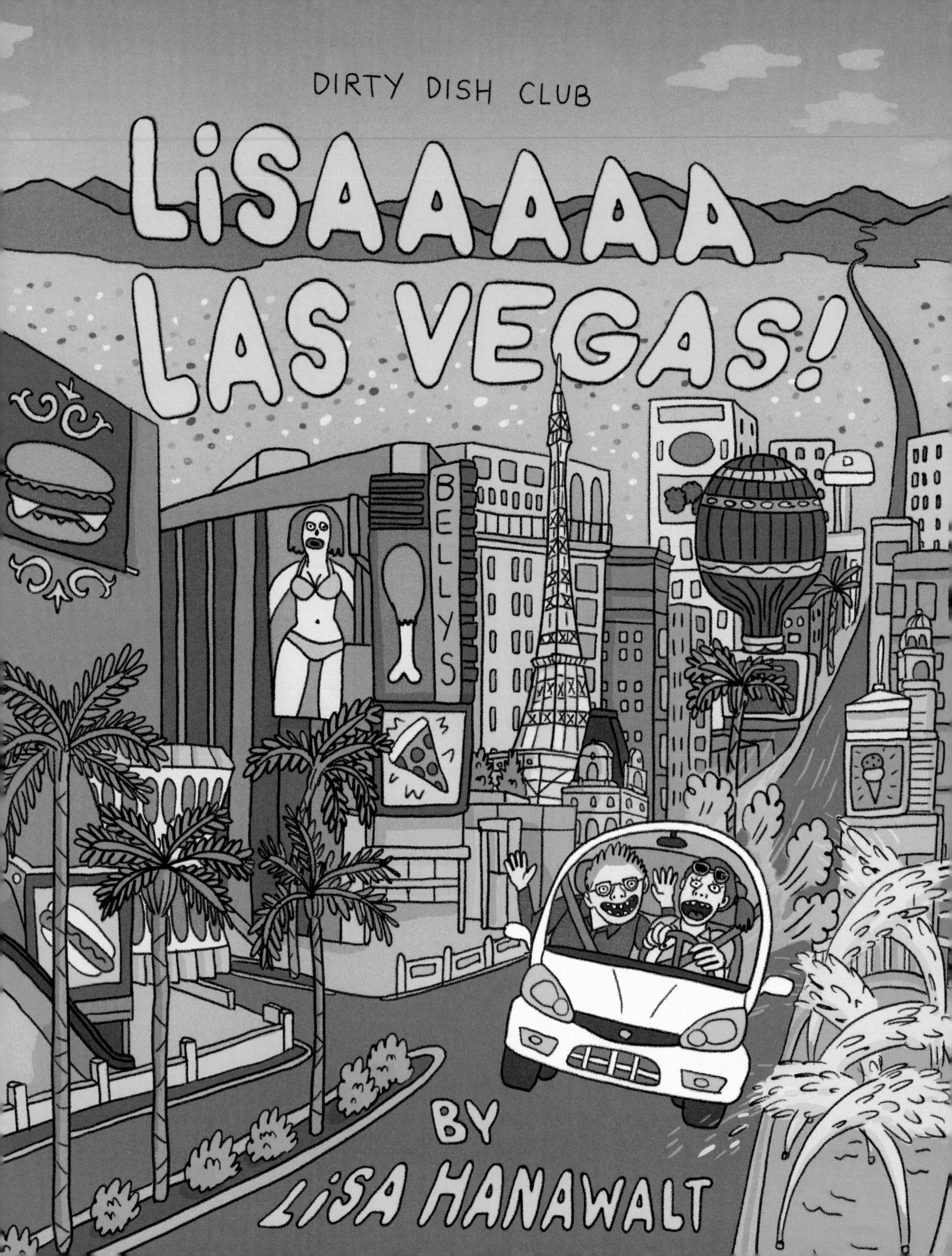

DIRTY DISH CLUB
LiSAAAAA LAS VEGAS!
BELLYS
BY
LiSA HANAWALT

LUCKY PEACH BOOKED A HOTEL ROOM FOR ME AND MY BOYFRIEND AT THE COSMOPOLITAN ON THE VEGAS STRIP AND INSTRUCTED US TO GORGE OURSELVES. EASY!

WE KNEW ABOUT THE COSMO BECAUSE WE'D SEEN THEIR INSANE AD PLAYING CONSTANTLY ON TV. IT'S A FLASHY MISHMASH OF MODELS AND MISBEHAVIOR SET TO A REMIX OF MAJOR LAZER'S "ORIGINAL DON," A SEXY, POUNDING, DANCE-PARTY SONG THAT MAKES YOU FEEL LIKE AN OBNOXIOUS AND MORALLY BEREFT PERSON FOR LISTENING TO IT. WE BLASTED IT ON REPEAT ON OUR WAY TO VEGAS, AND IT BECAME OUR ANTHEM OF EXCESS. I EVEN MADE UP CHANTS TO GO WITH IT.

WE'RE SUCKING UP RESOURCES. WE'RE TREATING MONEY LIKE A TOY AND EATING TOO MUCH FOOD. WE'RE PLAYING THIS DUMB SONG TOO LOUD. WE'RE WOLF OF WALLSTREETING!!

VEGAS HOTELS USUALLY HAVE THEMES. CIRCUS CIRCUS IS A BIG TOP; THE PARIS AND THE VENETIAN ARE EUROPEAN. THE COSMOPOLITAN'S THEME IS MORE SUBTLE: "YOU'RE INTERESTING AND RICH!" IT'S PERFECT FOR YOUNG NARCISSISTS LIKE OURSELVES.

THERE ARE CRYSTAL CHANDELIERS AND STRINGS OF SPARKLY GLASS BEADS DANGLING FROM THE CEILING. A FRANK SINATRA-TYPE GUY IS SINGING CLASSY JAZZY TUNES ON A STAGE WHILE PEOPLE MILL AROUND. FLAT-SCREENS IN THE ELEVATORS AND LOBBY SHOW ANIMATIONS OF BUGS MORPHING INTO STEAMPUNK GEARS. IT'S VERY EFFECTIVE AT MAKING THIS PLACE FEEL SPECIAL, BUT WITH A TOUCH OF OLD-SCHOOL VEGAS GLAMOUR.

THERE ARE LITTLE HERDS OF BROS AND BACHELORETTES GRAZING AROUND, AND WE PASS A MAN IN SCRUBS CARRYING A LARGE PIZZA.

A PIZZA DOCTOR??!!

OUR HOTEL SUITE IS PALATIAL. IT TAKES EIGHT FULL SECONDS TO SPRINT FROM ONE SIDE TO THE OTHER AFTER REMOVING ALL YOUR CLOTHING, SWINGING YOUR PANTS ABOVE YOUR HEAD, AND YELLING, "GOODBYE FOREVER, PANTS!" PLUS THE BALCONY HAS AN AMAZING VIEW OF THE STRIP.

THE WICKED SPOON IS THE COSMO'S BUFFET, AND IT'S FANCIER THAN WHAT I'D IMAGINE FOR AN ALL-YOU-CAN-EAT VENUE. THERE ARE CLASSY AMUSE-BOUCHES AND TEENY-TINY PLATES THAT SUBLIMINALLY DISCOURAGE GUESTS FROM BEING HORRIBLE GORGE-BEASTS.

OH HO, BUT YOU CAN STILL GO SO GROSS HERE IF YOU WANT TO. THERE'S A MOUNTAIN OF CRAB LEGS THAT BACHELORETTES ARE GRABBING AT. THERE'S A FULL BUTCHER SHOP IN HOUSE—LIKE, THEY CHOP UP ENTIRE COWS AND PIGS IN THE CASINO—SO THE BUFFET HAS FRESHLY SMOKED PORK BELLY, STEAK, AND BONE-MARROW CHUNKS.

THERE'S A BIG, BEEFY CUSTOMER LOADING UP HIS PLATE WITH FRIED CHICKEN, PIZZA, MAC-N-CHEESE, SLIDERS, AND WHATEVER THE HELL ELSE, AND WHO CAN BLAME HIM FOR GOING A LITTLE NUTS? WHETHER YOU'RE THIS BIG GUY OR A SNOTTY FOODIE, YOU CAN FILL UP HERE. THERE'S SOMETHING FOR EVERYONE.

I START OUT KINDA HEAVY WITH A GIANT MEATBALL AND A MINI SHEPHERD'S PIE. THEN I GO REAL DAINTY WITH A DELICATE SHRIMP CEVICHE AND A MINI NICOISE SALAD WITH A QUAIL EGG. THEN I DON'T KNOW WHAT HAPPENS—MY PLATE IS A BLUR OF STEAK AND CRAB LEGS AND SOME KOREAN BULGOGI THAT IS TOO CHEWY TO DO ANYTHING WITH BUT SUCK ON.

I TRY ONE SCOOP OF AN ARTICHOKE SALAD THAT IS PAST ITS PRIME AND NEEDS TO BE SPIT OUT, THEN QUICKLY ERASE THAT ERROR WITH A

HOTTEST VEGAS TRENDS: PEPLUM TOPS AND CRAB LEGS

SAMPLING OF OLIVES AND CHEESES. BUFFET FOODS ARE HIT OR MISS AND OFTEN LUKEWARM, EVEN AT A FINE ESTABLISHMENT LIKE THIS, BUT THERE'S SO MUCH OF IT, AND IT'S CONSTANTLY REGENERATED SO THERE'S NO CHANCE FOR DISAPPOINTMENT TO TAKE HOLD.

EVERY DESSERT IS FANTASTIC. TWENTY DIFFERENT KINDS OF TART AND CAKE, PLUS INTERESTING GELATO FLAVORS. HEAVEN.

THE BUFFET STAFF ANTICIPATES HOARDING BEHAVIOR, SO THERE ARE NO PAPER NAPKINS ANYWHERE FOR CARRYING FOOD AWAY. I WANT TO SLIP A COFFEE-FLAVORED RICE KRISPIE TREAT INTO MY PURSE, BUT THE ONLY OPTION IS TOILET PAPER, WHICH... NOPE. DO I THINK ABOUT IT? YES. DO I BRING MY RICE KRISPIE TREAT ALL THE WAY INTO THE RESTROOM BEFORE SUMMONING A SCRAP OF DIGNITY? GET OFF MY BACK!

THE NEXT MORNING, WE GO TO THE OLDER BELLAGIO HOTEL FOR THEIR BRUNCH BUFFET AND HAVE TO WANDER THROUGH A CASINO TO FIND IT. ON THE WAY THERE, WE GET LOST IN AN ATRIUM DECKED OUT TO CELEBRATE THE CHINESE LUNAR NEW YEAR OF THE HORSE, AND IT'S MAGNIFICENT ENOUGH TO MAKE ME EXCLAIM "OH F*****CK!" IN FRONT OF A BUNCH OF SURPRISED TOURISTS.

THIS BUFFET HAS MUCH MORE STANDARD FARE THAN THE WICKED SPOON. THE MOST EXCITING THING IS THE CONGEE PORRIDGE. AND THERE'S AN OMELET STATION WITH CRAB OMELETS. WHY AM I SO CHARMED BY THE ABUNDANCE OF CRAB IN VEGAS?

I REALIZE ANOTHER BENEFIT OF BUFFETS: YOU CAN EAT LIKE A COMPLETE IDIOT HERE.

EVERYONE ELSE IS SO FOCUSED ON LOADING UP THEIR PLATES THAT NOBODY WILL STOP TO ASK YOU WHAT THE FUCK YOU'RE DOING LADLING SOUP DUMPLINGS ONTO PILES OF BACON. I DO THIS, AND NOBODY NOTICES. THEN I EAT IT, AND NOBODY STOPS ME.

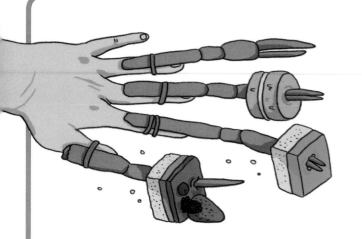

YOU CAN POUR THREE DIFFERENT FLAVORS OF SYRUP INTO THREE MUGS, CARRY THEM TO THE OMELET STATION, GLARE AT THE COOK, AND SAY, "MAKE ME A THREE-SYRUP OMELET." YOU WILL NOT BE ASKED TO LEAVE.

YOU CAN STICK PETIT FOURS ONTO THE ENDS OF CRAB LEGS, TIE THEM TO YOUR FINGERS, AND RUN AROUND CALLING YOURSELF EDWARD CAKECRABHANDS, AND YOU WILL SIMPLY BE OFFERED MORE CRAB.

THERE ARE NO CONSEQUENCES TO MY ACTIONS HERE, AND IT'S INTOXICATING.

WE TRY TO WALK OFF OUR BRUNCH BY BROWSING HIGH-END SHOPS AT THE NEIGHBORING ARIA MALL, WHERE I DISCOVER THAT LUXURY GOODS HAVE A LAXATIVE EFFECT. I SEE A PRADA SKIRT WITH A HUMAN FACE PRINTED ON IT, AND MY GUTS CRAMP INSTANTLY.

WE HIT THE HOTEL GYM IN THE AFTERNOON, STILL FULL OF BUFFET, AND I SLOWLY PRANCE UP AND DOWN ON AN ELLIPTICAL TRAINER WHILE PLAYING MAHJONG ON THE ATTACHED SCREEN. LIFE IS GOOD HERE.

IN THE EVENING WE GO UPSTAIRS TO JOSÉ ANDRÉS'S RESTAURANT, JALEO, TO MEET RENATA, THE COSMO'S PUBLIC-RELATIONS MANAGER. JALEO ISN'T TECHNICALLY ALL YOU CAN EAT, BUT RENATA ORDERS US UNLIMITED COCKTAILS AND STUFFS US WITH A MILLION DIFFERENT DISHES OF INVENTIVE AND EXTRAVAGANT FOOD.

PRADARHEA

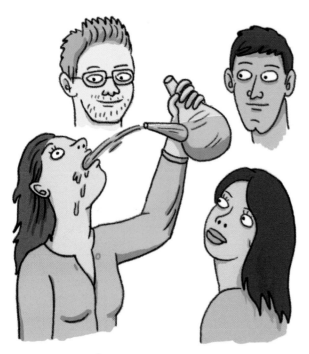

PORRÓN MORON

SHE ALSO ORDERS A PORRON PITCHER FULL OF BEER. IT'S A TRADITIONAL SPANISH THING AND THE RESTAURANT IS CLEARLY PROUD OF IT, BUT IT FEELS LIKE A FRATBOY-ISH STUNT YOU HAVE TO DO. YOU HOLD IT ABOVE YOUR MOUTH AND POUR THE LIQUID DOWN YOUR THROAT IN AN ARC WITHOUT TOUCHING IT TO YOUR LIPS. IT'S VERY URINAL.

I RESENT HAVING TO TRY THIS FOR THE FIRST TIME IN PUBLIC BEFORE PRACTICING IT ALONE, AND OF COURSE I SPILL BEER DOWN THE FRONT OF MY BLOUSE. ONLY LATER, AFTER I'M ALREADY DRUNK, DO I TRY THE PORRON AGAIN AND DO WHAT I FEEL MUST BE A REALLY AWESOME JOB.

WE TALK TO RENATA FOR AN HOUR, WHICH IS TOO LONG BECAUSE I ONLY HAVE LIKE TWO QUESTIONS AND THEY'RE BOTH ABOUT GUESTS BEING ASSHOLES AT THE BUFFET.

I SHARE MY FANTASIES OF "HOTEL GUESTS EXPLODING AFTER EATING TOO MUCH," WHICH I THOUGHT WE'D BE ON THE SAME PAGE ABOUT, BUT ACCORDING TO RENATA IT ISN'T AN ACTUAL PROBLEM.

I TRY A NEW ANGLE TO SEE BEHIND THE SCENES OF THE BUFFET KITCHEN, BUT RENATA INSISTS THAT ALL I'D SPY BACK THERE IS DISHWASHING. EITHER SHE'S TELLING THE DULL TRUTH, OR SHE'S HIDING SOMETHING WILLY WONKA-ESQUE.

MY PERSONAL GUESS? GUESTS WHO ATE SO MANY CRAB LEGS THEY TURNED INTO CRAB PEOPLE!! AND THEY ARE ADOPTED AND FORCED TO WORK IN THE CASINO KITCHEN.

I'D BETTER TAKE IT EASY ON THE SEAFOOD.

DO GUESTS EVER OVERDO IT AND GET KICKED OUT?

WHAT DO YOU MEAN "OVER-DO IT"?

UHHHH

WEE!

OOF!

WE SPEND OUR LAST FEW HOURS IN VEGAS GAMBLING AT THE SLOTS AND BLACKJACK TABLES.

LOOK, I WISH I COULD SAY WE WENT INSANE AND BLEW HUN-DREDS OF DOLLARS AND THEN EARNED IT ALL BACK! BUT IN REALITY WE BET LOW, MADE LOW WINNINGS, AND BASICALLY BROKE EVEN. EATING IS THE ONLY THING I LIKE TO DO TO EXCESS. I CHOOSE TO GAMBLE WITH MY GUTS! LP

INFECTIOUS CONFECTION

by **Harold McGee**

I've recently come across a fringe fermentation method that, unlike the breads and brews and yogurts and pickles and misos we know and love, isn't run by the usual benign microbes. The engine behind this fermentation method is *Clostridium perfringens*, a close relative of bacteria that cause botulism, tetanus, and food poisoning. It can eat flesh. It gives gas gangrene its name by causing putrefying flesh wounds that bubble and foam with flammable hydrogen. And it can make something surprisingly delicate and tasty.

Illustrations by Victor Kerlow

As befits a nasty pathogen, *Clostridium perfringens* grows aggressively. Its cells can divide every ten minutes, a handful turning into trillions of hydrogen makers overnight. That hydrogen gas can leaven dough just as yeast-generated carbon dioxide does. The result is something known as "salt-rising bread." A century ago, a scientist went so far as to bake bread leavened with *Clostridium perfringens* drawn from an infected wound, in what the *West Virginia Medical Journal* called "perhaps the most macabre experiment in culinary history."

And so I present to you an all-you-can-eat story not about the limits of stomach capacity, but about the far shores of edibility.

The origins of salt-rising bread are unclear but seem to lie in the nineteenth-century American frontier, where it was likely difficult to obtain fresh yeast or keep a bread starter cool and regularly fed.[1] The salt-rising process produces a leavened loaf from grains and water in about eighteen hours. The name is misleading, because salt doesn't play a major role. (Perhaps "salt-rising" was just a way of saying "yeastless-rising.") The real key to the process is heat: scalding-hot liquid to start with, then a feverish but *perfringens* friendly 100 to 115 degrees Fahrenheit for the starter, sponge, and dough.

Of course there are many different recipes and contradictory advice on the details, but the basic process begins with making an unusual starter. You boil milk or water, pour it over some cornmeal and/or wheat flour and a little salt, and let the hot mix sit in a warm place overnight until it gets bubbly and smelly from bacterial growth. Cornmeal and milk accelerate the process and help flavor the bread, but they're not essential. You mix the starter with additional flour, water, and baking soda into a batter-like sponge, and keep it warm for a few more hours until it, too, swells with bubbles. Then you add enough flour to make a dough, shape it, put it in a pan, and keep it warm for another few hours until it has doubled in volume, at which point you bake it.

The result is a tight-grained, dense yet tender loaf with an unusual aroma that's usually described as "cheesy." The social historian J. C. Furnas, who learned to love salt-rising bread as a child in the early twentieth century, wrote that "the flavor was once well defined by my sister as like distant dirty feet," but to his older and more discerning self it tasted "as if a delicately reared, unsweetened plain cake had had an affair with a Pont l'Eveque cheese." In my experience, salt-rising breads made with milk smell like a combination of swiss and parmesan—sharp rather than stinky. Milk-free salt-rising breads tend to be pungent in their own less cheesy way, though one of them, my all-time favorite so far, came out with a wonderful washed-rind aroma.

This curious flavor variability in salt-rising breads comes at least in part from variability in the microbes in the flour and cornmeal that we select to do the fermenting. And the selection process is pretty drastic. You notice that the recipe starts with scalding-hot liquid poured onto the dry ingredients. This step kills all of our familiar friendly yeasts and lactic acid bacteria, and, in fact, most microbes of any kind. The survivors are those bacteria that happen to be present as dormant and tough spores, which are actually stimulated by the high heat to germinate when the temperature drops back down to livable levels.

Does that situation ring a warning bell? It should. The standard recipe for salt-rising bread instructs us to do something we're warned against in the name of food safety: leave thoroughly cooked foods to sit in a warm place for hours. Cooking kills bacteria that are already active, but spores survive and are stimulated to grow—and grow fast—when the food temperature drops from piping hot to warm. That's exactly how *Clostridium perfringens* ends up being a common cause of food poisoning. And yet in salt-rising bread we make a point of encouraging it.

The realization that the salt-rising bacterium was a form of pathogen came in 1923, when a USDA microbiologist named Stuart A. Koser analyzed commercial salt-rising starters. He found that they were teeming with *Clostridium perfringens*, then called the Welch bacillus, a microbe already known to be very common in soil, water supplies, and foods, and especially numerous in the human intestine and in sewage. It hadn't yet been connected with food poisoning, but it was implicated in gangrenous flesh wounds. So Koser checked to see whether bakery loaves of salt-rising bread contained any of the bacillus. Indeed they did, but in the form of spores rather than live cells. He tested these bread strains on guinea pigs and found that they didn't cause gangrene.

Koser then wondered if a known disease strain could grow well enough in dough to leaven it and so pose a hidden hazard to the

[1] Salt-rising bread has remained surprisingly obscure—even Sandor Katz omits it from his 2012 magnum opus *The Art of Fermentation*—but the tradition has been kept alive in and around the Appalachian region. There are recipes in *Joy of Cooking* and other comprehensive sources, and Susan R. Brown maintains a website devoted to it at *home.comcast.net/~petsonk*.

Salt-rising bread is most conveniently started in the evening to bake late the following afternoon.

The body-heat fermentation temperature is essential for *Clostridium perfringens* to thrive. Before you start, calibrate the low end of your oven thermostat to hold a constant 100 to 110 degrees Fahrenheit, or set up a water bath and check its temperature regularly.

SALT-RISING BREAD

MAKES 2 8½"×4½" LOAVES

To make the starter

· 1 C cornmeal
· 1 T sugar
· 1 t salt
· 2 C milk

Combine dry ingredients in a bowl or large jar. Bring milk just to the boil and pour over dry ingredients. Mix briefly, then cover loosely and keep warm, 100 to 110° F, for 8 to 10 hours.

To make the sponge

· 1 t baking soda
· 1 C water, warmed to 120° F
· **the starter**
· 2 C all-purpose flour

Add the soda and water to the starter, then stir in enough flour to make a thick batter. Cover and keep warm again for 3 to 4 hours, until the batter is spongy with bubbles.

To make the bread

· 1 t salt
· **the sponge**
· 3 to 4 C all-purpose flour

1. Stir salt into sponge, then knead in enough flour to make a resilient dough. Divide the dough between 2 greased loaf pans and allow to rise in a warm place until the volume has significantly increased, 2 to 6 hours.

2. Preheat oven to 425° F. Bake the loaves for 45 minutes or until nicely browned. Remove loaves from pans and cool on a rack.

consumer. So he obtained a bacillus culture from the army that had originally been taken from a soldier's infected wound. It was called the "Silverman" strain, probably after the soldier or his doctor. And Koser made bread with these wound bacteria.

"The salt-rising bread prepared with the Silverman strain compared favorably in size and texture with that prepared from the [commercial] starter," he reported. Regrettably but understandably, he didn't report on the flavor. Less understandably, he didn't test the wound-risen bread for toxicity. But his creepy experiment made clear that there were different strains of the bacillus with different toxicities, and that though the strain in the commercial breads was relatively innocuous, it was possible that other breads might contain a dangerous strain.

It wasn't until the 1940s and '50s that scientists recognized *Clostridium perfringens* as a leading cause of foodborne illness as well as wound infections. Since then, they've found that there are at least five major types of the bacterium that produce different toxins and cause different kinds of disease. Their surveys have also found that most samples from the general environment don't produce the toxin that causes food poisoning.

The safety of salt-rising bread was revisited in 2008 by a physician at West Virginia University and a microbiologist at the University of Pittsburgh. Professors Gregory Juckett and Bruce McClane noted Koser's "macabre" but inconclusive 1923 experiment, and set out to determine whether salt-rising bread "should be viewed as the Appalachian equivalent of fugu, the poison-laden pufferfish of Japanese gourmands."

They analyzed a number of bread starters and found that all of them contained strains of *Clostridium perfringens* type A,

the group associated with food poisoning rather than wound infection. But none of these strains actually produced toxins. Given that finding, together with the fact that both toxins and active bacteria are inactivated by the heat of baking, and the lack of any known cases of the bread causing illness, Juckett and McClane concluded that "it seems reasonable to continue the consumption of this delicious old-fashioned bread."

Good! It also seems reasonable to begin exploring new possibilities for this old-fashioned and unusual process. Where familiar fermentations convert food carbohydrates primarily to alcohol or to lactic or acetic acid, *Clostridium perfringens* produces a cocktail of organic acids that includes acetic and lactic but also butyric—the characteristic sharp smell of aged cheese—as well as propionic—typical of Emmental-style swiss. A hot loaf of just-baked clostridium bread emits enough of these volatile acids to sting the inquiring nose. Milk in the starter seems to boost the butyric, but I've found that even dairy-free breads can sometimes be good and cheesy. It should be possible

to select clostridium cultures and starter ingredients to produce distinctive flavors reliably.

The most useful practical survey for the salt-rising experimentalist is a 2002 article by Reinald S. Nielsen in issue 70 of *Petits Propos Culinaires,* the quirky small-format journal published in the UK by Prospect Books. Nielsen had started making salt-rising bread in the 1950s, and over the years collected and tested old recipes and sent samples to a microbiology lab for analysis. He discovered that cornmeal is a far richer source of *Clostridium perfringens* than wheat flour, but that various materials can serve as slow but workable sources of starter microbes. Not just all kinds of grains, milled or flaked, conventional or organic, including packaged breakfast oatmeal and shredded wheat, but even bark from oak and black locust trees. Taste-of-place fans take note: *Clostridium perfringens* is everywhere. The possibilities are endless.

If you do give clostridium bread a try, a word of caution: Don't lick the spoon or nibble the raw dough. Just in case. Remember which family of microbes you're playing with. **LP**

LOOK AT A ALL THE

by **Jamie Feldmar**

It's tough to keep track of all of the things humans can eat. The list is constantly changing. With each passing year we invent new chemically engineered edibles, while every now and again we eat some poor plant or animal into extinction. We consume record-breaking amounts of some foods today—corn, meat, and sushi, for example—but far less of others—think barley, hedgehogs, and all but one kind of banana. To put things into some context, and to give you an idea for both the multitude of choice and the narrowing of choices we make, here are a few visual representations of how consumption has evolved since the dawn of mankind.

Children of the Corn

The U.S. is the world's largest producer of corn—32 percent of the world's corn supply is grown here. Over the past fifty years, while the amount of cropland has stayed nearly the same, farmers are now planting more corn than ever, often at the expense of less profitable "small grains" like oats, barley, and rye. Of all that corn, about 40 percent of it is used as animal feed; 30 percent for ethanol fuel; 10 percent is exported; and 12 percent is consumed by humans, either directly (corn chips) or indirectly (high fructose corn syrup).

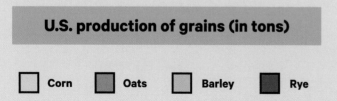

U.S. production of grains (in tons)

☐ Corn   ◼ Oats   ☐ Barley   ◼ Rye

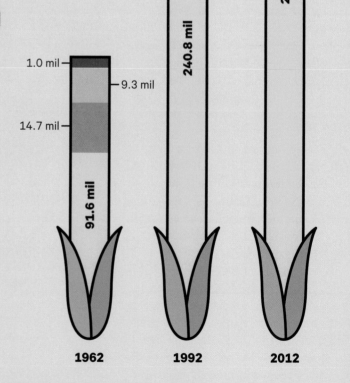

1962 — 1.0 mil, 9.3 mil, 14.7 mil, 91.6 mil

1992 — 290k, 4.3 mil, 9.9 mil, 240.8 mil

2012 — 176k, 930k, 4.8 mil, 273.9 mil

Source: Food and Agriculture Organization of the United Nations (FAO); National Corn Growers Association 2013 Report

THiNGS YOU CAN EAT!

Illustrations by Helen Tseng

Top Banana

Humans eat nearly 100 billion bananas every year. 99.9 percent of them are Cavendish bananas. Cavendish are efficient to grow and easy to ship, but there are more than 1,000 other banana varieties, many of which are grown and eaten in local markets in Africa and Asia.

And while the Cavendish control the market, until 1960, the 20th century was actually dominated by another banana: the Gros Michel (aka "Big Mike")—a breed that was ultimately rendered virtually extinct by a deadly fungus called Panama disease, a nasty virus that enters banana roots and fatally chokes off their water supply. Since then, the Cavendish have ruled, but that breed is currently threat–ened by a new strain of a deadly fungus called... Panama disease.

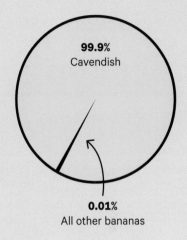

99.9% Cavendish

0.01% All other bananas

Goldfinger
Appearance: Small and hefty. Developed as as a potential disease-resistant alternative to Cavendish.
Tasting Notes: Sweet-tart apple flavor when ripe. Can be eaten green when cooked.

Praying Hands
Appearance: Two adja-cent banana bunches fused together, resembling clasped hands. Separate with a knife when ripe.
Tasting Notes: Medium sweetness, orange/peach notes. Eat cooked or fresh.

Rhino Horn
Appearance: Curved and elongated, can grow up to two feet long (the longest banana in the world).
Tasting Notes: Very sweet, alleged "cookie-dough-like consistency." Eat raw or steamed.

Dwarf Red (aka Dwarf Jamaican Red or Dwarf Red Dacca)
Appearance: Small and slender, with deep red/maroon skin when ripe.
Tasting Notes: Creamy, very aromatic, orange notes. Eat cooked or fresh. Also frequently sold dried.

Blue Java (aka Ice Cream or Hawaiian Banana)
Appearance: Silver-blue skin, white flesh.
Tasting Notes: Vanilla fla-vor, ice cream-like consist-ency. Eat cooked or fresh.

Musa Basjoo (aka Japanese Banana)
Appearance: Small and green.
Tasting Notes: Inedible. The plant is cultivated for appear-ance and to make fibers used in kimonos and paper.

Lady Fingers (aka Sugar Bananas or Niños)
Appearance: Short and chubby, thin-skinned.
Tasting Notes: Delicate and very sweet. Best eaten fresh.

Burro (aka Chunky Banana)
Appearance: Short and blocky, almost rectangular with straight edges.
Tasting Notes: Starchy and slightly acidic. Good fried.

Pitogo (aka Ugly or Ping Pong Banana)
Appearance: Round, stubby fruit ranges in size from a ping pong to tennis ball.
Tasting Notes: Creamy and firm. Good for frying.

1000 Fingers
Appearance: Solid green plant with hundreds of 1- or 2-inch fruits. Stems can grow up to 8 feet long.
Tasting Notes: Fragrant and sweet, slightly acidic. Eat raw or cooked in butter.

Source: Koeppel, D. "Banana: The Fate of the Fruit That Changed the World." Penguin, 2008; various banana enthusiast message boards

The History of Meat

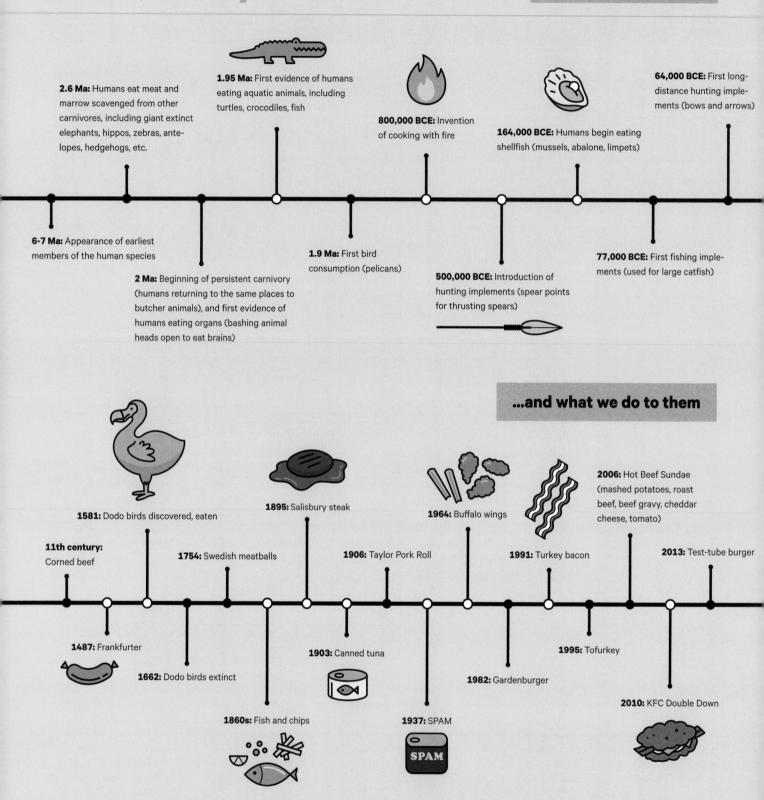

2.6 Ma: Humans eat meat and marrow scavenged from other carnivores, including giant extinct elephants, hippos, zebras, antelopes, hedgehogs, etc.

1.95 Ma: First evidence of humans eating aquatic animals, including turtles, crocodiles, fish

800,000 BCE: Invention of cooking with fire

164,000 BCE: Humans begin eating shellfish (mussels, abalone, limpets)

64,000 BCE: First long-distance hunting implements (bows and arrows)

6-7 Ma: Appearance of earliest members of the human species

1.9 Ma: First bird consumption (pelicans)

77,000 BCE: First fishing implements (used for large catfish)

2 Ma: Beginning of persistent carnivory (humans returning to the same places to butcher animals), and first evidence of humans eating organs (bashing animal heads open to eat brains)

500,000 BCE: Introduction of hunting implements (spear points for thrusting spears)

...and what we do to them

1581: Dodo birds discovered, eaten

1895: Salisbury steak

1964: Buffalo wings

2006: Hot Beef Sundae (mashed potatoes, roast beef, beef gravy, cheddar cheese, tomato)

11th century: Corned beef

1754: Swedish meatballs

1906: Taylor Pork Roll

1991: Turkey bacon

2013: Test-tube burger

1487: Frankfurter

1662: Dodo birds extinct

1903: Canned tuna

1982: Gardenburger

1995: Tofurkey

1860s: Fish and chips

1937: SPAM

2010: KFC Double Down

Sources: Food and Agriculture Organization of the United Nations (FAO); Earth Policy Institute; interview with Dr. Birana Pobiner, Smithsonian National Museum of Natural History; foodtimeline.org

Humans have a long history of eating our fellow animals. In 2007, total meat consumption in the U.S. hit a historic peak of 55 billion pounds (that's about 270 pounds of meat per person that year), compared to less than 10 billion pounds (115 pounds per person) a century earlier. Here's how we arrived at our current carnivorous state.

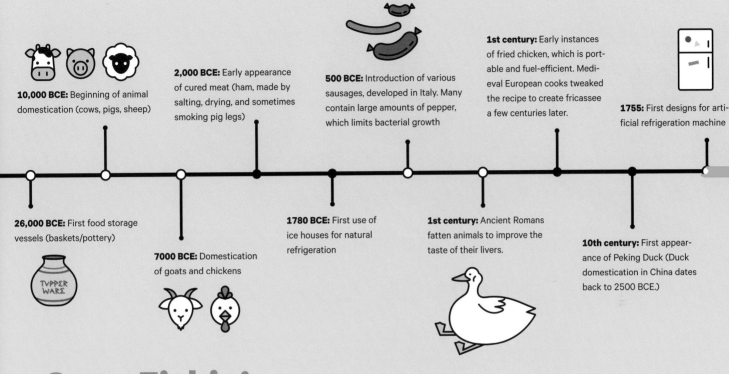

10,000 BCE: Beginning of animal domestication (cows, pigs, sheep)

26,000 BCE: First food storage vessels (baskets/pottery)

7000 BCE: Domestication of goats and chickens

2,000 BCE: Early appearance of cured meat (ham, made by salting, drying, and sometimes smoking pig legs)

1780 BCE: First use of ice houses for natural refrigeration

500 BCE: Introduction of various sausages, developed in Italy. Many contain large amounts of pepper, which limits bacterial growth

1st century: Ancient Romans fatten animals to improve the taste of their livers.

1st century: Early instances of fried chicken, which is portable and fuel-efficient. Medieval European cooks tweaked the recipe to create fricassee a few centuries later.

10th century: First appearance of Peking Duck (Duck domestication in China dates back to 2500 BCE.)

1755: First designs for artificial refrigeration machine

Gone Fishin'

Kawafuku, the first sushi restaurant in America, opened in L.A.'s Little Tokyo in 1966, and our hesitating acceptance of raw fish has grown into an ocean-decimating fixation since then. The number of sushi bars in the U.S. quadrupled between 1988 and 1998, and raw fish on rice can now be had in gas stations, convenience stores, and airports everywhere.

Odds of spotting specific fish on a sushi menu

95% Tuna

93% Salmon

86% Eel

45% Hamachi

Mackerel: 42%	**Snapper:** 29%	**Smelt:** 22%	**Escolar:** 8%	**Halibut:** 7%	**Bonito:** 6%	**Tilapia:** 2%
Whitefish: 30%	**Flounder:** 25%	**Bass:** 13%	**Striped Bass:** 8%	**Sea Bass:** 7%	**Flying Fish:** 4%	**Grouper:** 1%

Sources: FoodGenius; Hsin-I Feng, C. "The Tale of Sushi: History and Regulations." Comprehensive Reviews in Food Science and Food Safety, vol. 11, 2012.

ALL YOU CAN EAT ON

There aren't many all-you-can-eat buffets in Manhattan, but hidden behind scaffolding on 7th Avenue, marked with half-lit signage, is Midtown Buffet. Inside, steel pans line two aisles with the basics of a Chinese buffet: hot and sour soup, sushi, fried rice and noodles. There are chicken nuggets next to the egg rolls and slices of cantaloupe arrayed aside a sea of red jello cubes.

The crowd on a recent Sunday afternoon, after lunch and before dinner, was mixed: a mother-daughter duo who spoke Spanish and got identical plates of food; a couple of hungry-looking single men; a family of four with screaming kids; tourists with curious faces.

I sat there with my "free" Coke, wondering what I'd eat next. I glimpsed some crab legs and some delightfully greasy roasted duck. I was already obsessing over my choices while working on my plate of salad. The waitresses vacillated between intense boredom at the afternoon's slow crowd and rushing at lightning speed to clear plates off tables whenever guests got up. I wondered if they'd take my plate if I went to stockpile some duck before finishing my current course. Moreover, I wondered, how do these places survive?

Later I asked the manager this very question. He laughed and handed me a piece of paper with a number.

"Try to call the boss," he said.

OMICS

by
Bourree Lam

Illustrations by Helen Tseng

On the many occasions I phoned, the voice on the other end would always ask, "Why?" Each time, I left my number and was told: "Mr. Chen will call you back if he wants to." After many calls and many messages, none of them returned, I finally gave up on Mr. Chen.

Buffet businesses are rife with secrecy: hard numbers about profit margins are extremely hard to come by, and many business are scared you want to talk health safety or whom they get their raw materials from, and at what price—information they regard as trade secrets.

But the basic economics of a restaurant are like those of any regular business: the cost of inputs must be less than what customers pay for the outputs. The difference between the two is the profit margin. Full-service restaurants have to balance sales with what they spend on food and alcohol, labor, rent, and incidental costs.

The variables at an all-you-can-eat (AYCE) buffet are different from those at a traditional restaurant. The demand for waitstaff is usually greatly reduced: customers line up to serve themselves. The kitchen staff cooks from a prescribed menu daily, and at places like AYCE shabu-shabu or Korean barbecue places, businesses save further on cooking costs as customers cook their own food as part of the experience.

Though buffet operations don't have to deal with finicky guests sending their orders back to the kitchen (log that under incidental costs), they do have to deal with another kind of tough customer: the kind who want to bankrupt them with their stomachs.

"We specifically refer to our 'all-you-care-to-eat' items in this way because we do not want to encourage our guests to intentionally overeat," says Kerry Kramp, chief executive of Sizzler. "Sometimes guests misperceive these types of promotions and they take it as a challenge to potentially overconsume. That is not what we hope for and the majority of our guests greatly appreciate the flexibility to have a little more of their favorite menu items. We never create 'consumption challenges' and that is why we basically refer to these as 'all you care to eat' versus 'all you can eat.' People can eat a lot of food if they are not feeling like there is a value to the actual item."

Sizzler, once a buffet-focused chain, has moved away from that model since the nineties. But its salad bar remains AYCE, and Sizzler continues to offer special items such as

steak and riblets that can sometimes still be purchased as AYCE. As far as dealing with those customers trying to "beat the buffet," the maxim is this: it's all about the average.

For every big, hungry guy or gal who can really eat his or her weight in crab legs, buffets count on a few who won't. It helps that buffets appeal to groups: a big family might have one super eater, but Grandma or your toddler brother will probably under-eat.

The other key metric in buffet economics is managing waste. Ovation Brands—previously Buffets, Inc.—owns more than 330 buffet restaurants in thirty-five states; it's the parent company of Old Country Buffet and HomeTown Buffet. Each year its restaurants serve forty-seven million pounds of chicken, six million pounds of steak, and eighty-five million dinner rolls to one hundred million customers. Though the company has suffered some setbacks (Buffets, Inc. filed for bankruptcy in 2008 and 2012), it is currently reporting the strongest sales numbers in seven years. And it got there by really getting to know its waste numbers.

Michelle Gessner, senior vice president of administration for Ovation, emphasizes the importance of portioning as a means of minimizing waste. "Every item will have anywhere from 5 to 25 percent waste, even with the small pans. Whenever you're doing more than one serving, you're going to have waste." Once upon a time, her company made one large pan of chicken potpie. Nowadays it makes single-serving pies in place of the big one.

Ovation Brands collects data weekly on waste in its restaurants. From there, the numbers are plugged into a computer for modeling based on time of year. Projections are made for the number of customers expected, along with what they'll likely eat.

"We know pretty well how much food will be consumed on any particular day," says Gessner. "We use far more fish products on the weekends, more salads at the beginning of the year. Meatloaf and fried chicken are the most popular items."

The introduction of the AYCE buffet in America is most often attributed to Herbert McDonald, an entrepreneurial casino publicist. It is said that McDonald started the cheap casino buffet tradition at the El Rancho Vegas in 1956. From McDonald's 2002 obituary in the *Las Vegas Sun*, we get a look at the American AYCE buffet's simple origins: "One night while working late at the El Rancho Vegas, the first hotel on what would become the Strip, McDonald brought some cheese and cold cuts from the kitchen and laid them out on the bar to make a sandwich. Gamblers walking by said they were hungry, and the buffet was born."

The Las Vegas buffet has evolved over time. The priority in the early days could be boiled down to one word: cheap. The original twenty-four-hour Buckaroo Buffet at the El Rancho had AYCE salad, cold cuts, and hearty entrées like Salisbury steak for just a dollar. The trend caught on fast: other Strip casinos offering AYCE Chuck Wagon Buffets with seafood and cold cuts sprang up. By the turn of the century, the cheap buffet had become an archetype of the Las Vegas business model: lure visitors in with cheap entertainment—say, AYCE prime rib—and hope to snare them at the tables on their way through the casino floor.

In an article for the website *Vegas Inc*, Ed Komenda, a gaming reporter at the *Las Vegas*

Sun, wrote, "Throughout the '80s, '90s, and early 2000s, buffets were among Las Vegas's biggest loss leaders. That's when gambling revenue still reigned on the Strip."

But the model has shifted. Las Vegas buffets today push the Vegas indulgence factor.

"The buffet at Bellagio was the pioneer in the revival of the modern-day buffet," says Edmund Wong, Bellagio's executive chef.

Fifteen years ago, Bellagio was the first hotel on the Strip to make the buffet a big, fancy deal—offering caviar on Fridays, for instance. After it came the Wynn and Caesars—both of which offer a staggering 500 items in their respective buffets.

And they're no longer cheap. A weekend dinner will set you back $53.99 at the Bacchanal Buffet at Caesars. So the question becomes: Do Las Vegas buffets make money as independent operations, or are they still just a draw to get hungry gamblers in the door?

Though none of the casinos I interviewed would reveal earnings numbers for their buffet operations, their chefs were aware of strategies for turning a profit. The secret is tactical presentation: placing appropriate side dishes near entrées (you'll definitely want some mashed potatoes with that) or well-manicured fruit near sophisticated desserts.

"Buffets are not known as moneymakers per guest. It's all about volume levels," says David Snyder, executive chef of Wynn Las Vegas. "When writing buffet menus, the key is having your costs correct, having the correct amount of high-cost items compared to lower-cost items."

David G. Schwartz at the University of Nevada's Center for Gaming Research, which does scholarly research into gambling and gaming issues, speculates that at least some buffets are able to meet the bottom line. "It's hard to say for sure because I don't see their balance sheets. At some casinos on the lower

end, they probably don't make money. But when you're hitting at a higher price point, it's likely that there's some profit."

All this talk of profitability demands a further question: Are customers "profiting" in the all-you-can-eat system?

Economists will tell you that more choice is better (though researchers like Columbia University's Sheena Iyengar have found in recent studies that too much choice can be paralyzing). And that certainly seems to be one big reason people go to buffets. I asked what draws people to AYCE buffets on Chowhound and got 300 replies in a week.

Laliz: "When there is a large group, then everyone can find something they will eat or enjoy. I also very much enjoy the 'show' of people and what they choose. Kind of like looking at others' shopping carts in the grocery store."

mrsphud: "I can have all the protein I want—sliced meats, chicken, etc. and the family can have whatever else they might be interested in."

However, while more food choices in unlimited quantities sounds like a great deal, when the effort to maximize value exceeds satisfaction (because you've stuffed yourself silly), marginal utility—the difference between what you're putting in and getting out of the buffet—will be negative. In other words, if you eat past the point of comfort, the buffet is a losing proposition. This is the calculus that people forget when they try to get their money's worth from AYCE. If you try to beat the buffet by busting your gut, you will fail. But if your particular bag happens to be mixing a little caviar with your crab legs and egg rolls, you just might leave the casino on top. **LP**

Carbo-loading with America's swingers

GREAT FOR LARGE GROUPS

Text and photographs
by **Naomi Harris**

It was eight o'clock on a Saturday night when we turned into the strip mall parking lot in Fort Lauderdale. Most of the storefronts were empty with FOR RENT signs in the windows except for one unit at the end of the mall where an illuminated red sign read TRAPEZE. This is where I would attend my first swingers party.

I had moved to Miami in December 1999 to pursue a career in photography. Florida is a hotbed for news. I arrived in the middle of the Elián González debacle; I was there for the hanging-chad fiasco and the anthrax-mail scare. My personal motivation for moving south, though, was the snowbirds; I wanted to document those senior citizens who migrated to the warmer climate for the winter. When I wasn't photographing them or chasing the news, I would hang out at a beach called Haulover.

Haulover was a nude beach. And while not all nudists are swingers, it's pretty safe to say that many swingers are nudists.

I would situate myself with the same group of regulars: Larry, an older gentleman who specialized in sensual massages on the beach; Captain Richie and his wife Judy who lived on their boat; Paula, a diabetic, who would inject insulin as casually as she'd apply sunscreen; and Ron, a New Yorker who'd retired to Fort Lauderdale to dedicate himself to his tan.

As I lounged, au naturel, I would often hear chatter about "special" parties that I was never invited to. I reasoned that it was because I was thirty or forty years younger than most of my beach friends. But one afternoon, Ron asked me if I'd like to be his date to a swingers club that night. Single men weren't permitted so he needed me to act as his "key." No strings attached, of course—I could do whatever I wanted or nothing at all. Ron knew I was a photographer and would probably find it interesting.

I'll try anything once. I asked Ron what one wore to a swing club. He told me to "dress to impress," and

that he'd pick me up at seven so we could get to the buffet early. Buffet?

We parked the car in the lot of the strip mall, entered through a frosted glass door, showed our IDs, paid the entrance fee, and entered a large room with an empty dance floor to the right and a buffet to the left. Ron wasn't messing around. He made a beeline for the food: macaroni salad, potato salad, coleslaw, rolls, scalloped potatoes, slices of cake, cookies. At the far end was a rather stout man dressed in a starched white jacket complete with a chef's hat standing in front of a carving station: roast beef. And sure enough there was already a snaking line of hungry swingers in front of the glowing red heat lamps.

Were it a few hours earlier, we might all have been in line at the bank or the supermarket. It was a perfectly ordinary, average-looking crowd save for the men's shiny club shirts and the women donning micro-mini dresses and six-inch Lucite heels. Otherwise you might confuse any of these people for your accountant or dentist—hell, they probably *were*. I joined them in piling plates high with a variety of salads, sides, and hot beef.*

They sat around tables ravenously polishing off their dinners from paper plates. Those who had finished eating began milling around the dance floor, while others returned for seconds. Gradually the party picked up, as my fellow partygoers began to bump and grind to "Da Ya Think I'm Sexy" and "Electric Boogie." I started noticing couples heading toward a door that led to a locker room.

In order to enter the back playrooms, one was required to be in an appropriate state of undress: nothing but a towel and a smile. I was eager to head to the back, partially out of curiosity but mostly so I could get out of my "sexy jeans" and let my stuffed body breathe.

I won't bore you with the details of the Rob Ford–ian feast of flesh that transpired over the next few hours. The participants seemed unencumbered by the massive banquet of minutes ago. I observed quietly from the corner, burping and wishing I had an Alka-Seltzer.

At about quarter to two I told Ron that I had had enough of the sex smorgasbord, and was ready to go home. We retreated to the locker room, got dressed, and headed back to the main dance room. The dinner buffet had been cleared away and the pudgy meat-carver was nowhere in sight, but a new table had been set: breakfast. There were assorted pastries, croissants, cereal, and fruit. An urn of coffee gurgled next to the prune Danish. As we exited the club, my last view was of a fully naked woman wearing only stripper heels, fixing herself a bagel with a schmear. 🄻🄿

*I would go on to publish a book called *America Swings* (Taschen), for which I traveled all over the U.S. to more than forty parties over the course of five years, photographing swingers at play. The parties almost always began with a similar Dionysian feast—I never got a straight answer why.

Classic AYCE Challenge
NUMBER ONE

Eat one tablespoon of cinnamon, ALL AT ONCE

Illustration by Ian Huebert

INSA

by **Chris Ying**

Photographs by Gabriele Stabile

ANE

is a word I hear a lot. It has crept out of the swamp of hyperbolic surfer–snowboarder rhetoric——along with *rad(ical)*, *gnarly*, *sick*, *killer*, etc.——onto the shores of wider use. Restaurant people use it in various adjectival and adverbial configurations: "The duck is insane!" "These canelés are insaaaaane." "We insanely ordered too much food." (Also "We ordered insanely too much food.") $\rightarrow$

To be colloquially as opposed to clinically insane implies something so fantastic in quality or outlandish in quantity that it shatters rational expectation. In its splendor or munificence, the insane thing may drive us to senseless, unhealthy behavior. Sports fandom is insane. To the sports abstinent, those of us who bind ourselves emotionally to our teams—whether for geographic, nostalgic, or less explicable reasons—may appear deranged in the way we live and die with the outcome of largely meaningless competitions. But this means nothing to the sports fan. The joy of watching your team win is euphoric, and is amplified by how hard you have supported your squad. To leave a game early, even in the face of insurmountable odds, is

unthinkable to a true fan. Showing up early is equally important. That's where tailgating comes in. As Warren St. John tells it:

> In the early '70s, some mad football fan someplace … got it in his head to drive a motor home right up to the stadium on game day, probably for the simple reason that motor homes have bathrooms and therefore provided this fan and his beer-drinking buddies the luxury of a place to take a leak during their pregame tailgate party.

And so tailgating grew from beers and barbecue in the parking lot to a days-long ritual.

> RVs completely changed the fan experience. Before, football games were circumscribed events. They took place inside

> a stadium on Saturdays and lasted about three hours, after which everyone went home. Logistical problems like traffic, the need for tickets, the need for those bathrooms—set games off from the rest of life. RVs blew open the experience. The event was no longer confined to three hours—it could last three days.

St. John is the author of *Rammer Jammer Yellow Hammer*, an entertainingly self-conscious book about being a fan of the University of Alabama football team. A blog entry late last year for the *New Yorker* singled out college football as "perhaps our most insane cultural institution." The writer, Reeves Wiedeman, was writing specifically about the Iron Bowl.

The Iron Bowl—the annual clash between the University of Alabama Crimson Tide and Auburn University

Illustration by Helen Tseng

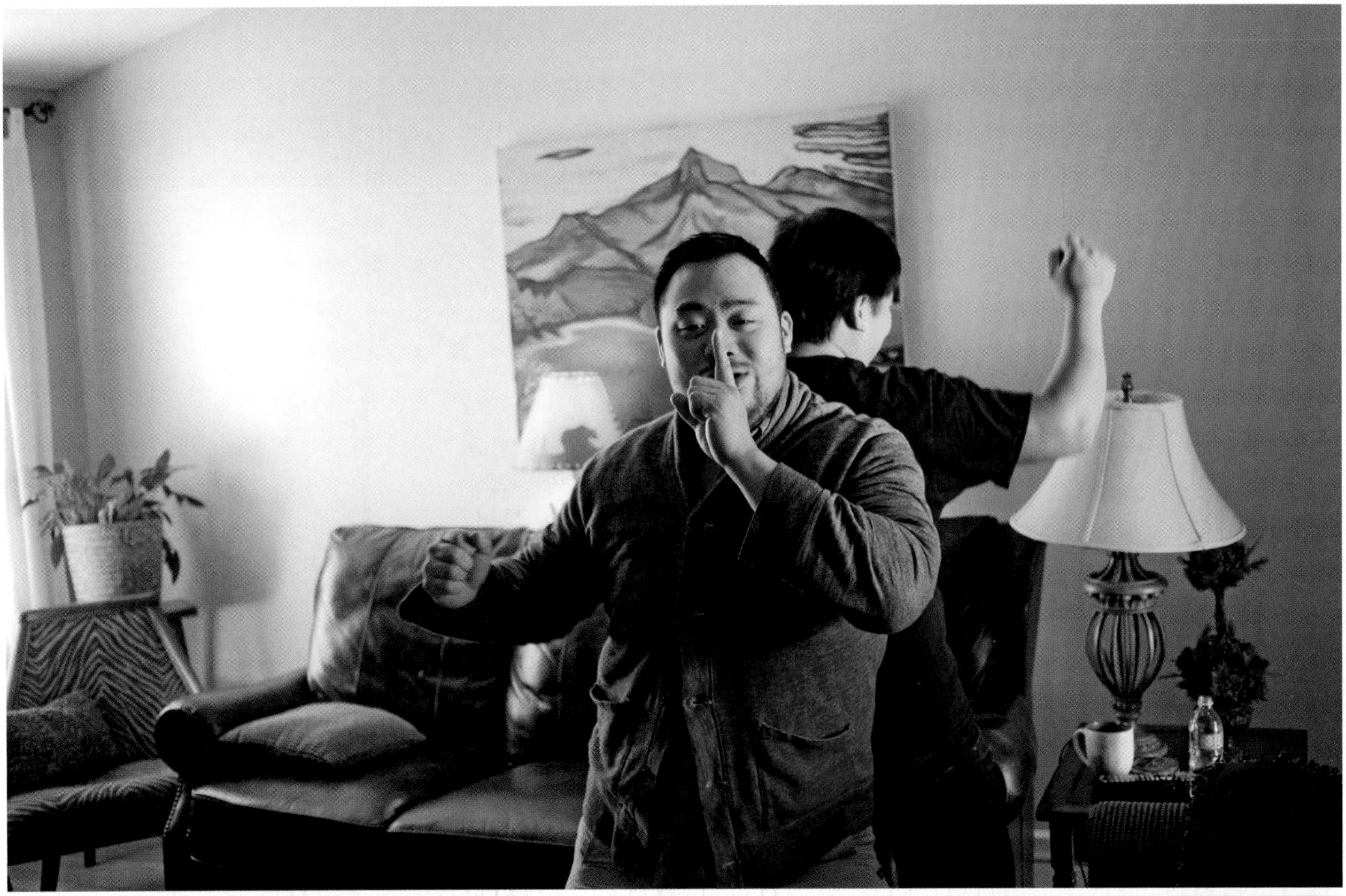

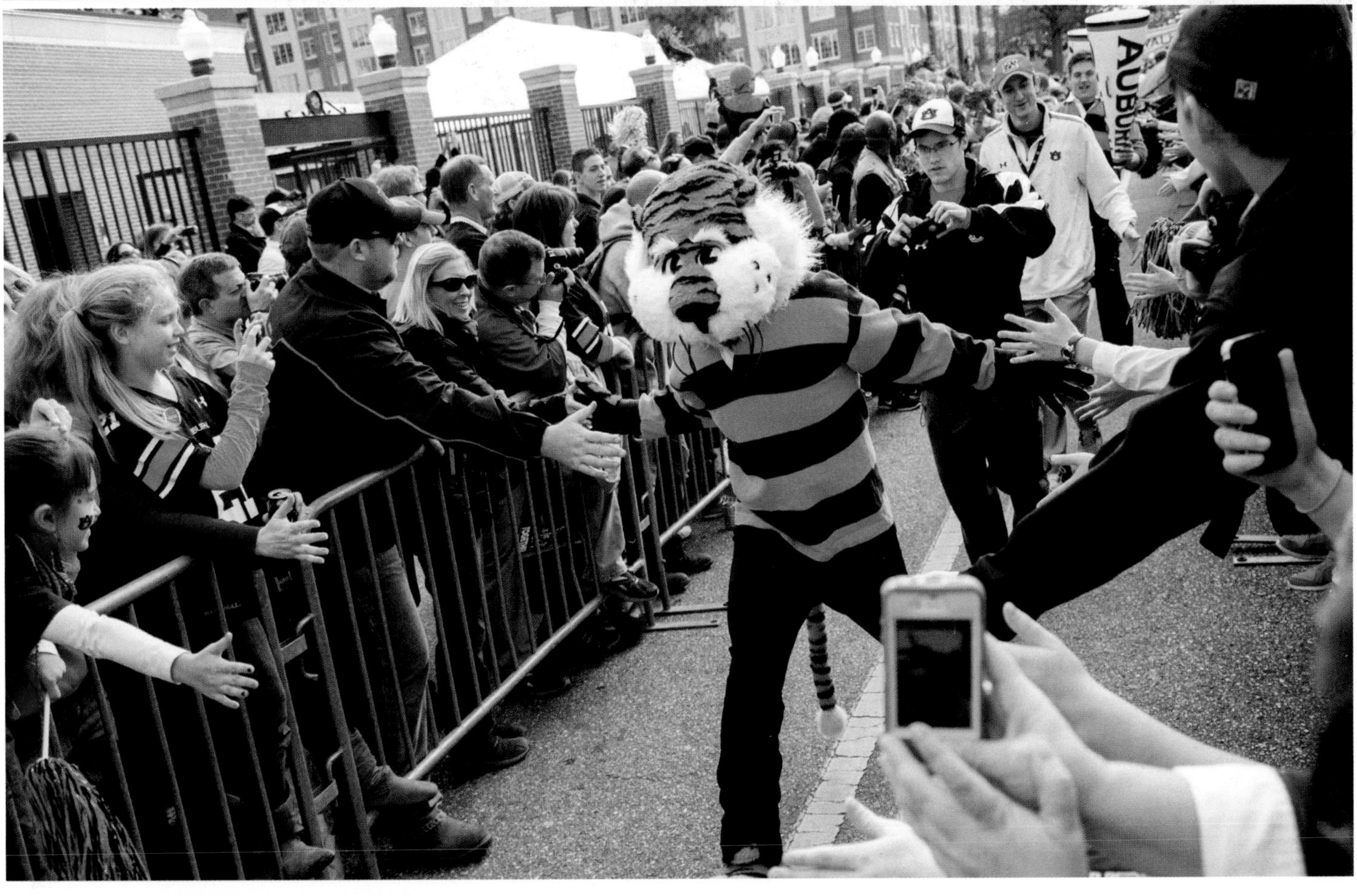
AUBURN

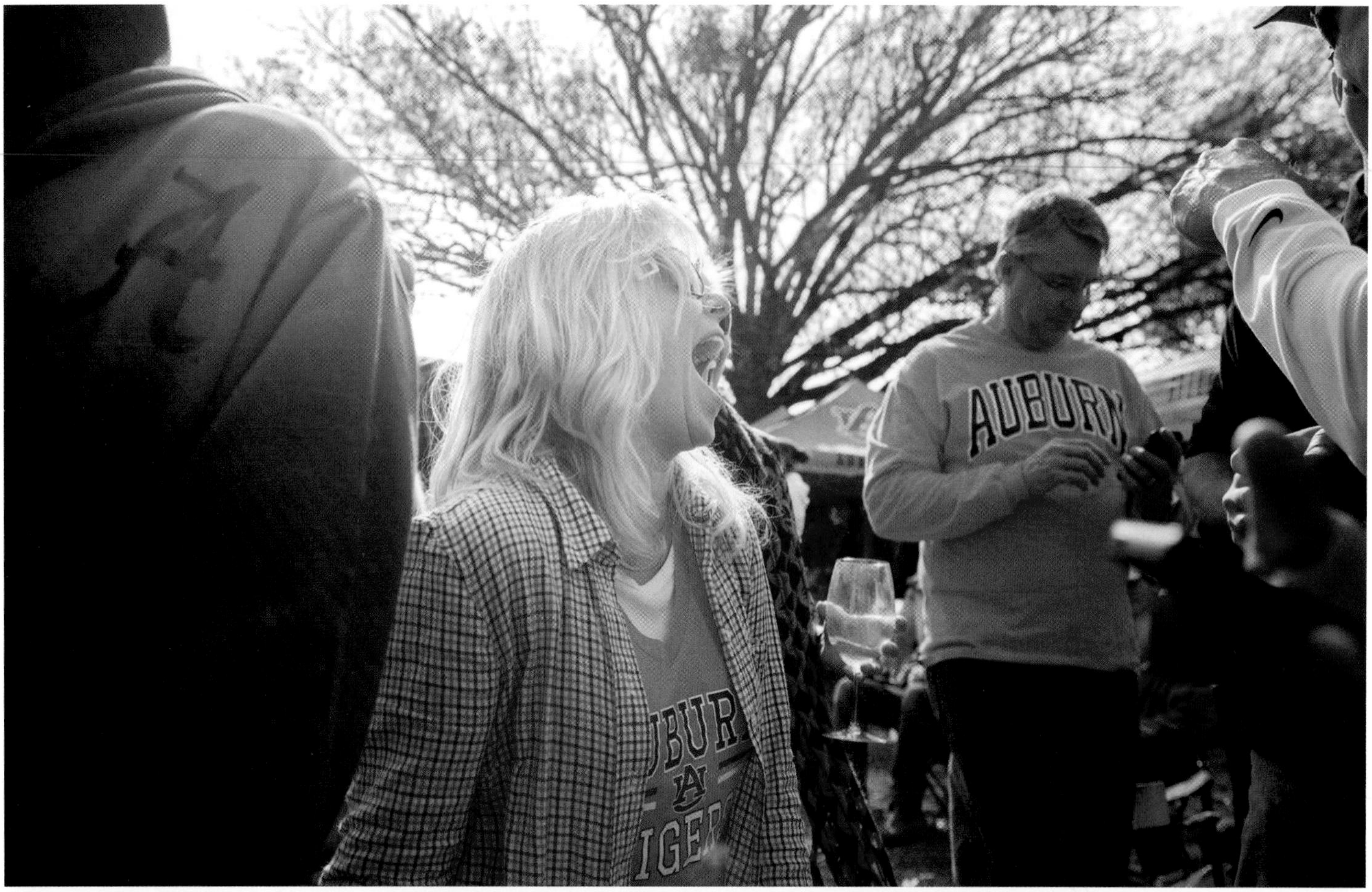
AUBURN

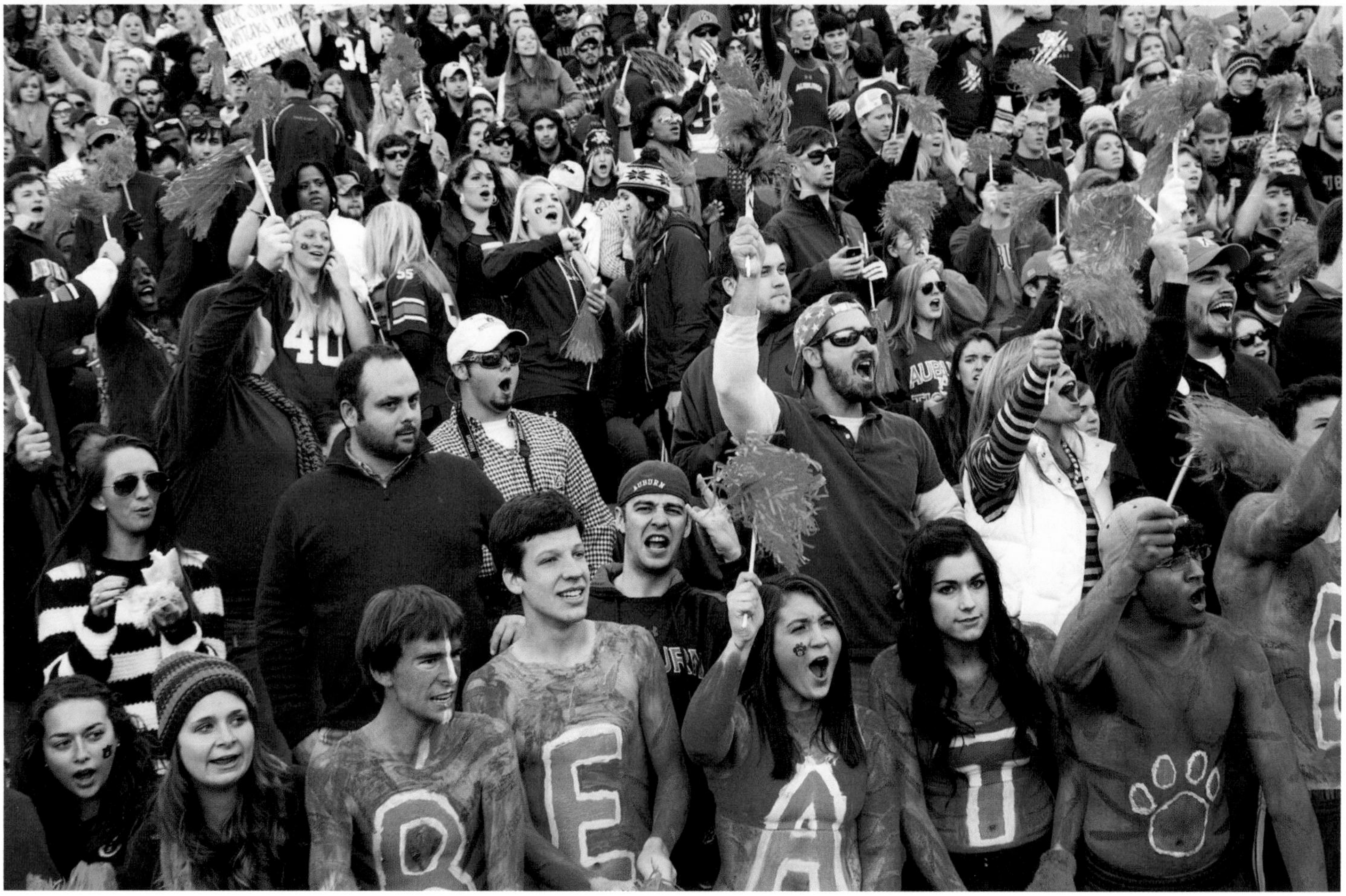

Tigers—is one of the premier events in college football, a spectacular intersection of fierce internecine rivalry and not having much else to care about. There are no Big Four professional sports teams in Alabama, so these two titans share the full attention of most of the sports lovers in the state.

It has been said that the college towns of Auburn and Tuscaloosa, which alternate as the site of the Iron Bowl, come to a standstill during game week. Weddings and funerals make way. Businesses close early. The Iron Bowl is colloquially and DSM-5 insane. Dave Chang and I, being great admirers of sports, eating, and people acting crazy, flew to Auburn to take in the spectacle in person.

During Iron Bowl week, the citizenry is so focused on the game they pay attention to little else. They certainly didn't flinch when two conspicuously oversized Asian men showed up in very not-Asian Auburn the day after Thanksgiving to visit a school neither of us attended to watch a football game neither of us had any stake in. "You guys here for the game? Cool."

We were, by association, fans of Auburn. (Dave's assistant, Kat, went to Auburn, and she arranged the trip to her alma mater.) But our explicit reason for coming was the tailgating—we'd been told that the schools of the Southeastern Conference have refined tailgating to an art. That was enough to sell us. Dave and I graduated from two schools without great football traditions. Mine at Berkeley was stronger than Dave's at Trinity College, but as far as tailgating goes, they might as well have played in the same peewee division.

On our first night in town, with visions of legendary excess dancing in our heads, we crammed ourselves into a frat party that appeared to be extracted directly from an *American Pie* movie. Students were spilling out of a barnish building, perched on windowsills and atop tables and railings, watching four rappers on a raised stage. The musicians played to the grinding, hormonal sea of bodies, at one point unleashing the Auburn version of "Sweet Home Alabama," in which "Fuck you, Alabama / War damn eagle"[1] is wedged in place of the chorus.

But conspicuously absent from the party were the overflowing rivers of booze we thought we'd encounter. I had expected more from my first SEC frat party. I'd imagined keg stands and boat races and cans smashed against foreheads. I thought I'd learn at least one new way to quickly force a twelve-ounce beer into my body.

The beverage drought, along with Dave's realization that he was twice the age of the other party attendees, pointed to our imminent skedaddling. For most of the walk home, Dave held forth about how he would have orchestrated the alcoholic feng shui for such a party. "At least fifty kegs, stationed at the three points of egress...."

On the way home, we stopped at Waffle House. Hash browns at WaHo formed one of two pillars of our daily bread in Alabama. The other was Chik-fil-A.

The part of me that cares about other humans recoils a bit at the idea of eating at a restaurant chain with politics that are openly and aggressively discriminatory. But Dave has a way of sweeping you up in hyperbolic endorsement when he wants you to make him feel better about doing something he knows is wrong too: "You won't care about civil rights when you got that biscuit in your hands." So we went to Chik-fil-A—numerous times. If you haven't had one, the namesake fillet is salty and a little bit sweet, the breading not aggressively crunchy, the spices passive and savory in a nonspecific way. It is eminently satisfying. The biscuit is the best vehicle for the chicken, but you can also try it on a bun, squishy and soft as it is. The truth is that everything in a Chik-fil-A sandwich, whether bun, biscuit, or bird, is essentially the same texture—a fact that comports well with the company's well-documented homophobic politics. It's a guilty pleasure.

It took me a while to identify what I found unsettling about Auburn.

It wasn't the usual Southern stereotypes that tend to furrow the eyebrows of big-city Yankees traveling below the Mason-Dixon. Sure, the trucks are big and decorated with Stars and Bars—the cars in general all seemed to be modified from their factory default. But that's to be expected. We were likewise unfazed by the fact that we came across only two other Asian people the whole time we were in Alabama. The city of Auburn is a shade over 5 percent Asian. The undergraduate population of the university is 2.1 percent Asian (421 students) and 85.3 percent white (19,799 students).

What's unsettling about Auburn is this: there are no weirdos. Where are all the disaffected stoners, goths, punks, and geeks? Where are all the people we hung out with in college? Dave and I are already

---

1 Auburn's team is the Tigers, but they are just as closely associated with the battle cry "War eagle" (or, at extra-feverish moments, "War damn eagle"). Auburnites greet each other by saying, "War eagle." You can also deploy "War eagle" to thank people for small favors—opening a door, giving you directions. I was half surprised that neither of the premeal prayers I witnessed in Auburn was concluded with "War eagle."

anomalous among our own kin,[2] let alone amid all these happy white kids. During our stay in Auburn, we never met anything short of the most courteous, welcoming people one could hope to encounter, but that made our presence feel all the more incongruous. In addition to kind of being weirdos, we're also kind of assholes.

Chief among the not-assholes were the Burketts, a family of peanut farmers from Donalsonville, Georgia, who have a daughter who's a Tigerette (a sort of cheerleader–student recruiter hybrid). They, along with the Carters—more peanut people from Georgia, but not *the* peanut Carters of Georgia—invited us to a tailgate at their RV, stationed a hundred yards from Tiger Walk, where the players file in from their buses to the stadium to the thrill of thousands of gathered fans. (The football team spends the night before each home game in an out-of-town hotel to shield them from distractions.)

The spread comprised all the sustenance a Tigerette requires to smile and cheer and generally be ebullient about all things Auburn. Tigerettes, it would appear, are predominantly powered by sugar. There were pancakes and pecan French toast, mayhaw jelly, a honey-baked ham, and "crack dip," a cloying mortar of cream cheese, brown sugar,

and crumbled Heath bars. Plus Oreo pops, which are sort of like Oreo meatballs. To make them, you mix ground-up cookies with cream cheese, form the mixture into balls, and then dip the balls in melted chocolate. They become "pops" if you impale them with sticks.

My sweet tooth is small and undeveloped, so I stuck to inspecting the savory offerings: sausage, cheese, and egg strata; sausage balls; smoked hot links; shrimp and grits; cheese wafers. Dave, I think, shares my general aversion to sweets. He took a bite of an Oreo pop that was given to him, and then surreptitiously stuffed it in my hand as if I were a dog under the table. Before I could object, I saw the gaze of our hosts falling on us, so I jammed the pop in my mouth along with another half-eaten one I'd already been stashing. I felt a tingle in my kidneys that I was sure meant Dave had just pushed me over the threshold into diabetes.

At another tailgate situated at a site on campus reserved for high-profile tailgaters, we spotted Pat Dye and spoke with Yann Cowart. Dye is the legendary coach after whom Auburn's field has been named since 2005. Cowart played for Dye as the center in front of Bo Jackson, and he cooked the ribs for the tailgate. I talked rib cookery with Cowart, who said the key to success was copious quantities of garlic powder and salt: "When you think you had enough, double it." I thought that was charming even if the ribs were unspectacular, so I pressed for more recipes.

A guy named Steve told me about his tomato grits. I had never heard of tomato grits, and thought perhaps I could break the story on them. "You start with quick-cooking grits, and boil them with milk and water. Then take a big number-ten can of Ro-Tel diced tomatoes, and cook

them with Kraft garlic cheese..." I jotted furiously, and Steve saw me struggling to keep up. "I'll tell you what. The easiest thing for you to do is go to *foodnetwork.com* and search for 'Paula Deen Tomato Grits.'"

There were rumblings from the early planning stages of the trip, all the way

---

2 Size is the most obvious anomaly. The apocryphal tale of Dave's relative largeness is that when he was young, he wanted desperately to be bigger than his brothers. In an impressive show of willpower, he drank a gallon of milk every day for something like five years, until he had blown past his siblings into the ninety-ninth percentile of Korean boys in Virginia. He says the milk was the cheap stuff—as in not from organically raised and pastured cows—and he attributes his success to bovine growth hormone. As for me, my parents owned ice cream stores for the first ten years of my life. I am much larger than my own brother, who did not spend countless hours skulking around the back room of Baskin-Robbins, gobbling down sundaes. I suppose I'm also a product of BGH.

until kickoff, that we'd get to meet Bo Jackson, Auburn's favorite alum and perhaps the most physically gifted athlete of all time. Standing on the sidelines before the game, our handler/host Wendy said that Bo might come out of the tunnel for a chat, but if he decided not to, our meeting just wasn't going to happen. Sort of like Punxsutawney Phil on Groundhog Day. It seemed to me to be a mistake to give Bo the choice of whether or not to meet us; I was confused why he'd want to. But I was feeling lucky that day, and I told our photographer Gabriele as much.

Part of what makes sports worth watching and why it's seen as a crime to leave the stadium early is that at any given game, there's a chance you'll witness something incredible: a physics-defying play, a miracle comeback, a last-second winner, an unbreakable record broken. But the odds are not in your favor. In reality, most games unfold as predicted—that's why sports gambling and analyzing sports statistics are such big-money endeavors.

We had more or less struck out with the tailgates. I feel guilty saying it, as our hosts were supremely generous. The food was plentiful and quaintly homemade, but nothing had been especially insane. I don't know exactly what I'd had in mind. Some blend of Memphis in May and Oktoberfest, I suppose—a cloud of smoke hanging in the air above hundreds of roasting pigs, girls flashing, beer slicking the asphalt, drunks fighting. I assumed the tailgates would be rowdier, that I'd see more Alabama fans being harassed. In the student union, a long line of Tigers stood politely waiting for the restroom with a few Tide fans. I wanted them to block those bozos from peeing! But these weren't the hooligans of *Among the Thugs*. They were nice people not overdoing it too much before the game. Hell, I would've settled for a redneck calling me a racist epithet. At least it would've been a story.

As kickoff approached, I was nervous about how uneventful things had been so far, and perhaps that anxiety fueled my faith that we'd see something special on the field. Anyway, we never met Bo. But we did pose for photos with Nova, the actual war eagle that hypostatizes Auburn's rebel yell.

The Iron Bowl is always significant to Alabamians, but the buildup to this past November's encounter was amplified to a national frenzy because both teams were in the hunt for the national championship. Alabama is almost always in that discussion, but the Tigers were a surprise—a shock, really. Last season they were 3-9, and nobody expected them to be legitimate contenders. But here they were, number four in the country, and likely destined for the big dance

if they could eke out a win against their bitterest rival.

If you have even a passing interest in football and you haven't seen this game, it really is worth watching in its entirety. Those who saw it will be able to recall the details from memory for at least the next five years, as I will for you now. We'll jump in about three minutes into the fourth quarter. A 99-yard Alabama touchdown knocks the wind out of the Auburn crowd. A roar of cheers rings out from the northeast corner of the stadium, where the visiting fans are corralled, but otherwise it's eerily quiet. Time bleeds excruciatingly from the clock until finally Auburn ties the game with forty-one seconds remaining. Alabama receives the ensuing kickoff, and manages to move the ball 33 yards on three plays. There's a moment of relief when everyone thinks that time has run out with the score tied. We'll win it in overtime. But Alabama's veteran coach Nick Saban appeals to the officials to check the replays, he's pretty sure his guy was pushed out of bounds with one second left on the clock. The refs confer and decide to award Saban his one second and a chance for a game-winning field goal. This is it, we Auburn fans think. This is how it ends—that crafty wolf Saban is going to steal it. The teams line up for the try, and Auburn's coach Gus Malzahn takes a time-out to ice the kicker. I'll take this post hoc time-out to mention that all of this is taking place two weeks after what Auburn fans thought would be the most jaw-dropping, jumping-up-and-down-on-the-couch moment they'd experience this season and possibly their whole lives: a 73-yard, game-winning Hail Mary that was deflected by two colliding defenders, then juggled

for what seemed like an eternity before ultimately being brought in and taken to the house by speedy wideout Ricardo Louis. Back at the Iron Bowl, the kick is true but short. Cornerback Chris Davis is waiting at the back of the end zone for this very possibility. The ball is catchable and technically returnable, so he cradles it under his right arm, and takes seven or eight strides to the right before cutting back left. One or two Crimson Tide players manage swipes that make fleeting contact with Davis as he flies down the sideline. It takes the crowd until Davis is at the 30 to realize what's happening—it's not often one sees a field goal attempt run out of the end zone—and it's not until he's at midfield that we entertain the possibility that maybe he's going to make it all the way. Somebody has grasped onto my shoulders, and I can't tell if I'm jumping up and down or being bounced like a baby in this person's arms. And then Davis is gone, 109 yards for the win. And suddenly we are all infants, screaming and crying and bouncing.

Before the game, Dave had asked the usually bubbly Wendy if we could storm the field when Auburn won, and she had replied soberly, "No, we don't do that." But we did—there was no stopping us, along with most of the Auburn-favoring crowd. Once you're on the field, there's really not much to do but will yourself into absorbing as much of the moment as you can. I plucked a few blades of grass from the 50-yard line and put them in the folds of my hat.

Gabriele is Italian and finds the rules of American football mystifying. Later, as we filed out of the stadium, he asked, "So what we saw tonight, does this happen often?"

Not really, Gabri. It happened exactly one time, just now.

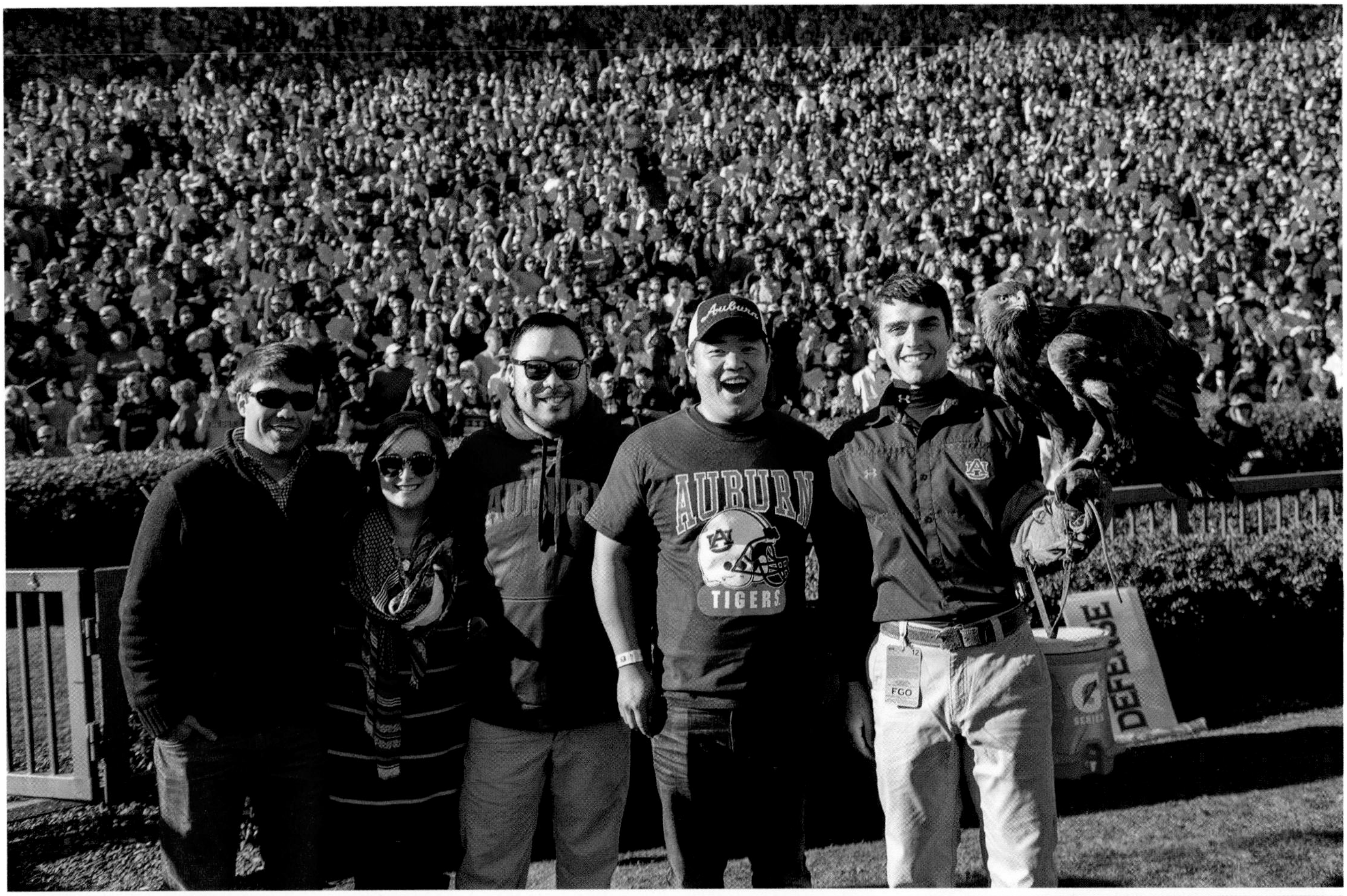
Auburn
AUBURN
TIGERS
DEFENSE
FGO

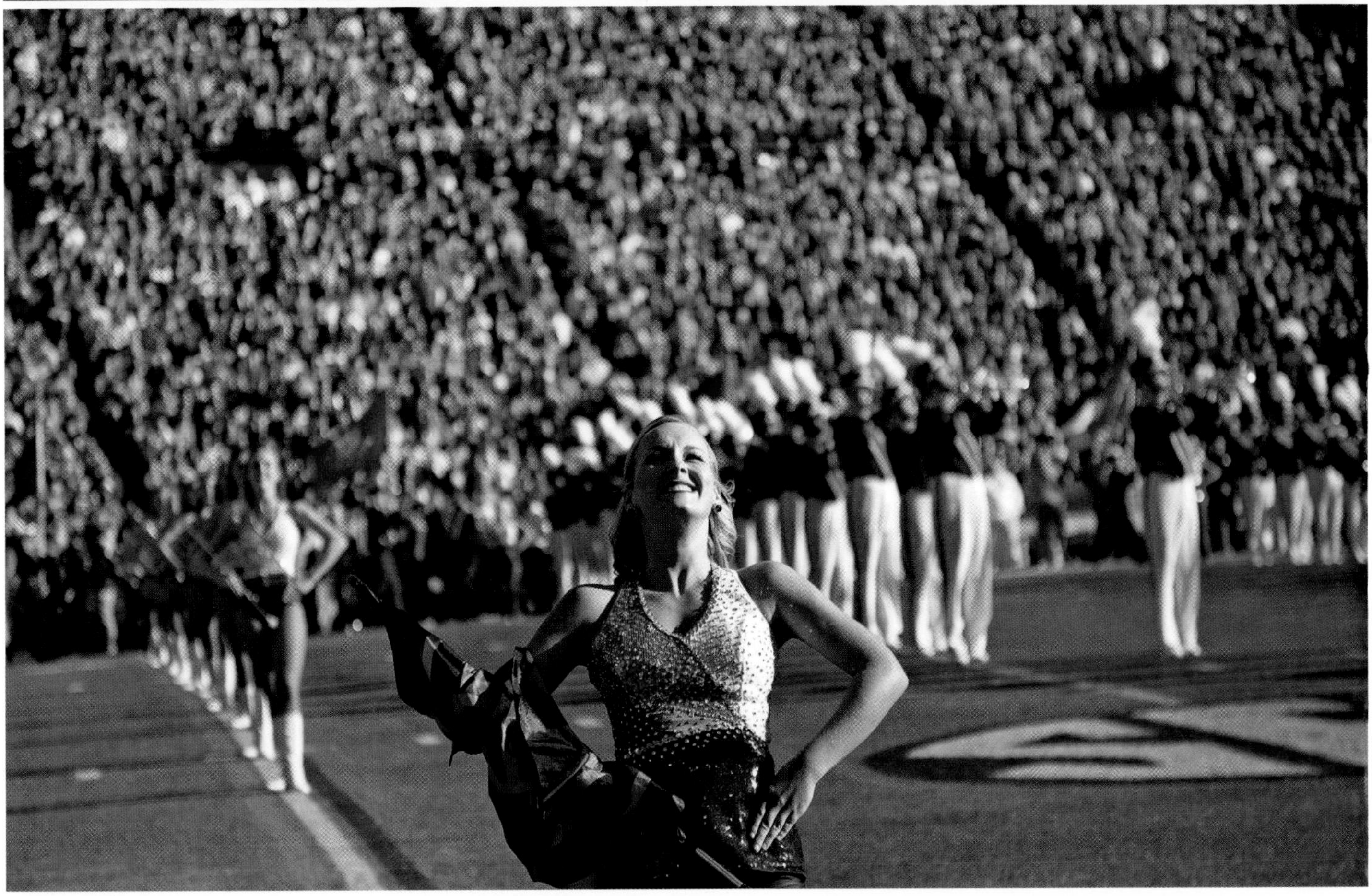

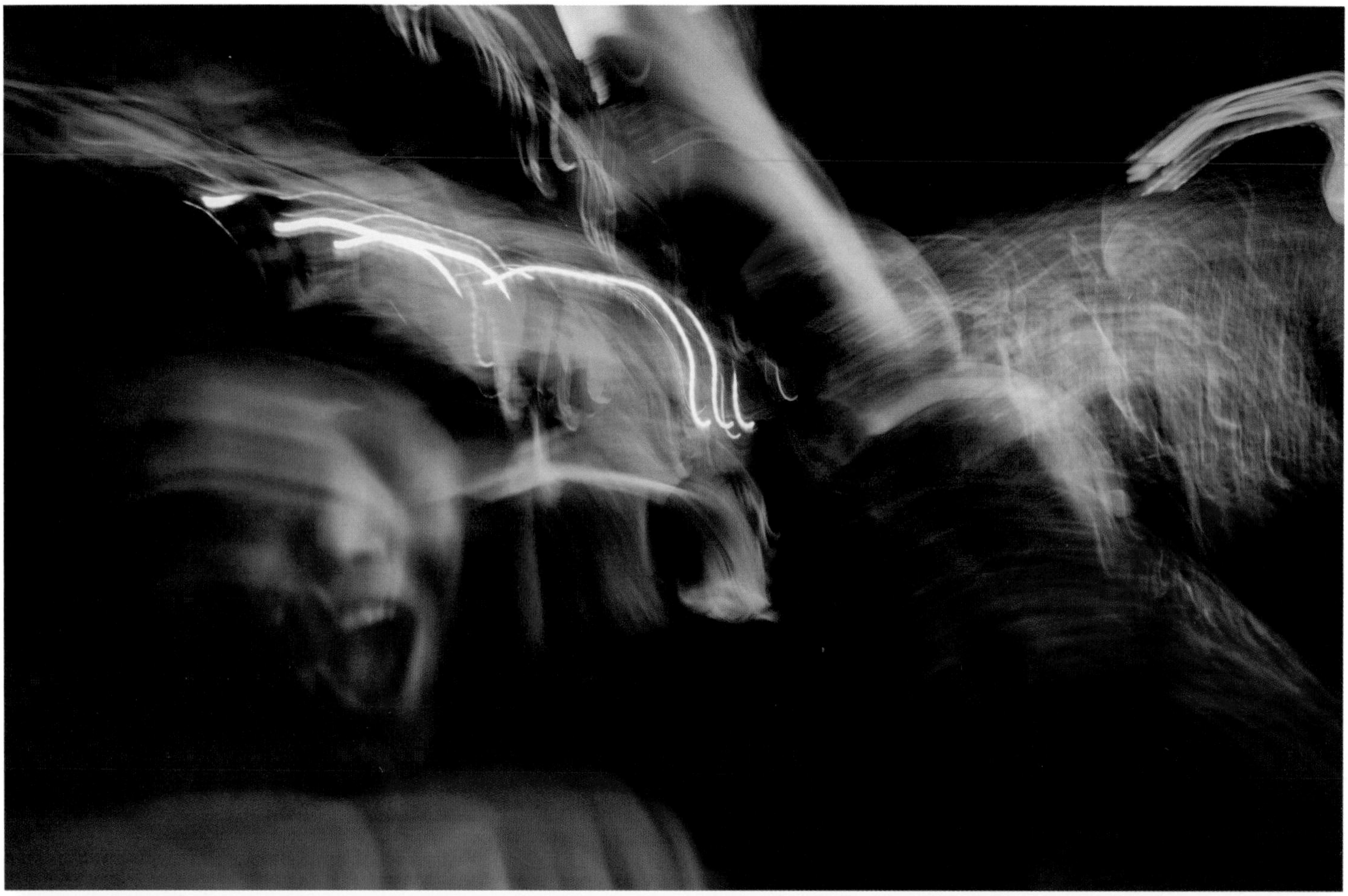

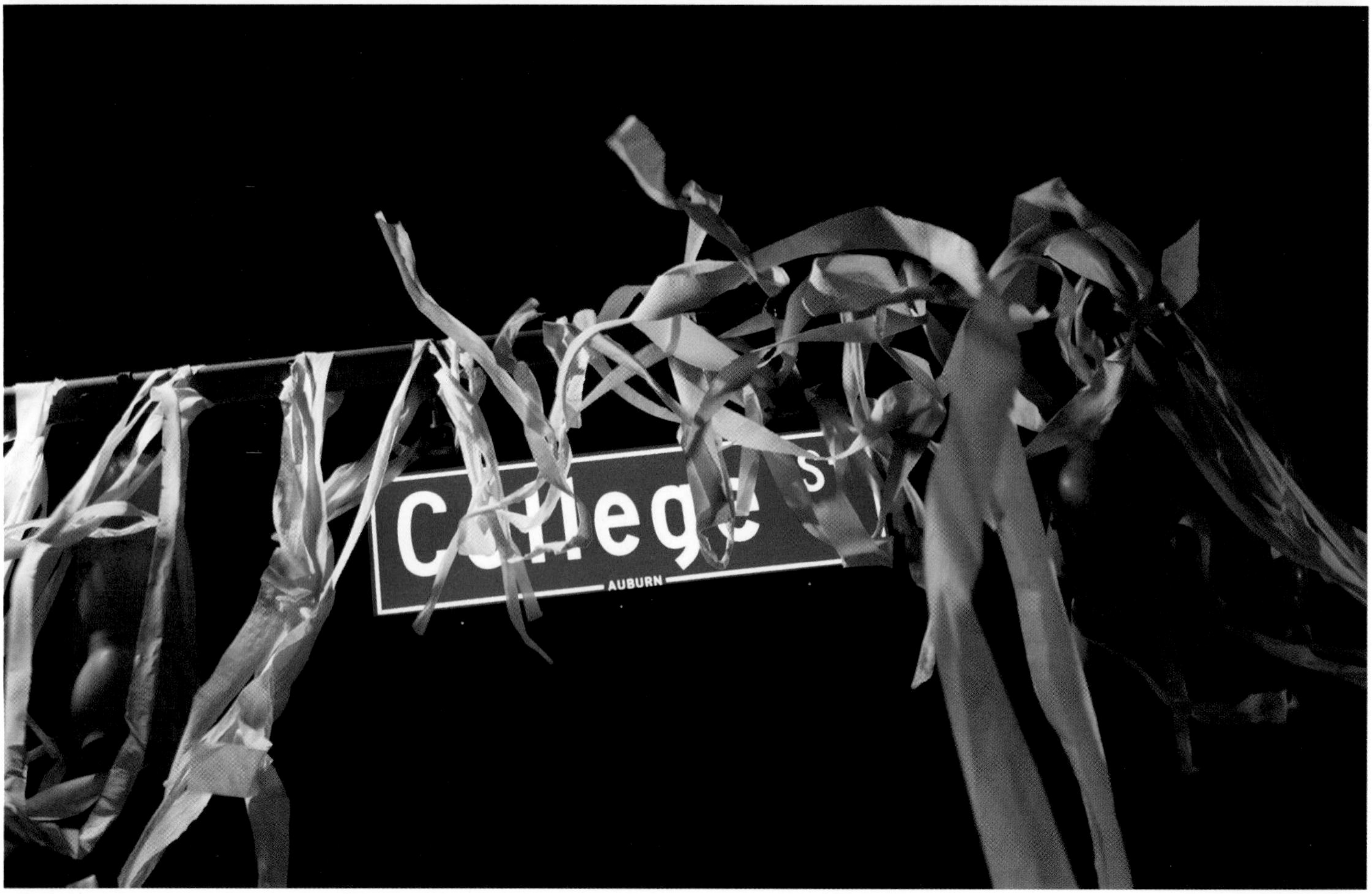
AUBURN

We thought for sure that the entire town would burn to the ground. We had front-row seats for the aftermath of the biggest victory in Auburn history, and if the campus had been swept off the earth in a tidal surge of ecstasy, we would happily have let ourselves be carried away with it. So we walked to Toomer's Corner, where, until recently, everything good at Auburn was celebrated by veiling a pair of ancient oak trees with thousands of rolls of toilet paper. An unhinged Alabama fan put an end to that tradition, though, by dosing the trees with enough herbicide to kill a forest, and the oaks were felled last April. But the fans still gather, undeterred, to heave rolls of two-ply over everything in sight.

From there, we considered heading to the hayfields, the epicenter of Auburn tailgating. We'd visited earlier in the day, and gawked at the thousands of RVs that had been parked bumper to bumper for as long as a week ahead of the game. The fields have the look of an internally displaced persons' camp but the sort of meticulous zeal of a comic-book convention. If we wanted to see insane, for sure that's where it'd be.

Ultimately we decided that we should see what the kids were up to. We stopped in to a frat house where the boys were somehow celebrating without booze. We quickly moved on. Kat's brother was still an undergrad living in a frat-ish house near campus—perfect. They were poor students, though, so they probably wouldn't have much beer either. No problem—we stopped in at a liquor store and bought 120 cans from a very sour shopgirl who'd been rooting for Alabama.

We arrived at the house, hoisting the beer over our heads, thinking we'd be received like returning conquerors. But the denizens of the house were unmoved. A kid muttered, "Holy crap" from his supine position on an air mattress on the floor, but otherwise nobody deigned to join us. Kat and I played the most sullen game of beer pong while Dave checked his e-mail. We left the beer for the house and headed for Chik-fil-A.

I've had some time to consider how little drinking we encountered in Auburn, and I still haven't figured it out. Were we just unwelcome narcs? Were kegs being rolled into closets and bottles emptied into toilets the moment someone caught wind that the old fogies were on their way? The day after the game, Dave and I questioned a bartender at the worst chicken-wing shop in America. He pointed to the Southern Baptists. (In a survey conducted by the Princeton Review, Auburn had emerged as the most conservative student body in America.) "Drinking is a sin," the bartender said. "People drink, but they don't flaunt it."

Later on the night of the Iron Bowl, Gabri and I stopped by the hayfields to see if we could catch some drinkers in the act. But aside from a few scattered night-cappers huddled around fires, the place was quiet. Everyone was ensconced in their RVs or else partying in secret, somewhere we couldn't find.

Kat had scored our tickets and access to the game through a friend whose father was a big donor to Auburn athletics. We couldn't leave town without paying a visit to our benefactor, so after the failed party and sandwiches at Chik-fil-A we hitched a ride from Kat's friend's dad to his house for a late-night snack. It was two days after Thanksgiving, so on the menu were turkey-day leftovers, which I was happy to find, as I'd missed out on my own leftovers to be in Auburn. Kat's friend described one dish as his "not-Chinese grandmother's Chinese chicken salad." I can never resist Chinese chicken salad, no matter how not-Chinese it is.

We sat together in yet another sleepy living room, and I surveyed my placid surroundings. Everyone was so happy to have won. They were tired and hoarse from screaming, but still buzzing. And I realized that there's no single team or endeavor that my entire collective family and friends get behind. I don't think I share a common rooting interest with more than two people. In fact, I generally get more pleasure from my friends' teams losing than from mine winning. Maybe that's why we drink so much beer when we watch sports. One of us is going to lose, so the only way for us all to be happy is to be drunk together.

We rewatched the "Kick Six" a few times from the DVR, and Dave kept whispering to me that this man was very important and very wealthy, and could I eat with a fork and not my fingers for fuck's sake? Show some respect. He was the reason we had tickets to the best game of college football we'd ever see. The seats we had were thanks to his season tickets. I couldn't help but think that the home we were in was not as lavish or gigantic as I'd imagined from a big-time Auburn booster. There were, what, four bedrooms? That was barely enough for his family of six.

Kat's friend's dad drove us home. On the way, I asked, "So how long have you been living in Auburn?" trying to get a sense of our bighearted sponsor. He responded matter-of-factly, "Oh, I don't live here. This is a house we keep for game days."

Insane. **LP**

USiNG THE SQUiRREL GOD GiVES YOU

by
**Padgett
Powell**

Sometimes I have to stop in a grocery store——I like a country IGA——and get me the small handsome bottle of Goya extra-virgin olive oil, I don't know why. Sometimes I have to go out in the yard and shoot the squirrels, I know why. Once a squirrel poked his face out of the hole he'd eaten in my Rubbermaid garbage-can lid to get the chicken feed inside the garbage can, before Wal-Mart ruined Rubbermaid——don't watch the *Frontline* on that or you will be *incensed*——and I at last deployed some of the no-pain-no-gain martial-arts skills I have sweated into myself, tearing the medial meniscus in my knee and rupturing the radial sagittal band on my right hand's middle knuckle and so forth, and popped the squirrel back into the can with a hammer fist. I then induced him to leave the

hole and took aim with my pistol loaded with .22-long rat-shot shells, but he froze, with genius, behind my chicken-waterer, a $150 industrial appliance that a squirrel knows a man is reluctant to shoot through. No matter how bad the man wants to shoot the son of a bitch eating his irreplaceable Rubbermaid feed bins and his feed, the son of a bitch eating the cans and the feed knows the man won't shoot. He calculates his next move, and when he makes it, the man will humiliate himself one way or another, shooting the waterer after all, or shooting the roof of the coop, or shooting his own toe, or hand, or face, or dog. He will not shoot the squirrel.

His humiliation will grow along these lines until he supplements the .22 with the 28-gauge Ruger shotgun with the handsome slender English stock, a gun as elegant as

Illustration by Hannah K. Lee

an egret, and begins, ever so incrementally, to reduce the humiliation by pushing the squirrel through the one-way membrane unto Death.

Optional: Sharpen you a basketball-inflating needle and insert it into your squirrel once he's on the Other Side and inflate him to the size of a cane toad, robbing him of dignity. But let's be clear about something: this is a majestic creature, superior to your athleticism and to your wits on your feet, and if you make him look like a toad and a little blood spittles out of his orifices when you apply the air, that is really no derogation or detraction from the glory of this animal at all, so now proceed.

Not optional: Squirrel fur is perfumy and sheddy. A good small hunting knife, such as those you might get from Wayne Hendrix in Allendale, South Carolina, or Bob Dozier in Springdale, Arkansas, is contraindicated. Get you some good scissors and insert a sharp tip into the skin—if you have cane-toaded the squirrel the skin will be loosened—at where the waist would be were the squirrel wearing a shirt and pants, and cut this waist around him, or her (look later for fetuses), and then with good old-fashioned slip-joint pliers get a grip on the shirt and a grip on the pants and remove them just as you would the shirt and pants from a tiny child. Skinning is done. I have saved you a lot of homespun, down-home old-boy perorating, and I have spared you the quaint unworkable instructions in the otherwise eminently sane and dependable *Joy of Cooking*, complete with its Gorey-like cartoon of boot on squirrel tail on the ground. Tail on ground don't work in the hands of the neophyte. Shirt and pants do. This will take thirty seconds, though budget considerably more time in cleaning the corpse, because, while the cleaning proper is quick, you may slip up and

start to marvel at things that will throw you into the God versus Darwin versus neither debate if you are prone to it, such as the fetuses, or the huge and finely veined cloisonné testicles that look like a big, pretty delicious-looking bean or nutmeg in cross-section, or the impossible deltoid muscle extending from navel to shoulder that accounts for this animal's unequaled and humiliating vertical-climbing acceleration and power. A squirrel is a *man*! It is a tiny robust *bear*! Extract the little musk or scent glands allegedly in the small of the back and under this deltoid muscle in the armpit (where it is hard to locate a defined gland but there is discolored-fat-looking stuff, get it out). Now we ready.

Your naked tiny child will look like a skinned puppy, which will give you pause, or not. Puppies are probably delicious. These *faux* puppies certainly are. I spare us the tacky calling of them "tree rats," et cetera. Grant us relief. Cut into anatomical units that make sense and can be browned evenly (if you can accept uneven browning, or want to use a lot of oil, leave the puppy whole), season with salt and pepper, brown them up. If you have been hunting diligently and have a lot of squirrel in the freezer, I find that "sixteen squirrel" has a kind of natural-law feel to it, like a peck or a furlough or a pound.

Put them aside, on a plate where you can look at them and consider eating them in this state, very tenable if you have taken them past light browning and if you can do tough (not that tough, try them). Into the pot put copious onion and parsley. (I like prodigious parsley, it is rendered invisible anyway.) Put the squirrel back in, add some stock to braising level, cover this dish, ought to be a Dutch-oveny kind of unit, put in oven under 300 for two hours or so. Go outside in the yard with or

without gun and get any chanterelles might be out there, or some other mushrooms won't kill you, put them in with the squirrel at end.

Cook some rice. I hope you have a proper steamer but almost certainly you do not. Edwin Poulnot III in Charleston, who used to sell them to me as the last gasp of Kerrison's Department Store, has stopped answering his phone and I am afraid may have passed on. Peter Patout of New Orleans, whose famous Campeche chair I am trying to write a piece on, when I shamed him for making such a huge to-do about rice-eating in Louisiana without his having a proper steamer, found some nice steel ones at the Crystal Rice Plantation of Crowley, Louisiana, called the Blue Rose Stainless Rice Cooker. Lay these squirrel that have been responsible for so much humiliation and God's or Darwin's or neither's glory over some of the rice with mushrooms you have found or not and see if they are not really good.

Let's say you do not like the idea of whole pieces of rodent on rice: okay, fair enough. Bone the braised squirrels and put the meat into a Brunswick stew, such as James Villas's in his *Stews, Bogs, and Burgoos*; it's an aggressive recipe with bacon and a ham hock and okra in it. Or use the squirrel in a gumbo—I'd go with Paul Prudhomme on the gumbo because Villas has the inane idea that a gumbo roux should never be dark; use the squirrel for the chicken in Prudhomme's chicken-and-andouille gumbo, and make that roux as dark as Hershey's syrup. In either the stew or the gumbo use the squirrel-braising liquid, which will be nuclear heavy, as stock. I sometimes never open my Goya oil bottles, so handsome and well shaped, little golden statues, but it's always good to have some fresh oil on standby, just in case, as the Russians say. ∎

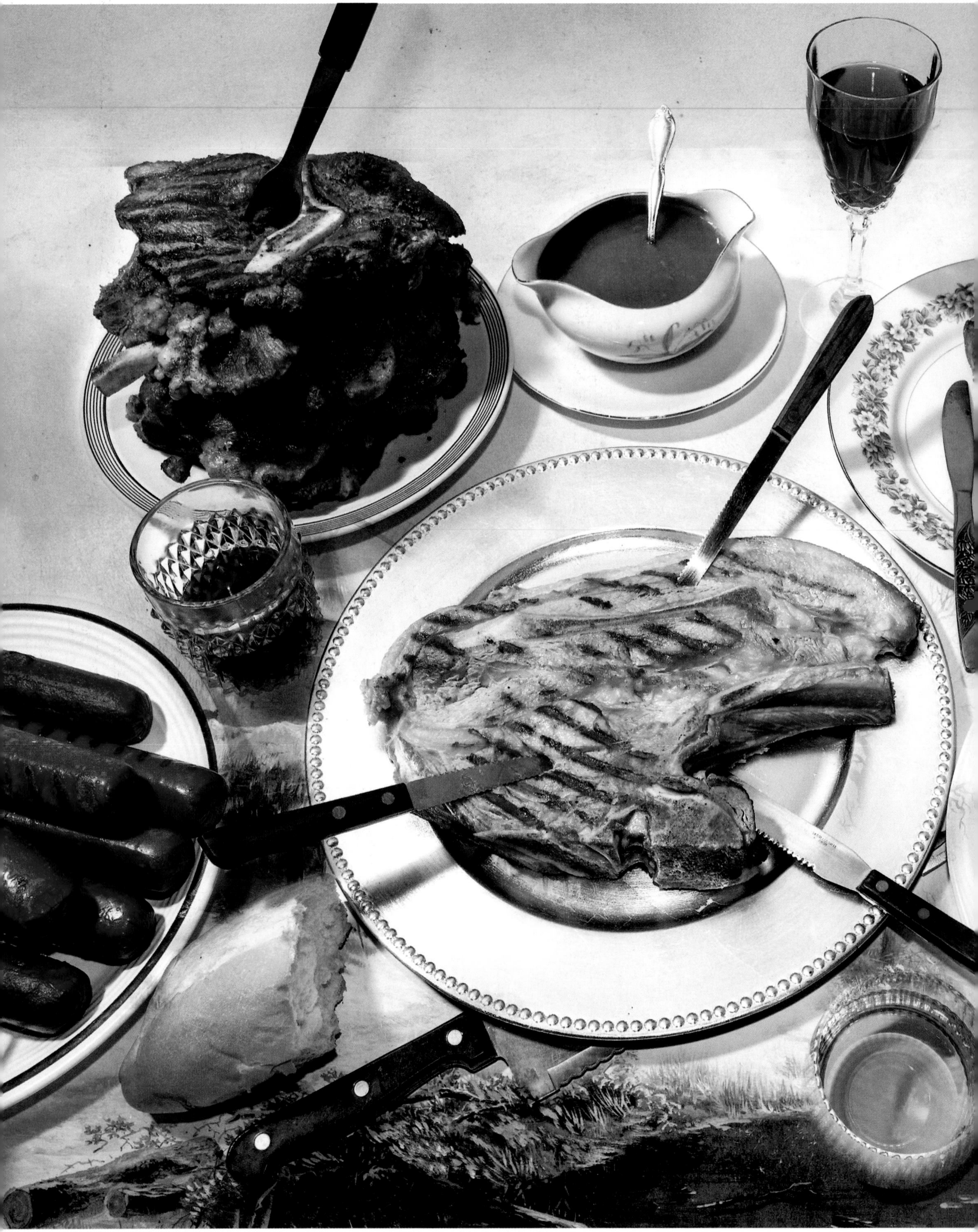

The Order of Good Cheer, OR:

ANOTHER WORLD

by **Adam Leith Gollner**

Photographs by
Meiko Takechi Arquillos

On a Sunday morning last December, much of my atomized nuclear family assembled for a Christmas celebration a few weeks before the actual feast day; we mark occasions not based on calendrical orthodoxy, but around one another's schedules. My mom greeted us with hot farls of Irish soda bread and a mint-flecked salad of chopped plums, grapes, and blueberries in sweetened lime juice. The main dish was her recent breakfast specialty: panettone French toast with thick-cut bacon from the Boucherie de Tours, suspended in lagoons of maple syrup.

My brothers and I complained about the heaviness of the meal as we laid waste to the spread.

"It's light," my mom protested.

"It's pretty decadent," we assured her.

"I mean the panettone's light to begin with," she clarified. "It's airy! But I guess you're right: once you add the eggs and the cream and the butter and you fry it up..."

"And drench it in syrup," I said, doing just that.

This got us talking about Quebec's tradition of sugaring off, and the specific dishes made during the *temps des sucres*, when fresh sap is gathered from maple groves. Each winter, "sugar shacks" (*cabanes à sucres*) serve up bottomless portions of fat-packed sausages, lardy baked beans, and *oreilles de crisse* (deep-fried skin-on curlicues of salt pork, known here as "Christ's ears" because of their auricular shape and French Canadians' religious weirdness)—all of it hemorrhaging *sirop d'érable*, the mahogany blood of our forests.

Variations on those classic dishes are a large draw at chef Martin Picard's Cabane à Sucre Au Pied de Cochon. The enormous more-than-you-can-eat meals served there, as well as at his original Montreal restaurant, Au Pied de Cochon, are largely responsible for having put Quebecois cuisine on the world map. The other main attraction in town, Joe Beef, is also infamous for offering unwieldy helpings of demented Franco-lardcore fabulations like foie-gras Double Downs, garbage-can-smoked salmon, corn-flake-coated eel nuggets, deep-fried lobster Monte Cristo sandwiches, and omelets cooked in a wheelbarrow.

When chefs here decide they like you, they say, "We're going to kill you." They seem constitutionally incapable of restraining themselves to the merely humongous.

The quality of the food, alas, is as otherworldly and perverted as the quantity, which leaves unwittingly masochistic diners fording their way through never-ending piles of heavily heavenly carnage.

How did we come to be such a gouty outpost? On Christmas day, over yet another multi-course dinner with cousins, aunts, and uncles, my father ascribed Quebec's foodicidal tendencies to "the squirreling instinct." He hypothesized that the Siberian winters drive people to eat continuously and voluminously just to deal with the brutal, barren, Arctic iciness. But, he added, there's more to this situation than a simple layer of blubber; otherwise all Nordic peoples would be famed for their voracity.

The real reasons for our gluttonous inclinations are wrapped up in the past. As this province's license plates state, *Je me souviens*—"I remember."

One spring night a few years ago, I took a close writer friend and his new girlfriend to eat at Joe Beef. They were in Montreal for a few days together and wanted to go somewhere special on their first night here. We started with a platter of oysters, snow crab, Matane shrimp, raw clams, and other sweet-fleshed springtime shellfish. Umpteen courses later, my friend turned to me and said, "I think this is the happiest I've ever been in my whole life."

He isn't the first out-of-towner to react that way. Montreal has a long tradition of offering dining experiences so memorably excessive visitors can't even compare them to anything else. "Upon the whole," wrote Lord Dalhousie of England, in a diary entry from 1824, "I don't recollect having ever spent a more pleasant or more interesting day than that with the Beaver Club."

The Beaver Club was a gentleman's dining club and social association for the top fur-trading barons of Montreal. The organization formed in 1785 and "it entertained in a brilliant, expensive, and noisy manner." Beaver Club meals traditionally began when a flaming boar head was carried in on a red velvet cushion with lit camphor in its gaping maw. Eye-witness descriptions of what would transpire next include: "heavy debauch" "feats of eating," "wild carousel," and "extravagance and hilarious mirth."

Celebrants kicked things off with a clubby cocktail such as an Athol Brose (whiskey mixed with Scottish oatmeal-infused water and honey) or some mahogany liqueur (two parts gin, one part molasses, shaken with ice, and served up). The great Canadian cooking authority Jehane Benoit found a traditional, handwritten Beaver Club menu at her grandfather's house in 1914, featuring dishes like braised venison and bread sauce, *Chevreuil des Guides* (a deer stew), venison sausages with wild rice and quail, partridge "du Vieux Trappeur," pickled turnips, "sweet peace" applesauce, and bag pudding (*see recipes, page 54*).

Beaver Clubbers were also, in that era's parlance, "bon vivants of the first water." At one of their gatherings, nineteen members consumed a bottle each of port, alongside twenty-nine bottles of Madeira, fourteen bottles of porter, twelve quarts of ale, as well as brandy, gin, and cigars. That they had copper-plated stomachs isn't that surprising, but for a bunch of Canadian woodsmen they were also intimately versed in the *ars coquandi*. Just as wine nerds today can differentiate between a Volnay and a Pommard (and The Beaver Club's "offerings to Bacchus were neither poor in quality nor limited in amount"), some club members knew the produce of the Great Lakes so well they could identify the provenance of a particular fish simply from its flavor.

When Joe Beef's weirdo-savant co-owner David McMillan went to cooking school, he and all his classmates hoped to one day become chefs at The Beaver Club, which remains to this day an excellent, expensive restaurant inside the Queen Elizabeth Hotel.[1] Although he never ended up working there, McMillan did look to Quebec's storied culinary past—and his own childhood—when opening

Joe Beef, named in honor of a nineteenth-century tavern famous for having a menagerie of animals in the basement.

"When I was a kid, all my neighbors ate and drank too much," McMillan explains. "I spent a lot of time in a cabane à sucre owned by some family friends, the Whittomes. Old man Whittome was a cook in a lumberjack camp. He'd lost his hand in a logging accident, and his arm ended in a claw. A stainless-steel metal claw. He was an excellent cook, and he owned a personal cabane where he made syrup, and we were always there eating sugar-shack food."

The food at Cabane à Sucre Au Pied de Cochon isn't too different from what McMillan ate at chez Whittome. "Martin is doing his take on the meals he had when visiting family-owned sugar shacks as a kid," McMillan says. Both he and Picard are threading their own narratives into this province's half-forgotten history. And although few people realize it, there is an actual context for the level of dissipation they offer. It goes way beyond the Beaver Club, the weather, and the maple cabanes. Yale historian John Mack Faragher notes that New France's hedonistic blowouts of the early 1600s were in "striking contrast to the drab piety of the New England pilgrims." And Canada's archival records are indisputable: even at their most buffoonishly extravagant, Montreal's modern-day lumberjack chefs are still going easy on us compared to their forebears.

Immoderation has always been practiced and celebrated here, whether on the French side, the English side, or by the First Nations who preceded both. Quebec's name is derived from the Algonquin word *Kebec*, meaning "where the river narrows." This is the story of how it became a place where the belly

---

[1] Their mushroom festival, held each autumn, stands out in a city renowned for its festivals—whether it be jazz, lobster, comedy, souvlaki, cars, or poutine.

widens—where, as the Quebecois like to say, *"on s'bour la bedaine."*[2]

"The meals of the French in Canada, if I may permit myself to say so, are habitually overabundant," wrote the explorer Pehr Kalm, in his 1749 account of life in the colony. Kalm was of Swedish-Finnish background; he knew how people usually eat in cold climates—and it wasn't anything like what he saw in Nouvelle France. Meals here regularly stretched to twenty or thirty courses. A section title in the first chapter of Jean-Marie Francœur's history of early Quebec gastronomy (*La Genèse de la Cuisine Québécoise*) is, simply: *L'Excès*. Excess: it's the essential ingredient in our food culture's beginnings.

The first few attempts at a permanent agricultural settlement here failed due to the churlish winters and Europeans' ignorance of scurvy. "I grew up in Cap Rouge, near Quebec City," McMillan explains. "That's where Cartier and the others ate conifer buds when the natives helped them understand that you need vegetables to survive the winter. The Frenchmen were just eating boiled meats and slowly dying. Cedar and pine teas kept them alive."

They learned countless other skills from the Amerindians in those early years. Perhaps the most crucial, in terms of establishing a successful colony, was the ability to eat way too much food. "We passed this winter most joyously, & fared lavishly," recalled Samuel de Champlain of 1606, the first year Nouvelle France became a continually inhabited colony. Among the early settlers were

wealthy aristocrats, magistrates, and clergymen. These fat cats had learned from their predecessors' mistakes, and they weren't setting up here bereft of gourmet provisions. Behind their missionary motives, they intended to create a New World version of rural Champagne, with seigneurs, lords, and bourgeois landowners overseeing *habitants* whose toil would make them even richer than they already were. They came equipped to spread God's word through the wilds (and exploit the resources, *bien sur*) in grand French style.

Around ten years ago, McMillan and Picard were contacted by historians working on a book about how Champlain instituted "the art of living with *gourmandise*." (It was published in 2005, in French only, as *Le Menu Quotidien en Nouvelle France*.) "When Hélène-Andrée Bizier [one of said historians] called me, she goes, 'We've got the register of what Champlain brought over on his boat,'" McMillan recalls. "She was like, 'You might be surprised to know how they were eating.' I found that register more than interesting. I was *shocked*. I thought they had maybe a barrel of apples and some hard tack. I never realized that they came over with *jambon de Mayence* and *six* other kinds of hams, that they had casks of Gascony wine and Spanish wine, that they had olive oil, anchovies, raisins, almonds, oranges... It was insane."

The French *explorateurs* found themselves (and their well-stocked larders) in a hunter's utopia bursting with game animals, wild fowl, and "so great multitudes of certeyne bigge fysshes." Crabs, clams, and sea urchins could all be hoisted out by the barrel-load. They quickly discovered local delights like bear spareribs, elk steaks, and prime beavertails.

The woods on Île d'Orleans, next to Quebec City, were festooned with such a profusion of wild grapes that they named it "The Island of Bacchus." (Not that they were running low on fuel for their bacchanalia: cellars here were so well stocked with clarets, ports, and Rhenish whites that sommeliers were soon

---

2 *On:* "we." *Bourrer:* "to stuff or completely fill by shoving in." *La bedaine:* "the paunch."

employed to organize the bounty.) While hardship and poverty were lethal and grueling for the lower classes, the upper crust in New France "had as much if not more food on their tables than French nobility," notes Jean Soulard, chef and author of *400 Years of Gastronomic History in Quebec City*. "They certainly weren't missing anything in terms of ingredients." They had truffles, spices, turtledove pastries, white-cod sausages, wheels of cheese, rose water, dried fruits and nuts, among countless other delicacies. Historians of the era delighted in listing all the *munitions de bouche* being devoured here in the middle of nowhere.[3]

These inventories took on a particularly well marbled hue around the holidays. *Réveillons*, the traditional Christmas celebration here,

---

[3] Including the stale bread, gluey black lichen, tree bark, melted snow, boiled moccasins, britches, and leathery moose skins that harder-up pioneers resorted to in lean times.

started after Midnight Mass. Feasts began at two in the morning, with endless successions of *tourtières, cipailles, ragoûts de pattes et de boulettes,* roast geese over apples, *hare civets,* chimney-smoked pork legs, eel tarts, and more. The revelry would end after dawn, whenever everyone's relatives finally conked out. "My grandma's réveillons were fucked and fuck off," McMillan explains. "So much food, way too much booze, too many people. French-Canadian celebrations are always like that: people sitting on top of milk crates and things that aren't chairs. You always have a drunk uncle who makes a deer box out of himself and some cousins that start making out." This tradition, still alive in parts of the province, only began to wane when religion lost its hold on the populace during the Quiet Revolution of the '60s.

The influential French chef François Vatel[4] visited Montreal in 1665 and experienced one of these all-night Christmas gatherings, finding the cavalcade of ortolan pâtés, young-pigeon pies, haunches of Bayonne ham, and heaping bowls of candied-lemon rind to be "most impressive."

Quebecois writer Narcisse-Henri-Édouard Faucher de Saint-Maurice (1844–1897) described old Christmas réveillons as being straight out of "Gargantua's dreams." It's an important designation. Nouvelle France itself has always been Gargantuan at its center, argues the historian Jean-Marie Francœur, who says that Rabelais' spirit can still be found "everywhere in our culture." (McMillan and Picard aren't the only ones emblematic of this.)

The heart of Rabelais' oeuvre is clogged with descriptions of food: his *Pantagruel* told of a country whose inhabitants, the Gastrolators, worship their stomachs as their god—and he provided page after page of descriptions of the culinary offerings they made. That vision seems to have taken root in New France—a land whose very discovery influenced Rabelais' writings. He met Jacques Cartier in the 1540s and transposed a number of passages from Cartier's *Voyages* into his own works, which were widely read by settlers.

Quebecois French today is a language that has more in common with Rabelaisian French than it does with contemporary Parisian French. It's filled with still-utilized archaisms—something awesome is *écœurant* (nauseating); a car is *un char* (a chariot); the look of love is *avoir les yeux dans la graisse de binnes* (to have one's eyes in the fat of beans); something that isn't bad is *mieux qu'une pipe d'un veau* (better than a blowie from a calf); the worst swear word is *tabarnak* (tabernacle, the small cupboard where consecrated hosts are kept)—that are the Francophone equivalent of using Shakespearian slang today. A key Quebecism is the term *sarf* (also spelled *zarf,* or *safre*), which refers to someone with an insatiable appetite. It pairs with another Rabelaisian expression, *escornifleur,* which translates to a "greedy feeder, or smell-feast; one that carries tales, jests, or news from house to house, thereby to get victuals."

Montreal has always been a sarfing paradise. "Few places are so advanced in all the luxuries and comforts of high civilization as Montreal," commented the British physician John Jeremiah Bigsby, in his 1850 book *The Shoe and the Canoe.* Add to those culinary

---

4 Vatel, the inventor of Chantilly cream, later killed himself by driving his sword through his own heart when an order of seafood failed to be delivered in time for a banquet.

Cooking with the
BEAVER CLUB

These recipes were written by the Quebecois culinary authority Jehane Benoît (1904-1987) who based them on a Beaver Club menu she found on a parchment in her grandfather's attic in 1914. I, in turn, found these in the basement stacks of McGill University's library in a long out-of-print magazine called *Canadian Collector.* —**ADAM LEITH GOLLNER**

Braised Venison in Bread Sauce

"It is still possible to have venison, and it is a beautiful meat. If venison is unsustainable, substitute marinated boned leg of pork."

1. Wipe the meat with a cloth dipped in red wine vinegar.

2. Cut the thinly sliced salt pork into strips and spread on top of the boned meat. Roll the meat tightly and tie with butcher's twine.

3. Blend together the flour, salt, pepper, marjoram (or oregano) and spread over the meat.

4. Melt the diced salt pork in a heavy cast-iron pan; brown the roast in the fat over medium heat.

5. Add the red wine, orange juice, and grated apples. Stir, cover, and cook over medium-low heat for 2 to 3 hours, depending on the tenderness of the meat. Baste and turn 3 or 4 times during the cooking period.

6. Strain the gravy and serve separately.

> **INGREDIENTS**
>
> **4 to 6 lbs** boned deer loin or leg
> **+** red wine vinegar
> **¼ lb** fatty salt pork, thinly sliced
> **¼ C** flour
> **1 t** salt
> **½ t** pepper
> **1 t** marjoram (wild oregano was used)
> **½ C** all-fat salt pork, diced
> **¼ C** red wine
> **¼ C** orange juice
> **2** large unpeeled apples, grated

luxuries the fact that Quebecers (like the British) used to have pitiable dental care. In Bigsby's time, almost everyone here lost their teeth by the age of thirty. Think about it: those with means would dine hard and fast while they still had chewing capacity. (After that, they'd predominantly eat pea soup, a meal so widely consumed amongst French Canadians that the Anglos called them, pejoratively, "pissous.")

All of which is fine, but to properly understand this place's culinary culture requires examining the traditions of those whose land the French invaders claimed under the auspices of their one and only God. The Hurons, Iroquois, Algonquins, Cree, and other tribes here all overate ritualistically, and their behavior was keenly noted by settlers—for a Quebecer is a European who learned how to survive in the wilderness by emulating (and, ultimately, decimating) the First Nations. There's widespread denial among the French majority here about their "Indian" roots. They like to see themselves as *pure-laine*—untainted thoroughbreds—rather than cherishing their cross-pollinated past and present. The truth is, miscegenation made Quebec.

As wide-eyed arrivals, the French were initiated into the rites of smoking tobacco and drinking the blood of caribou (the Mi'kmaq name for reindeer). They shot the rapids in canoes and stumbled through the tundra in snowshoes. They learned to eat things like *sagamité*, a proto-polenta dish, and *rubaboo*, a maize-and-bean porridge larded with bear fat or *pemmican*, a kind of berry-infused venison jerky. They discovered the taste of sunchokes, chipmunks, pumpkins, cranberries, maple sap, and corn—still called *blé d'Inde*, or Indian wheat—in Quebec. But most of all, they came to realize that feasting is a way of life here.

The European newcomers closely observed the consumption patterns and dietary habits of the First Nations from the start. It was clearly possible not just to make do here, but also to do so very well. The easiest half of the year was from May to October. During those months, the natives fished cod, oysters, shellfish, sturgeon, and other seafood from their well-supplied, pristine waterways. Wild strawberries, raspberries, blueberries, and other small fruits blanketed the open spaces, as did a cornucopia of novel root vegetables, squash, grains, and legumes. Come autumn, the aboriginals ate birds of passage such as woodcocks, snipes, and long-tailed partridges. As it grew colder, they'd head upstream, to the eel-spawning grounds. With winter descending, they hunted venison. They'd then go ice fishing for *ponamo* (now called tomcod, or frost fish) and baby turtles. "Never had Solomon his mansion better regulated and provided with food, than are these homes and their landlords," concluded Father Pierre Biard in *The Jesuit Relations* of 1616, a report on happenings in the colony.

So well provided-for were Canada's indigenous peoples that they regularly held banquets described by witnesses as being "on a scale of extravagant profusion." There were mystical and religious components to their festal gatherings, as well as medical aspects. They believed that fist-sized demons of illness inhabited the bodies of the sick, and that overeating forced the djinn-like ailments out of them. "In some cases, the imagined efficacy of the feast was proportioned to the rapidity with which the viands were dispatched," wrote the nineteenth-century Massachusetts historian Frances

Bread Sauce

"Bread sauce has long graced the English table. Well done, it is the best of sauces with game, and surely it was popular at the many Beaver Club dinners."

1. In saucepan, bring milk and the onion, stuck with the cloves, to boil over low heat. Simmer over low heat for 10 minutes.

2. Add the bread cubes and stir well. Simmer over low heat 10 minutes, stirring once or twice.

3. Remove onion. Stir mixture.

4. When ready to serve, add butter, cream, salt and pepper. Beat with the spoon over low heat until creamy. Serve.

INGREDIENTS
1 C milk
2 whole cloves
1 small onion, peeled
1½ C crustless cubes of bread
1 T butter
1 T cream
+ salt & pepper to taste

Chevreuil des Guides

"This was a favorite dish. Pieces trimmed from the roast were used. This recipe calls for two pounds of meat, but can be easily doubled."

1. Pick over and wash the beans, then soak them in cold water for 12 hours. There should be 4 to 5 inches of water over the beans.

2. In the morning, place the beans and what is left of the water in a tall pot. Add beer, bay leaf, and salt pork. Stir and add the carrots, onions, savory, salt, pepper, and molasses. Cover and bake for 2 hours in a 300°F oven.

3. Stir well and add the deer meat. Mix cover and cook another 2 hours at 300°F. After one hour, stir and add cold tea or hot water if the beans seem

Parkman, in his magisterial seven-volume study *France and England in the New World.* "The spectacle then became truly porcine."

Not only was feasting capable of healing the infirm, Huron shamans claimed it could even restore life to the dead. Entire communities took part in extended banquets involving disturbing amounts of food, exhumed corpses, nudity, and sacrificed dogs. There were so many types of these "momentous ceremonies" that the French couldn't document them all.

"As regards feasts, it is an endless subject," lamented Jean de Brébeuf, a Jesuit missionary whose eventual martyrdom made him the patron saint of Canada. Brébeuf was a strong leader, sharp-minded and upright—"like a dammed-up torrent, sluiced and guided to grind and saw and weave for the good of man," in Parkman's words. In paintings, his angular cheekbones frame eyes that seem to be peering into some other dimension. He was gravely perturbed by the festivals he witnessed, and he deemed "savages" (the term he used in his writings) to be "slaves of the belly and of the table."

Brébeuf came over in 1625, tasked with converting Hurons to Christianity. He displayed a facility for communicating with those whom he was evangelizing, and in the course of the fifteen years he spent among them, he assembled a French-Huron dictionary, documented their mythologies, and became intimately familiar with their customs. Brébeuf's writing, explains his biography, "establishes the picture of the Hurons at the time when they were still themselves, before successive epidemics, war, and massacres had reduced them to the state of human wrecks." His contributions to *The Jesuit Relations*, which chronicle everything he'd learned about the Huron civilization, contain vivid descriptions of their feasts and celebrations.

Of all their revels, the most magnificent were those dubbed *festins à tout manger* (all-you-can-eat feasts). At these dreaded occasions, the "game of teeth" would last for twenty-four straight hours, sometimes longer. The rule was simple: everything cooked had to be eaten. They would prepare twenty whole deer and four bears at a time, or a hundred and twenty giant salmon alongside "fifty great fish, larger than our largest Pike in France." Participants would be served portions large enough to keep them eating from morning until night. As soon as they'd finished the food in front of them, they'd be given more. There was no choice but to keep going, even as they vomited out the contents of their swollen stomachs. To throw food into the fire or to the dogs was an unforgivable sin. To not finish was inconceivable, a dire insult to the spirit world, a portent of calamity and misfortune.

A feaster could hire another person to help consume their helping, but in the end, all the meat in the kettles had to be polished off by the members of the clan. These rites were observed not just by the Hurons, but also by many other tribes. Some celebrants actually died while struggling through the *festins à tout manger*. Others injured themselves internally. "Their ostrich digestion was sometimes ruined past redemption by the excess of this benevolent gluttony," remarks Parkman.

All this medico-mystical feasting had no effect whatsoever on the lethal diseases and viruses that the Europeans brought with them from the land beyond the sunrise. Between 1634 and 1640 one in two Hurons died. (By the end of the

---

dry. When the meat and beans are tender, serve. This dish can be cooked the day before, and cooked beans and meat left on the kitchen counter, covered. To serve the next day, check liquid in beans—it is sometimes necessary to add a cup or two of water. Cover and heat 1 hour at 300°F. *Super!*

INGREDIENTS

3 C "yellow-eyed" beans ("*haricots à oeil jaune*")
2 lbs venison, cut into cubes
4 C beer
2 bay leaves
½ lb salt pork, diced
2 large carrots, diced
4 large onions, thinly sliced
1 t summer savory
2 t salt
1 t pepper
1 C molasses

Pickled Turnip

"Wild game or bird could not be served without pickled turnips. For many years I have made these in late autumn, when turnips are best."

1. Fill jar with sliced turnips. Mix remaining ingredients together and pour over the turnips. Cover the jars and leave in refrigerator for 2 to 3 days before serving.

INGREDIENTS

4 to 5 C turnips, peeled & thinly sliced
1 C sugar
1 C water
¼ C wine vinegar
1 T coarse salt
¼ t yellow food coloring
1 T fresh ginger root, grated

eighteenth century, native populations had dwindled by as much as 90 percent.) Neither side yet understood that small pox, measles, and other illnesses were to blame. But as it became evident that the white men had brought on these outbreaks, many converted "heathens" renounced Jesus. Crosses were torn down and chapels burned to the ground. Huron "witch doctors" believed Brébeuf possessed a charmed cloth responsible for the pestilence. Their lives in danger, he and his fellow black gowns were branded as sorcerers and banished from Huronia. Elders warned them that hatchets might split their head in two at any moment. They held a farewell feast, as done on the eve of a Huron citizen's death, which allowed them to flee safely.

After experiencing visitations from the Virgin Mary ("no longer a dream, but a visioned presence") and seeing a massive cross looming over the snowy forests ("large enough to crucify us all"), the exiled Brébeuf ended up being tortured to death by the Hurons' primary enemies, the Iroquois. They "baptized" him in boiling water, cut off his lips, pierced his side with a spear ("Now you are opened like JESUS!"), stuck a hot iron down his throat, burned him with a necklace of red-hot tomahawks, cut chunks of flesh off his body (which they ate before his unflinching eyes), then scalped him, exposing his brain, and finally— because he exhibited no pain during these tortures—ate his heart.

"Imagine what life had been like in France before they came over to the new world," says McMillan. "Most of the settlers had probably spent their whole lives hungry, only visiting back-alley dentists, having diarrhea forty-nine weeks out of the year. They couldn't drink water, they were always croaking from dysentery. They basically only ate heavily salted, preserved meats. Like, you'd eat ten meals a week of bread with salted dried pork, which through a whole lifetime must've been ridiculously terrible. I wonder if the average Frenchman ever even ate fresh meat? But that's what they did here. It must've been odd to them."

The French first settled in Acadia.[5] The land's name can be traced back either to the Mikmawisimk word akàdie ("place of abundance"), or to the Greek Arcadia, the pure and bountiful region where Pan frolicked alongside his nymphs. The Canadian Acadian landscape around Port Royal was unspoiled, and plentiful in the summertime, but the winters were so deathly that the French failed several times in their attempts to start settlements here.

As a way of keeping spirits up in weather cold enough that settlers' blankets would become fringed with icicles made from their congealed breath, Champlain proposed that a feasting club be established. They called it L'Ordre du Bon Temps—the Order of Good Cheer (or of Good Times). There were fifteen members. Each of these chevaliers was appointed to be in charge of food preparations for one day out of fifteen, throughout the entire winter. Whoever was the host for the day would, alongside their chef, provide a feast of fresh meats at both lunch and dinner.

The members immediately started trying to outdo each other. In Marc Lescarbot's first-person account of France's ventures into the New World (History of New France, published in 1609) he wrote, "There was no

---

5 Today just over the Quebec border in Nova Scotia. The Cajuns of Louisiana were once the Acadians of New France.

Partridge "du Vieux Trappeur"

"Partridge were numerous and when found, were kept frozen in a barrel of snow. At the beginning of their trips, the voyageurs carried cabbage in large black wooden barrels insulated by a heavy layer of wool. The favorite liquid was a 'strong and a mild,' scotch or brandy mixed with cider."

1. Melt the salt pork in a heavy saucepan.

2. Split the partridges in two and leave whole, tying the legs. Roll in flour and brown in melted salt pork over very low heat, 25 minutes. Remove the partridges from the saucepan as they brown.

3. Add the cabbage and onions to the remaining fat. Cover and cook over medium heat, stirring often, until the vegetables are tender, approximately 25 minutes.

4. Set the partridges in the cabbage. Add salt, pepper, thyme, and the liquid of your choice. Cover and cook over very low heat for at least 2 hours, or until the partridges are tender. Serve.

Note: Stewing chicken, pigeons and pork filets may be prepared in the same way. Only the cooking time will vary.

INGREDIENTS

½ **lb** fatty salt pork, diced
4 partridges
4 **T** flour
1 large green cabbage, chopped coarsely
4 **to 6** large onions, sliced thin
1 **T** salt
¼ **t** pepper
½ **t** thyme
½ **C** liquid (white wine, red Burgundy, brandy, cider, apple juice)

one who, two days before his turn came, failed to go hunting or fishing, and to bring back some delicacy in addition to our ordinary fare." They ate spectacularly well in the dead of winter, dining on local caviar, dried-morel mushrooms, freshly caught larks, quails, bustards, duck, trout, otters, rabbits, porcupines, raccoons, even, Lescarbot says, leopards (likely meaning some form of lynx or cougar-like wildcat). For an idea of the amount of food being consumed, at some of the banquets, they'd share a full six sturgeons among the fifteen of them. The dishes were brought out in a procession led by the ruler of the feast, who would march into the dining room, wearing for that day the medallion of the order and holding its wand in his hand.

The meals, according to the chevaliers' accounts, were as fine as those served on the Rue aux Ours in Paris—and more copious. (In the sixteenth century, that street full of rotisseries, then known as Rue aux Oyers, was famed for the quality of its roast geese.) "Though the epicures of Paris often tell us that we had no Rue aux Ours," wrote Lescarbot, "as a rule we made as good cheer as we could have in this same Rue aux Ours... for of all our meats none is so tender as moose-meat (whereof we also made excellent pasties), and nothing so delicate as beaver's tail." Then came all the *gateaux*, *oubliés*, *échaudés*, *cache-museaux*, and other sugar-spun bonbons.[6]

6 Only the leaders of the settlement ate like this. Others had to make do with the ordinary rations brought from France, which were distributed fairly among the entire colony, as was the wine. The native populace quickly took note of the events, and would come by and watch the proceedings, just as the French watched them at their assemblies. "We always had twenty or thirty savages, men, women, girls, and children, who looked on at our manner of service," Lescarbot recalled. "Bread was given them gratis as one would do to the poor. But as for the Sagamos Membertou, and other chiefs, who came from time to time, they sat at table, eating and drinking like ourselves."

The Order of Good Cheer was a gastronomic, chivalric brotherhood with religious underpinnings. The Chief Steward, whose turn came once a fortnight, was called the "Architriclin." The term means "governor of the feast," but is also a reference to the banquet organizer in the wedding of Cana where Jesus transformed water into wine. The chevaliers of the Order intuited a connection between that miracle and their goals of transmuting Nouvelle France into an earthly city of God. Much in the way that aboriginals assigned incorporeal significance to their feasts, their European disciples viewed gorging as a sacred activity.

In his landmark study of the genesis of Quebecois cuisine, Jean-Marie Francoeur points out that the religiosity of the French colonists was intimately connected to their propensity for *la fine gourmandise*. To them, nourishing the body also meant nourishing the soul. They saw sensory experience as a trampoline capable of launching them beyond the terrestrial. The dining table was a doorway into the noumenal. At that time, pastry tables doubled as altars for communion. According to Antoine Furetière's dictionary, issued in 1690 and still considered by Francoeur to be the key to Quebecois French, the usage of the word *nappe* in the seventeenth century signified both tablecloth and liturgical cloth.

This overlap would have been evident to the Ursuline nuns who ministered to the colony. They put as much devotion into their cooking, Francoeur contends, as into their spiritual exercises. Sweets were their greatest form of prayer. As a result, they invented numerous desserts, including maple toffee, pumpkin pies with ginger, and the angelic fudge-like *sucre à la crème*. To this day, little coils of

cinnamon-flavored pie dough are called *pets de sœurs*, or nuns' farts.

If a conflating of the physical and the sacred was systemic to New France, it attained its most confused heights in Montreal. The adventurers who founded this town in 1642, three-and-a-half decades after Champlain laid claim to Quebec City, were acting on orders from above, on voices in their heads, on instructions received in dreams. The seed idea of starting an outpost on the uninhabited island of Montreal blossomed through a coincidental series of bizarre religious experiences. On multiple occasions in the years leading up to the founding of Montreal, different French-Catholic devotees[7] heard the voice of God commanding them to establish a colony at the base of Mount Royal and experienced inner visions of each other before actually meeting in real life.

One of these founders was Marie de l'Incarnation, an intensely mystical sister from the town of Tours who started seeing Jesus Christ in childhood in France. "Do you want to be mine?" he asked her, during one of the trancier phases of her youth. "Yes," she responded, breathlessly. The Lord promised to marry her, when she was ready. Later, he assured her that it had come to pass, that she was indeed his bride. He became a kind of living presence for her. She'd head off to church as though to a rendezvous with a paramour, speaking of him in sensual terms: "My love, my beauty, my Life! Come, let me embrace you, and die in your sacred arms." At times, spent

7 Including the nun Jeanne Mance, the priest Jean-Jacques Olier, and an enthusiastic tax receiver named Jérôme le Royer de la Dauversière who spent his spare time lashing his back and strapping himself into flesh-puncturing belts studded with thousands of thorn-like points.

with fatigue, she'd beg him to let her rest a little so that again she'd be able to give herself over fully to "his chaste and divine embraces." Just as the Order of Good Cheer members confused the terrestrial with the divine, Marie de l'Incarnation blended spiritual enthusiasms with sexual agitation.

At the same time, however, she was adept at taking care of business and at keeping things organized and orderly. Capable of balancing her visionary self with an equally pragmatic, practical side, she became superior of the Ursuline novitiate in New France—the ideal post for an erotically devout neat-freak who'd occasionally see her own body immersed in the blood of the Son of God.

On the boat ride over the Atlantic, an enormous iceberg with titanic intentions sped toward Marie de L'Incarnation. Catastrophe seemed certain, until the Lord heard her prayers and interceded. This was far from the last example of divine intervention reported among the colonists. *Voyageurs* battling lethal waterfalls would end up guided to safety by the Virgin Mother, who'd appear in a rainbow of spume like a hologram of Princess Leia. Cooks in the midst of preparing stuffed veal with creamed carrots would see Saint Joseph appear before their eyes. Miracles abounded.

Beatific visions, coincidences, and characters are how Montreal came to be—and they clearly informed the way we ate. The city was

founded on May 17, 1642. On that night, the travelers stepped onto land, singing hymns of gratitude. They sank to their knees among the acorns and the pinecones and the wildflowers. Colorful birds gazed down upon them from the treetops, oblivious to the profound transformations these newcomers were bringing. As twilight fell, millions of fireflies set the darkening sky aglow. The nuns caught a number of these and threaded them together into a garland of softly pulsating lights for the altar they'd set up to worship their God, the One who'd led them there, here, nowhere, on an island in a river with a mountain and winters and forests and wildlife and a civilization they knew nothing about. In another world.

Just as the French had their Ordre du Bon Temps, and the First Nations had their all-you-can-eat festivals, the British in Quebec also had a thing for sarfing, as evinced by The Beaver Club. Despite having an Anglo-Scottish ethos, its membership also included French-Canadians. Members had to have passed an entire winter—or more—in the interior wilderness. The convivium's bylaws stated the group's aim: "to bring together at stated periods during the winter season a set of men highly respectable in society, who had spent their best days in a savage country, and had encountered the hazards and hardships incident to the pursuit of the fur trade in Canada."

They had faced intense privation while in the bush. Being in the fur trade meant lengthy periods of solitude. While nature could be joyous and meditative, it was also easily bleak and arduous. They regularly went several days without a meal. Many died of starvation, or were murdered in the night. Should they survive, however, the early *coureurs de bois* (wood-running fur traders) would return to Montreal after enduring countless struggles in the Wendigo-haunted wilds, and find themselves bursting with new money, swaggering like aristocrats, spending lavishly on food, drink, and fashion. "They set no bounds to their riot," Parkman wrote. "Newcomers were bedizened with a strange mixture of French and Indian finery; while some of them, with instincts more thoroughly savage, stalked about naked."

They often went on such uncurbed sprees in the city that they'd soon lose all the money they'd amassed. They were the sort of men for whom "gratification followed desire with hardly a time interval," as

Charles Bert Reed, author of *Masters of the Wilderness*, put it. The Beaver Club became a way for the top tier of traders to blow off steam in a proper setting. Its motto, "Fortitude in Distress," could be read on the large gold medals that members wore around their necks, attached to a pale blue ribbon. The flip side of the medal depicted a beaver gnawing on wood, with the group's prized values, INDUSTRY AND PERSEVERANCE. At the end of the eighteenth century, with the defeat of the French by the English in North America, Montreal received an influx of WASP energy, and

found itself swarming with shrewd gangster-furriers. "They spend fast, play all the freaks, pranks, and street-fooleries, and originate all the current whimsicalities," wrote John Bigsby, in *The Shoe and Canoe*.

These fast-spending freak-players would show up to their Beaver Club gatherings wrapped in thick, luxuriant furs beneath which they were "richly adorned with ruffles and a profusion of gold lace, with knee breeches above their gold-clasped garters and silver-buckled shoes." They drank from crystal glasses and ate with crested silverware. An immense fireplace

sent waves of heat over the diners as the gluttony began. "On certain great occasions," added Bigsby, "the last plate put on the table before each member held a cheque for a sum of money."

Attendance was compulsory for members in good standing. (The club counted a membership of fifty-five, plus ten honorary places). The rumpus began around four p.m. Those with wives and children were allowed to call it a night around nine. At that point, the vibe turned "true Highland style," with all the alpha-dog fur traders competing to see who could drink the most and stay

up the longest and behave the wild-est. The meetings only ended when the final reveler could no longer sit up in his chair.

Colonel George Thomas Land-mann portrays a typical late eight-eenth century Beaver Club feast in his *Adventures and Recollections*: "By four o'clock in the morning the whole of us had arrived at such a degree of perfection, that we could all give the warwhoop," he wrote. "We all thought we could dance on the table without disturbing a single decanter, glass, or plate with which it was profusely covered; but on making the experi-ment we discovered that it was a complete delusion, and ultimately we broke all the plates, glasses, bottles, etc., and the table also, and worse than that, all the heads and hands of the party received many severe con-tusions, cuts, and scratches."

The Quebecois author George Moore Fairchild describes big men in various states of incapacitation ceaselessly pouring one another further intoxicants while partying well into the following day. "As each man fell off his chair and under the table the servants dragged him out and carried him out of danger of the broken glass, and there he slept off his deep potations, and the revelry went on." Those who had the foresight to consider the hangover in store for them would drop under the table "at an early stage of the orgy."

Staying up meant participat-ing in a special club game called "*le grand voyage*." The traders would arrange themselves on the floor of the banquet hall as though inside a long canoe. Then, taking what-ever paddle-like object was near at hand (a poker, a shovel, a broom, fire tongs), they'd start vigorously stroking their way down an imagi-nary river, chanting ("shouting at full voice") old voyageur songs. Soon they'd come upon choppy waterfalls,

and the leader would yell at them all to traverse the furniture in myriad contorted positions. The climax of the game involved climbing onto wine kegs in order to "'*saute*' the rapids from the table to the floor."

And that's how Que-bec food became Que-bec food. The way we eat here is steeped in archaic lore. *Je me sou-viens*. This land truly has—as sepa-ratists maintain—its own distinct culture. Perhaps the finest descrip-tion of that identity and how it dif-fers from that of the Englishness all around it, belongs to Parkman, the American historian who under-stood the French in Canada better than most other Anglos, better too than most Francophones. He knew that New Englanders were focused on material progress, on the steady rewards of patient industry, whereas the inhabitants of New France were a people "compassed by influences of the wildest freedom, whose schools were the forest and the sea, whose trade was an armed barter with sav-ages, and whose daily life a lesson of lawless independence." Ultimately, the once-powerful First Nations succumbed to the Europeans, even as the English defeated the French in the battle for control of North America. The rest is history, and that history is part of the reason Quebecois cuisine is so fascinat-ing today. That, and the storytell-ing—or, in David McMillan's words, the *tchatche*, the ability to talk a good game. Narrative matters here. We're a tale-loving nation of Rabe-laisian sarfs and escornifleurs. As Parkman concluded, "In every qual-ity of efficiency and strength, the Canadian fell miserably below his rival; but in all that pleases the eye and interests the imagination, he far surpassed him." **LP**

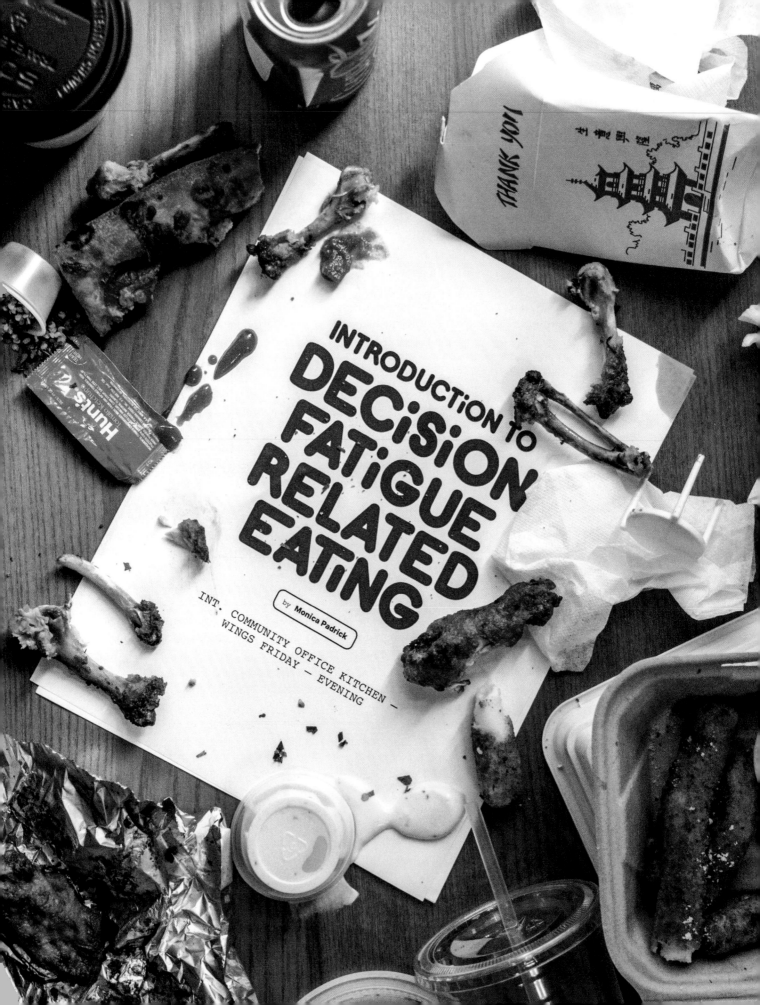

INTRODUCTION TO DECiSiON FATiGUE RELATED EATiNG

by **Monica Padrick**

INT. COMMUNITY OFFICE KITCHEN —
WINGS FRIDAY — EVENING

The kitchen is a large, fluorescently lit room lined
with counters and GIANT GARBAGE CANS teeming with PIZZA
BOXES, HALF-EATEN SANDWICHES, CUPS, NAPKINS, BONES.
There's all the usual office-kitchen stuff: refrigerator
full of yogurts and deli meats, a neglected coffee
maker, baskets full of bread-things, a sandwich press
with dangerous exposed coils and fossilized cheese, a
towering SHELF OF SNACKS, and underexplored cupboards
that have, like, muesli or whatever in them.

A long TABLE sits in the center of the room. Aluminum
takeout containers hold LITERALLY HUNDREDS OF COLD,
CONGEALED, BRIGHT-ORANGE BUFFALO WINGS next to waxy
bags of half-eaten CURLY FRIES. Styrofoam tubs stick
to the table with thick rings of RANCH DRESSING. There
is an untouched ROMAINE SALAD, and multiple untouched
CONTAINERS OF CARROTS AND CELERY. Maybe there are a
few fat MOZZARELLA STICKS left behind, but who are we
kidding, those go fast. The table has long been ignored,
a monument to some earlier, obviously shameful mistakes.

A WOMAN, 30, wanders in. She stands paralyzed in front
of the SNACK SHELF, with one hand hovering over an open,
oversize Tupperware containing what must be several
thousand pounds of PEANUT M&Ms. Her eyes wearily move
to the TUBS OF TINY COOKIES, passing easily over the
UBIQUITOUS RED VINES, before landing on a Costco-
sized carton of GOLDFISH. With a JOLT, she remembers
that there is a BOX OF JALAPEÑO-FLAVORED CHIPS above
the fridge. But also, there is a beautiful HALF-EATEN
HOMEMADE CAKE on a counter. And FRUIT SNACKS. And a
BASKET OF CANDY. And HUMMUS and CHOCOLATE-COVERED
ALMONDS. As she moves, zombie-like, her face betrays a
LIFETIME OF DIFFICULT DECISIONS.

A P.A. enters, hauling enormous bags of FRESH TAKEOUT.
The woman's face lights up.

                    P.A.
            Dinner's here, y'all.

This is the sort of unwatchable scene that could open a pilot for a television show about writing for television shows. I would go on, but the dialogue would drag, revolving around exchanges like "What're you getting for lunch today?" and "What's that smell?" and "Did someone throw out a tuna melt in the room?" and "Please don't fucking tell me we're out of chocolate-covered peanut-butter-filled pretzels again." Sure, there would also be some stuff about actual writing, maybe. *Maybe.*

Here's a thing about my job as a TV writer—most recently for the NBC sitcom *Community*—that really impresses my parents: I almost never have to buy my own lunch. (I think this is pretty standard at most shows, though I have also worked in cable and experienced the agony of buying my own sandwiches.) Once production on *Community* got underway and we got busy, I also never had to buy my own dinner. Or my own second dinner. Or, for that matter, whatever the midnight ice-cream meal is called. I assume some arcane precedent demands that studios pay for everything, no matter how decadent or stinky, and this has held up for generations of writing staffs pushing the limits of decency. I don't know. It feels like a bad idea to question it. All I know is, there was a cheerful, Georgia-bred, highly metabolized twenty-five-year-old who circulated menus, placed orders, and jammed his Mazda full of our food, always adding some extra group pizzas and orders of fried chicken and desserts, because he knew that short-term gratification is a great way to make friends.

There was always food at work. Sometimes the food was reasonable, and some of the more experienced writers knew how to tailor a menu for minimal bodily harm. But then, sometimes it was Wings Friday.

Wings Friday is exactly what it sounds like: hot wings, along with all their buddies in a hot-app sampler, every Friday. Midday, our boss at *Community* would call out "WINGS Fri-DAAAAAAY!" using a tone we called "football voice" in scripts when we wanted to identify lines of dialogue that should sound like something someone might shout during some kind of a game (there were not a lot of athletes in the room). For twenty-plus weeks, every Friday was Wings Friday, and every Wings Friday was a *Groundhog Day* of eater's remorse.

Quick sidebar about my personal relationship with hot wings: from age nine to age twenty-four, I was the sort of vegetarian who didn't eat land animals. I was pretty deep into my twenties when I first ate wings, and I remember them well. I was at Wogies in the West Village in New York and the wings' hotness level was "krazy [*sic*]." After that I started casually suggesting that my friends meet me at bars where I could get wings. Then I started just showing up at my local spot, Henry St. Ale House (which had perfectly good wings), sitting at the bar, pretending that I was waiting for someone, preemptively ordering the wings, and eating them all, alone.

I love wings. Everyone loves wings. They're the perfect food.

Wings Friday nearly ruined hot wings for me. Here's the thing I think none of us were willing to say, but everyone knows: wings don't travel well. They might have been piping hot from the fryer, crisp edges glistening orange with fat and hot sauce just twenty minutes beforehand. But by the time they hit the table, the trapped steam from takeout containers has rendered them a little soggy, a little rubbery, a little tepid, a little gross. We ate them anyway. A lot of them.

By seven o'clock or so, when the wings and mozz sticks and curly fries were finally tossed out to make way for dinner, all that was left was the dank, heavy smell of a post-apocalyptic Hooters. Dinner on Fridays was usually sushi, by the way.

Wings Friday started as a joyful, funny celebration and followed a classic joke trajectory from funny fun to funny death march and eventually, by the time Wings Friday was declared on the Tuesday before Thanksgiving so that nobody would be denied their wings that week, it was back to just being pretty funny. You could say, in the hero's journey of the hot wing, by the end of that third act, the wing was back to where it started, but something about it had changed.

We would have good food at *Community*, too, and a lot of it, from

nice restaurants we had never seen the insides of, but whose menus we knew by heart. Food wasn't just a perk that kept us complacent and forgetful that it was a Friday at nine and nobody would be going home any time soon. We also seemed to be feeding a different beast.

I asked a psychiatrist friend if she could help explain why, in my experience, the grazing going on in the writers' room seems to be not only a result of your everyday triggers— you know, proximity, access, trying to keep yourself from crying—but also the desperate need to stuff one's face whenever one is stuck on a story point or a joke, especially late at night.

It turns out the writers' room is the place to go if one wishes to partake of an environment where classic emotional eating collides spectacularly with something known as decision-fatigue-related eating—all with a blank check to pay for it.

Decision-fatigue-related eating is what one is compelled to do after constant decision-making. Constant decision-making causes your brain to crave glucose, and only when the glucose tank is refilled can you actually focus on figuring out whether we should say that Dean Pelton went to Dean Camp even though it's

completely fucking obvious that he's the *dean of a community college* and in order to justify to the audience why he'd want to improve the school the answer should be as simple as "it's his job" instead of "he just got back from Dean Camp and now he wants to impress his camp friends." *JESUS CHRIST.*

Anyway, this glucose thing might explain why, at about two a.m. one night, I witnessed one of my bosses, who is one of the most respected men in television, one of the smartest and funniest and sanest people I've ever worked with, stand up from the table, his eyes wild and desperate, as he called out, "We need pies, any pies, can somebody get pies?" He claims it was a well-timed joke. But the face-stuffing that ensued once the pies arrived was all too real.

Okay, so writing is just making endless decisions, and making too many decisions makes your brain crave sugar. But why, then, did we also seem to crave Miss Vickie's salt-and-vinegar potato chips? I'm no scientist, but I think it's because my colleagues and I have the extraordinary brains of unstoppable fatsos. "To make great art, you need great pizza," someone, I'm sure, has said. And for that reason, it's for the best that our struggle happens away from the lights and the camera and the action. 'Cause really, nobody should want to watch this:

```
INT. WRITERS ROOM — NIGHT

GROSSLY OVERFED WRITERS sit
around a table, pitching
PERFECT JOKES for the BEST
SHOW ON TV. The P.A. enters.

          P.A.
     Cookies are here, y'all.

          WRITERS
     Thank god. I'm starving.

END OF SHOW. [LP]
```

Illustration by Domitille Collardey

LE GRAND PRIX DE ALL YOU CAN EAT!

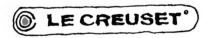

help pick the winner at lecreuset.com/lucky

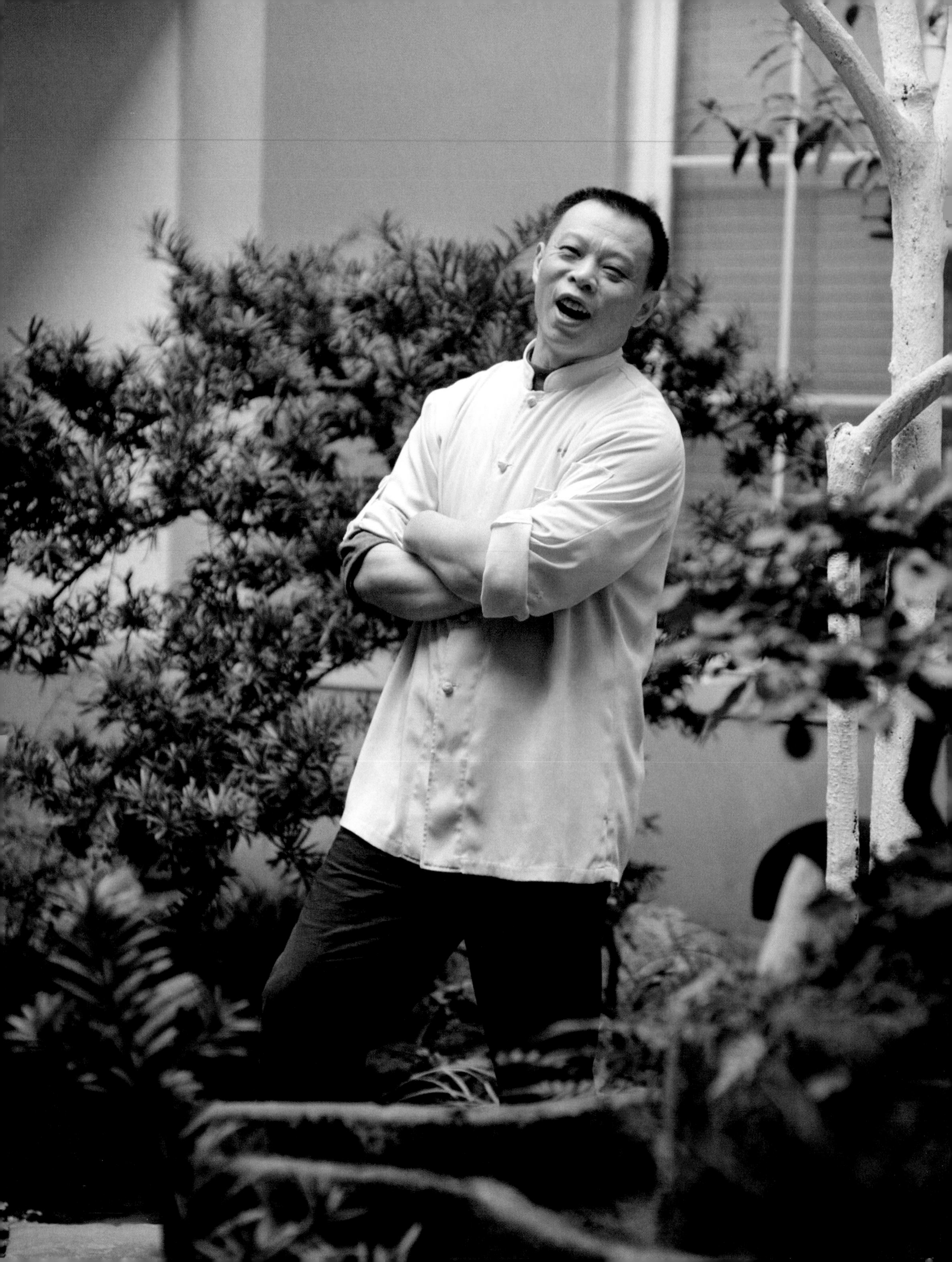

ALL YU CAN EAT

by **Fuchsia Dunlop**

Photograph by Andrew Rowat | *Illustrations by Jeannie Phan*

**O**ne evening in 2001 in the Sichuanese capital of Chengdu, a friend of mine led me through the corridors of a dull gray hotel into a private room with windows overlooking a car park. It was an unlikely location for an epiphany, but dinner that evening transformed my appreciation for Chinese food.

Eight of us sat down at a large round dining table, and a young chef called Yu Bo proceeded to light a fuse and blow our minds. There were forty-two courses, beginning with a checkerboard of sixteen exquisite appetizers served in little square dishes. Even back then, they were his calling card: "jade hairpins" made of intricately knotted flowering chives, bamboo shoots cut into "sparrows' wings," lemon-scented aloe vera. The main courses were equally astounding. A golden dome opened to reveal tiny morsels of bullfrog resting on a delicate egg custard. Slices of *konnyaku* jelly floated in an icy black tea with morsels of crisp apple and watermelon, presented in tiny crackle-glazed bowls. Languid honeyed rolls of catfish were displayed in an ornate lacquered box in the style of the Tang Dynasty. Between the main courses a series of soups and dainties were served, including a yolk-yellow imperial *geng* (a thick stew) floaty with tiny cubes of tofu, and chilled, flower-shaped cakes of sweet-pea jelly. Many of the serving vessels had been custom-made.

For years I'd dreamt of attending a proper Chinese banquet. Although I'd eaten food of extraordinary deliciousness during my several years of exploring

Sichuanese foodways, I'd never encountered the kind of banquet I'd read about in books. Half a century earlier, Chairman Mao had declared war on the fripperies of fancy dining. "Revolution," he said, "was not a dinner party." Over the course of the Chinese revolution, the educated, wealthy gentlemen who had sponsored elite gastronomy had fled into exile in Taiwan or seen catastrophic reversals in their fortunes—private restaurants had been nationalized and their "capitalist" owners persecuted. In place of epicurean feasts for discerning gourmets, restaurants were expected to serve "cheap and substantial food" for the common people.

By the end of the twentieth century, such revolutionary fervor might have abated, but the effects of Maoism lingered. Most of the smarter restaurants in Chengdu were decked out in a dull, Soviet-influenced style with a few Chinese characteristics, tableware was utilitarian, and the dining atmosphere invariably informal. In 2001, a feast in Yu Bo's private dining rooms stood out like a shimmering peacock in a field of geese. It wasn't just the delicate beauty of the food and the sheer multitude of dishes. Dinner there was a cultural performance, an opera as much as a meal. There were nods to imperial-court cookery and Chengdu street snacks, references to Chinese dynastic history and Japanese aesthetics. Dishes were served in porcelain tureens, bamboo baskets, and packages of silver foil tied with ribbon. Grand centerpieces alternated with little tidbits served in individual bowls. Yu Bo didn't see himself just as a cook, but as an artist with a personal vision of Chinese gastronomy.

Dinner that night was a lightning tour of the giddy heights of Chinese-imperial cuisine and the feisty flavors of Sichuan folk cooking, shot through with flashes of an unusual Japanese-influenced modernism. It was unlike anything I'd experienced in seven years of Chengdu eating. I emerged from the restaurant dazed and full of wonder. The heading in my journal for that night simply reads: Yu Bo: MIRACLE MEAL.

These days, Chef Yu is on the international map for the culinary cognoscenti. He's hosted Thomas Keller, Andrew Zimmern, Cecilia Chiang, and U.S. Ambassador to China Gary Locke. He's been featured on NPR, the BBC, and in the *Financial Times*. But in 2001 he was just a young maverick chef making his name with a new version of classical-banquet cooking. At the time, the Chengdu restaurant scene was lurching forward in a new atmosphere of economic reform. Shabby state-owned snack shops were reinventing themselves as modern fast-food restaurants, and borrowing tricks from the American chains. Sichuanese cuisine, until recently viewed as the poor relation of the swanky Cantonese, was on the up. The elegant Piaoxiang restaurant had given it a makeover, serving refined versions of traditional Sichuan dishes in newly glamorous surroundings. Baguo Buyi had caused a sensation with its reinvented rustic schtick: waitresses did their rounds in cotton smocks, dishes sang with the sour-spicy flavor of old-fashioned pickles, and there was even a fake tree trunk rising up through the dining room.

Finally, after decades of stultifying Maoist economics, entrepreneurs could make money. And yet here was one chef who didn't give a damn about commercial realities. Yu Bo buried his nose in old cookery books and pestered veteran chefs for their secrets. During our first meeting, he quoted Confucius as he explained to me it was necessary to become a good person if you wanted to be a good cook. While many of his contemporaries were falling into the arms of international

companies touting junky seasonings, he spent hours fiddling about with his ingredients, making stocks the expensive and old-fashioned way, and devising ever more dramatic presentations for his dishes. "What I want to achieve," he told me, "is perfection." While other restaurants were expanding into chains, Yu Bo was focusing his energies on only two or three tables in two private rooms decorated with vases, paintings, and calligraphies. Most people at that time thought he was crazy. "He'll never make any money," was the general view. But he was acquiring a loyal following among an elite of artists, intellectuals, and other gourmets.

When I met him that first evening, Yu Bo was an intense, somewhat coarsely spoken man with a ready laugh and manifest sense of his own amazingness. I remember him watching me as I ate, taking pleasure in my surprise and delight as the feast unfolded. He was trying to recreate, he said, the atmosphere of the pre-revolutionary days, when mandarins kept private chefs and entertained their cultured friends to elegant dinner parties. "It's a kind of *jin yi yu shi*. ('wearing brocade and eating jade')," one of my fellow guests explained to me—in other words, living in the lap of luxury. In the past, there had been a social chasm between the gentlemen gourmets who pondered and pontificated on the finer points of gastronomy and the chefs who slaved away at the stove. But Yu Bo was fusing the roles of both host and chef, craftsman and thinker. It was an unlikely choice of career for a high-school dropout who in those days described himself in that pejorative Chinese way as "a man without culture."

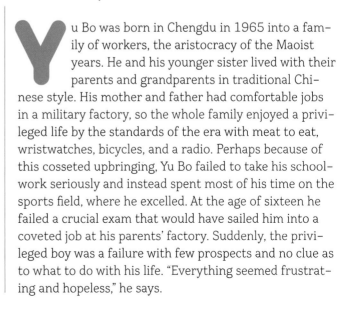

Yu Bo was born in Chengdu in 1965 into a family of workers, the aristocracy of the Maoist years. He and his younger sister lived with their parents and grandparents in traditional Chinese style. His mother and father had comfortable jobs in a military factory, so the whole family enjoyed a privileged life by the standards of the era with meat to eat, wristwatches, bicycles, and a radio. Perhaps because of this cosseted upbringing, Yu Bo failed to take his schoolwork seriously and instead spent most of his time on the sports field, where he excelled. At the age of sixteen he failed a crucial exam that would have sailed him into a coveted job at his parents' factory. Suddenly, the privileged boy was a failure with few prospects and no clue as to what to do with his life. "Everything seemed frustrating and hopeless," he says.

Left to right: The Chengdu team at the Third Chinese National Cooking Contest;
Yu Bo (second from left) with colleagues; Yu Bo and Dai Shuang

But Yu Bo had always been fastidious about food. His grandmother was a fine cook, and as a teenager he started dabbling in the kitchen: "just simple Sichuanese dishes, mostly vegetables with a little meat." In 1982, at the age of seventeen, he took a three-month elementary cookery course in the canteen of a hospital for contagious diseases, and was then assigned to a lowly role in the canteen of a silk-dyeing factory. "Life was really bitter," he says. "I had to get up at four a.m. and haul around enormous sacks of flour, chop vegetables. There was no chance to do any actual cooking. It was a miserable period, and I was desperate to escape."

In the end, he was rescued by his cooking teacher, who worked in a local-government office in Chengdu and offered him a job. Like most Chinese government bureaus, this place had its own canteen where officials could wine and dine their contacts, so the cooks were expected to lay on formal dinners from time to time. It was Yu Bo's first chance to learn about Chinese-banquet cookery. "There were only four of us in the kitchen, and it was hard work, but it gave me an understanding of basic cooking skills and I began to see my future as a chef," he says. His appetite whetted, in 1985 he managed, through a personal connection, to wangle a job as a skivvy in the kitchen of the Shufeng Garden, the recent reincarnation of a famous prerevolutionary restaurant.

Until it was demolished in the late 1990s, the Shufeng Garden was a little oasis of gentility in the center of Chengdu. You entered through a narrow passageway into a garden surrounded by private rooms built in the traditional style with wooden-latticework panels and a tiled roof. Banquets began with a selection of delectable appetizers served in a *cuan he*, a round, lacquered box holding a neat pattern of interlocking dishes. At that time, the fanciest restaurants in Chengdu were Cantonese, while the Sichuanese places tended to be riotous hot-potteries, fading state-run establishments, or white-tiled holes-in-the-wall. The Shufeng Garden was exceptional: it had an aura of elegant nostalgia and served polished versions of all the classic Sichuan dishes. It was where the Sichuanese authorities incubated their export-quality chefs: any chef who wanted to work abroad had to pass through its kitchens as part of their training. As soon as he crossed the threshold, says Yu Bo, he knew he wanted to work there, no matter how hard it might be.

It was at the Shufeng Garden that Yu Bo got serious about food and about life. He started out as a casual employee at the bottom of the kitchen food chain, so he had to work furiously to compete with his colleagues, all of them cooking-school graduates.

Photographs courtesy of Yu Bo

But he had the chance to learn from some outstanding chefs with expertise in various branches of the Sichuanese culinary arts. He clocked in early and left late, practiced his knife skills in his own time, and made cups of tea for his superiors. His hard work and respectful manner earned him an apprenticeship with Chef Zeng Qichang, an alumnus of the legendary Rongle Yuan restaurant.

Although his growing mastery of the arts of cold dishes was making his position at the Shufeng Garden more secure, Yu Bo's rebelliousness and individualism occasionally got him into trouble. "I wasn't very diplomatic and sometimes made people uncomfortable with my impulsive words," he says. "I spent my free time reading books and learning about classic dishes, but I also moonlighted making beautiful presentation platters for weddings and other special occasions, and my seniors weren't pleased. They began to worry that my heart wasn't in my job, that my 'body was in the camp of Cao, while my heart was with the Han'"—an idiom based on ancient Chinese military history that refers to the state of being in one place while longing to be somewhere else—"but my skills were making me more and more indispensable, so I kept my job."

In 1993 his fortunes took a turn for the better. He'd already been promoted to the role of a proper chef,

but that year he won a gold medal in a national cooking contest, and married the Shufeng Garden's accountant, Dai Shuang. Two years later, the two of them took over the management of the restaurant's branch in the nearby city of Dujiangyan, where they sharpened their business skills and Yu Bo began to make his name as a chef. After four years, they flew the Shufeng Garden nest altogether, acquiring the catering franchise of the Sichuan Film Company Hotel, where Yu Bo was free to indulge his culinary creativity in the hothouses of the private rooms where I first encountered him.

It's a measure of the traditional sexism of the industry, both in China and the West that Yu Bo alone is now showered with fame and glory. In fact, as Yu himself readily admits, the whole Yu Bo phenomenon is and always has been the Yu and Dai Show. "It was Dai Shuang's support that enabled me to win that gold medal in Beijing. And she is much better than me at handling personal relations," he says, in a tacit reference to his own hot temper and tendency to bluntness. "I would never have succeeded without her." Dai Shuang is not only a skilled administrator, but a clever cook and eater. And while Yu Bo may have the restless talent and relentlessly inquiring mind, she has a rich knowledge of traditional Sichuanese foodways. Many of the sublime old-fashioned dishes served in the restaurant come from her parents' and grandparents' repertoire.

There's the stew made of pork sourced from the Tibetan plateau, small cubes of layered belly meat simmered over a low fire for a day or more, with preposterous amounts of garlic that sublimates over the hours into a profound and sumptuous fragrance, invisibly infusing the meat. The tender pork is served with little *guo kui* flatbreads, as an elevated version of an old Chengdu street snack. And there's a nourishing split-pea soup with a hint of ginger: ochre yellow, a homely concoction fancied up in the restaurant through a garnish of miniature dough twists, fried peanuts, and pea shoots, and served in a magnificent pot.

One spring day a year or so ago, Dai Shuang took me to a local market where she reeled off recipes and folklore as we walked. We discussed the various greens, the thick mustard stems that could be pickled or sautéed with chili-bean sauce and Sichuan pepper; the fava beans that one might toss into a spicy salad with celtuce slivers and the local vegetable *ze'er gen*. She knew all the traditional admonitions: that eating alfalfa sprouts with alcohol would make a person sad, that spring onions were toxic in combination with honey. Another afternoon we sat in the courtyard drinking tea as she gave me, at my request, a long and fascinating disquisition on the subtleties of *kou gan* or mouthfeel, and the Chinese appreciation of texture.

In the restaurant, Dai Shuang often mucks in with the preparation, especially the skilled and intricate work of transforming chives into hairpins, or bamboo shoots into fans. On the road, when they've given presentations or laid on banquets abroad, Yu Bo and Dai Shuang do everything together, and there's little she doesn't know about the finer points of cooking and flavor. She shares her husband's commitment to Chinese and Sichuanese tradition: they are a team in every sense.

" I want the place to be like a *siheyuan*, an old-fashioned courtyard house, with a small patch of heaven above, somewhere I can entertain guests as if it was in my own home," Yu Bo once said of his dream restaurant. "And I want it to embody the culture of the Sichuan region, with its lacquer, silks, and miniature trees. I'm not interested in making a fortune; I just want a stable income so I can study cookery. My cooking master is always urging me to adapt my food to the market, but the market is a mess. I can't stand this popular style of cooking that is stuffed full of MSG and chicken powder. I think I should follow my own path—and I'm a stubborn man."

By 2001, Yu Bo and Dai Shuang had their first base, in a riverside house that formerly belonged to a Kuomintang general, and after a brief detour through another dreary hotel, in 2006 they fetched up in their current premises, tucked away at the head of the Wide and Narrow Alleys in the west of Chengdu. The entrance is discreet: a heavy, unmarked wooden gate, and beyond it an ornamental screen that masks the interior. But step beyond the screen and you're in a tranquil courtyard, with stepping stones leading over a pond to a wooden gazebo. Goldfish flit in the pond, and songbirds twitter in bamboo cages. You might linger here, sipping green tea and nibbling Xinjiang sultanas or roasted soybeans. After a while you'll repair to one of the six private rooms, where the ravishing display of appetizers awaits you. And then the show begins.

There is no à la carte menu at Yu Jia Chu Fang (Yu's Family Kitchen), just a fixed-price menu that varies with the seasons and the amount you wish to spend (a higher tariff pays for more exotic delicacies, like turtle skirts or matsutake mushrooms). The six private rooms can seat a maximum of seventy guests.

Yu Bo's cooking style is marked by a radical inventiveness that is grounded in a thorough understanding of Sichuanese tradition. In 2001, among the avant-garde concoctions and imperial classics on his menu were a few of the most famous Sichuan folk dishes, including *gong bao* (aka kung pao) chicken and fish-fragrant pork. The following year, such predictable dishes had disappeared as he forged new directions, plundering the traditional repertoire but always impressing his creations with a personal stamp. When he served Chengdu's camphor-and-tea-smoked duck, slices of it were suspended on red threads from a calligraphy-brush frame, and served with sweet fermented sauce and little flatbreads. The flavors of that old Sichuan favorite, twice-cooked pork, might appear in a dish made with crayfish. And the classic mapo tofu ("pock-marked old woman's tofu") was reimagined as a grand platter of cubed rice jelly in the traditional mapo sauce, embellished with fresh abalone.

He's never stopped reworking his tableaus of cold appetizers, which continue to embody the Sichuanese principle of *yi cai yi ge, bai cai bai wei* ("each dish has its own style, and a hundred dishes have a hundred different flavors"). Each dish is made with a different ingredient, in a different form, and dressed in a different combination of flavorings from the Sichuanese canon. And in 2002 he made the decision, startling by local standards, to make them entirely vegetarian.

"Anyone can make a delicacy out of lobster or abalone," he told me. "But I like to show it can be done with the simplest of ingredients." Some of his customers were affronted by the lack of meat, but Yu Bo didn't care; he had no intention of pandering to conventional tastes, and was unashamedly elitist. "It's about *yang chun bai xue* [literally "spring snow," and referring to highbrow art and literature]. My dishes are like fashions that are not worn by the common people."

There's a wit and playfulness to Yu Bo's cooking that recalls the magic and fun of dinners at the Fat Duck and El Bulli. One of his signature dishes is a porcelain jar of what look exactly like calligraphy brushes with a dish of red ink. But when you take one of the bamboo stems in your hand, dip the "brush" into the "ink" and then pop it into your mouth, you discover that it's actually a flaky pastry with layers mimicking precisely the hairs of a brush. Sometimes a potful of bamboo spills is served. Guests pick a spill, and eat the fragrant chunk of mushroom or fish on its end, before reading the riddle or challenge with which it's engraved: a drinking

game inspired by the dalliances of the characters in the eighteenth-century Chinese novel *A Dream of Red Mansions* (aka *Dream of the Red Chamber*).

To anyone familiar with the technological wizardry of creative cooking in the modern West, what is astounding about Yu Bo's kitchen is the lack of kit. There are no centrifuges or sous-vide machines, just a couple of microwaves, a liquidizer that's kept mainly in its box, and a coffee grinder for Sichuan pepper. Almost everything is done by hand, and using traditional methods. But then Chinese chefs have always managed to effect astonishing transformations of their food using simple tools and rich imagination, fashioning fish into noodles, chicken breast into "tofu," or bean starch into glassy sheets.

In the early days, one of the things that set Yu Bo apart from his peers was his open admiration for Japanese cooking. In a country where anti-Japanese feeling still erupts periodically in street protests, he refused to be a mindless patriot. He was frustrated at the nonchalance

RED-BRAISED PORK WITH GARLIC

DA SUAN HONG SHAO ROU

Aromatic longans bring a lovely sweetness to this dish. If you can't find them, you can substitute dates or just go without.

1 **Cut the pork into 1-inch cubes** and blanch in boiling water. Rinse and drain.

2 **Peel the garlic cloves,** keeping them whole. Use the flat side of a cleaver to crush the ginger and scallion slightly, to release their flavors.

3 **Place the pork in a clay pot** with all the ingredients and enough water just to cover.

4 **Bring the liquid to a boil over medium heat,** then cover and cook over extremely low heat for 10 hours, by which time the pork will be fall-apart tender and the garlic will have melted into the sauce.

5 **Before serving, remove and discard the ginger and scallion.** Garnish with more fresh scallion if you wish, and serve with plain steamed rice.

INGREDIENTS

1 lb boneless pork belly, with skin
3 heads garlic
1 small piece ginger, unpeeled
1 scallion
¾ C sugar, preferably rock sugar
¼ C dried longan fruit (fruit only, without pits)
1 T salt
8 Sichuan peppercorns

with which most Chinese people took their rich heritage for granted, and came to the conclusion that the Japanese were fifty years ahead of China in their culinary culture, partly because of their reverence for the past. "There's a conscientiousness to the Japanese that really impresses me," he said in 2002. "Everything looks perfect. They are concerned with sourcing 'green' ingredients, and their kitchen organization is rigorous, with strict rules on the preparation of food. And it's sad that the Japanese have more respect for Chinese culture than we Chinese do ourselves. When I visited Qufu, the home of Confucius, a guide there told me that when the Japanese invaded China they didn't damage the temple—the stone tablets were smashed by the Chinese during the Cultural Revolution."

Yu Bo says he was arrogant and narrow-minded when he started cooking, simply believing that Sichuanese cuisine was the best in China. Over time he came to see that other regional cuisines might have a lot to offer too. "I realized that you cannot resist change. And I wanted to use everything available to me to develop my skills, drawing on new ingredients and other cooking traditions."

His magpie approach to cooking has been encouraged by trips to America, Australia, and Europe. Few mainland Chinese chefs have dined at El Bulli, the French Laundry, and Tetsuya's, but Yu Bo is, by now, extraordinarily well-travelled. In 2004, I was with him on his first trip abroad, to California. I'd been asked to bring three Sichuanese chefs to a Worlds of Flavor conference at the Culinary Institute of America, and he came along with two other Chengdu chefs, Xiao Jianming of Piaoxiang, one of the outstanding chefs of his generation, and Lan Guijun of

TWICE-COOKED SWISS CHARD

HUI GUO NIU PI CAI

This is a reinterpretation of the Sichuan classic, twice-cooked pork, originally invented at a time when meat was a luxury beyond reach. Nowadays it's served as a "rustic" dish in restaurants.

1 **Cut the dark green chard leaves away from their stems.** Snap each stem into a few pieces, which will allow you to peel away and discard the stringy bits, as you would with celery.

2 **Bring a potful of water to a boil, add the stems and boil for about 3 minutes, until tender.** Add the dark green leaves and boil for another minute or so until they're just cooked through. Drain and shock under cold running water. Squeeze the chard leaves dry, and then cut them into bite-sized lengths.

3 **Heat a seasoned wok over a medium flame, add the oil, swirl it around, and then add the chili-bean paste and stir-fry until it smells delicious and the oil is richly red.** Add the garlic, ginger, and black beans, and stir-fry for a few moments more until fragrant. Then add the stock or water, bring to a boil, add the chard stems and leaves and stir to heat through. Finally, stir in the celery, cilantro, and scallion greens. Serve with steamed rice.

INGREDIENTS

1 lb thick-stemmed Swiss chard
3 T cooking oil (or 1½ T lard and 1½ T oil)
1½ T Sichuanese chili-bean paste (doubanjiang)
2 t garlic, finely chopped
2 t ginger, finely chopped
1 T fermented black beans
½ C stock or water
3 T celery stem (Chinese celery if possible), finely chopped
2 T cilantro, finely chopped
2 T scallion greens, thinly sliced

the Village Cook, then a wildly popular Chengdu restaurant that specialized in rustic cooking. For a week I was their guide, interpreter, driver, and co-presenter at the conference. I also felt duty-bound to give them a crash-course in what the Chinese call "Western food."

On the day after our arrival, in our motel in St. Helena, I fed Yu Bo and the others with morsels of all kinds of foods they'd never tasted before, including capers, olives, and aged parmigiano. We spent the days working at the cooking school, but in the evenings I brought them out to a few local restaurants and subjected them to a barrage of new dishes and ingredients. After the conference had ended, we lunched at Chez Panisse and dined at the French Laundry in Yountville. I wanted to introduce these three talented men to the premier restaurants of California, but my efforts were not an immediate success, as I've written elsewhere. The chefs were revolted by olives, disturbed by rare meat, and exhausted by the ordeal of a tasting menu that lasted four hours, an eternity by Chinese dining standards. Chef Xiao, the senior member of the group, complained that if he ate any more salad he'd "turn into a savage" (echoing the age-old Chinese disdain for raw foods). Over our dinner at the French Laundry, Chef Lan casually mentioned that when Chairman Mao had travelled to the USSR he had taken with him his own cook and food supplies. After only a few days of gastronomic adventures, they were all sick of novelty and dying for Chinese food.

But even then, with his first real exposure to Western food, Yu Bo's curiosity and open-mindedness were striking. As his companions soldiered on through that long dinner at the French Laundry with little apparent pleasure, he was rapt in concentration, exploring every sip and every bite. He was willing to try anything, and to admit that the foods he disliked were not disgusting according to any absolute standard, just incomprehensible in traditional Chinese terms. "It's all very interesting," he said of the food at the French Laundry. "But I simply can't say whether it's good or bad; I'm not qualified to judge." At Chez Panisse, he was prepared to eat a second raw oyster, a horror in Chinese terms, while Chef Xiao refused to try a single one. Yu Bo insisted that you couldn't critique Western food without understanding its cultural background, just as you couldn't understand Chinese food without an awareness of its cultural context.

On subsequent trips to Bolzano, Barcelona, Sydney, and London, I watched Yu and Dai eat with a critical eye that was a delicious riposte to the neglect of Chinese cuisine by the institutions of Western gastronomy. (Even this year, the San Pellegrino Asia's Fifty Best Restaurants included only three Chinese restaurants in mainland China; an earlier global list suggested that the best Chinese restaurant in the world was Hakkasan in London.) Dai Shuang was vastly amused by one American chef's opinion that Sichuanese food was too oily. "He complained," she said, "that our *shui zhu yu* [poached fish in a sea of sizzling chili oil] was oily—and then we watched him shovel a ton of milk and butter into his mashed potato! I pointed out that with Chinese food, if you use chopsticks you leave most of the oil on the plate, while you Westerners expect us to swallow it!"

Neither of them could understand why Western tasting menus were structured in blocks, with fish followed by meat and then a whole sequence of desserts. Chinese banquets, they pointed out, lacked these arbitrary borders between savory and sweet and between different classes of ingredients, so they could range more freely. They found the lack of variety in these blocks of related ingredients stultifying, and dismissed the tasting menu at one internationally renowned restaurant as so unstimulating by Sichuanese standards that it was "like drinking a cup of boiling water."

Yu Bo and Dai Shuang were eloquent on the subtle modulations of a good Sichuanese banquet, with its peaks and troughs, its carefully considered balances between salty and sweet, dry and wet, spicy and mild, hard and soft. Their views echoed those of another Chinese friend with whom I dined at the Fat Duck in England: amazed and delighted by the food, she was baffled by the way the feast ended with a nonstop parade of sweet dishes. "A Chinese banquet," she said, "should leave you feeling very *shu fu* [comfortable, well], not glutted like this." And I could see what she meant. For all the three or four dozen courses you might taste at Yu Bo's restaurant, you won't feel gouty or bilious after dinner.

All these foreign adventures have sprinkled their seasoning on Yu Bo's cooking. When, a few months after that first trip to America, he presented me with a new dish of spare ribs garnished with instant coffee powder, I did wonder if he might be losing his way, but happily this was a rare example of fusion confusion. One year after we'd been to El Bulli, he was serving spherified "pearls" of

jasmine tea on mother-of-pearl spoons (it turned out he'd been given a Ferran Adrià–branded spherification kit by an American chef based in Shanghai). On other visits, I've been served ice cream flavored with fruity, zingy Sichuan pepper, potato fries inspired by a visit to Heston Blumenthal's Hind's Head pub, and even a version of the roast potatoes I cooked for him once at my parents' home in Oxford.

Despite the modernist flights of fancy and the samplings from foreign culinary traditions, both Yu Bo and Dai Shuang are devout traditionalists, and the further they travel, the more they want to return to the simple, seasonal ingredients and hearty folk dishes that are the soul of Sichuanese cookery. So at their restaurant, you might taste expensive Chinese exotica, such as cloudlike snow frog ovaries served on a jade-green custard. But you'll also find elegant renditions of cheap, everyday dishes, like twice-cooked chards, a vegetarian riff on twice-cooked pork that was eaten when meat was scarce and people turned to eating plants that were normally fed to animals; or, in the right season, little tufted stems of *er cai*, or "son vegetable," served in their boiling water with a spicy dip. Perhaps loveliest of all, they've recently revived *tian shao bai*, a traditional Sichuan-feast dish of sliced-belly pork steamed with sweet-glutinous rice and black-sesame paste, and served with a sprinkling of sugar.

Twenty years ago, just about every neighborhood restaurant in Chengdu served fresh and delicious Sichuanese dishes. But ironically, just as the city has been hailed as a UNESCO City of Gastronomy, the traditional flavors of Chengdu are slipping away. The old lanes where peddlers plied their trades have been demolished, and replaced with the commercialized fakery of the Jin Li snack street. Ready-made sauces have infiltrated restaurant kitchens, and most young people, according to every chef and snack-maker I know, are unwilling to face the hardships of an apprenticeship in the arts of traditional cookery. Yu Bo and Dai Shuang's heroes are the shrinking band of artisans and restaurateurs committed to traditional ways of cooking and experts in Sichuanese foodways, like one old man who is, they say, a living dictionary of Sichuanese cuisine.

Yu Bo applauds the Japanese for their work in documenting Chinese food traditions, and decries the old-fashioned Sichuanese chefs who refused to hand down their knowledge, "keeping back a trick or two" (*liu yi shou*) for fear that their apprentices would steal their secrets and rival them in business. Yu Bo and Dai Shuang are both keen to research and preserve Sichuan's distinctive food culture. When Yu Bo won a cash prize along with his gold medal in Beijing, he says most of the other winners spent their money on new clothes for their wives. He called Dai Shuang and told her he was intending to spend it on a rare and valuable set of cookery books published in the 1980s (she approved of his decision).

"Sometimes modern techniques can destroy the quality of traditional dishes," Yu Bo says. "Take twice-cooked pork, for example. You need to cook it slowly, over a low flame, so the meat becomes fragrant and toasty—in restaurants these days they just 'pass it through the oil.' And, as one old chef taught me, if you add a dash of glutinous-rice wine to the wok, it softens the skin of the pork. But most chefs aren't interested in this kind of detail, in the theory of cooking, they don't reflect on what they are doing."

Visits to the United States have left both Yu and Dai with a sense of frustration at the lowly status of Chinese food abroad, and promoting the finest Sichuanese cuisine has become part of the purpose of their work. Yu Bo is critical of certain prominent Chinese chefs who he thinks are moving further and further away from their own traditions as they lap up new ingredients and techniques from the West: "We should start by understanding our own culture, and be proud of it."

Recently, Yu Bo and Dai Shuang have been on reconnaissance missions to Yunnan and Guizhou provinces in search of chilies—something of an irony for two Sichuanese restaurateurs. But they want to broaden their knowledge of chili cultivars, and to find new sources of chilies for their restaurant, because the paving over of the Sichuan countryside has devastated local fields. Ten or so years ago, I visited a chili market during the harvest season, where growers flocked with their bamboo baskets filled with long red chilies that were almost dazzlingly bright. Now, I hear, the whole area is covered with suburban villas. Golf courses, according to Yu Bo, have removed even more land from chili cultivation. And the loss of land isn't the only problem: in a society where babies' milk can be adulterated and even eggs may be faked, sourcing good ingredients is the biggest headache for any conscientious chef.

Yu Bo and Dai Shuang are also worried about the survival of their craft because good staff are so hard to find. Casual workers drift in and out like flotsam, but few young people, they say, are willing to commit to a life of kitchen toil. They've also been hit, like most luxurious restaurants, by President Xi Jinping's crackdown on corruption, which has led to a steep fall in official banqueting.

But still they soldier on, with their crazy determination and fastidious attention to detail. The food evolves, with new ingredients from other parts of China, and old Sichuan recipes rediscovered. In the fall of 2013, Yu Bo was experimenting with serving a liquid with every dish. The spicy rice jelly came with a single abalone steamed in clear beef consommé; rustic spiced chicken with a glass of fiery Maotai liquor; fish-fragrant shrimps with a cupful of mallow leaves in chicken broth. It was a lyrical dinner, perfectly balanced, and a very Sichuanese take on the Western convention of matching wines with every course.

Since those early days, when Yu Bo was a rebel on the fringes of the Chengdu food scene, he has been widely imitated. His checkerboard appetizers have appeared on menus in Beijing, and other "private kitchen" (*si fang cai*) restaurants have sprung up in his neighborhood. One year I was invited by a local food writer to a nearby restaurant that also sought to recreate the ambience of the lost prerevolutionary world of private dining. Although the setting was beautiful and the courses many and varied, the actual cooking was a smorgasbord of indifference. The menu incorporated rustic-Sichuanese dishes, modernist twists, Western and classical-Chinese references, and dramatic presentations, but it lacked the vision required to bring it all into focus. Compared with Yu Bo's, it was food with ambition but without love.

Yu Bo is fiercely competitive and ambitious, and his headstrong nature has caused occasional rifts with his peers. But his relentless individualism and refusal to toe any line of convention are also what make his restaurant exceptional. If you drop into Yu Bo's kitchen any morning, you'll probably find a young chef turning a row of stuffed buns the size of walnuts into "hedgehogs," using nail scissors to snip the raw dough on each one into more than a hundred tiny quills. Yu Bo will be overseeing proceedings, clarifying his stocks with minced pork and chicken, apportioning the turtle skirts and rare Yunnan mushrooms. Dai Shuang might be helping chief waitress Huang Wenyan plait the flowering chives into "hairpins," or counting out tiny hand-painted porcelain pots for the lunchtime service. More than a decade after Yu Bo first began stirring up the Chengdu gastronomic world with his glittering vision of pre-communist banqueting, the flame of his restaurant burns brightly amid the embers of Sichuan's grand old culinary tradition. **LP**

by
**Gideon
Lewis-
Kraus**

Illustrations by
Roman Muradov

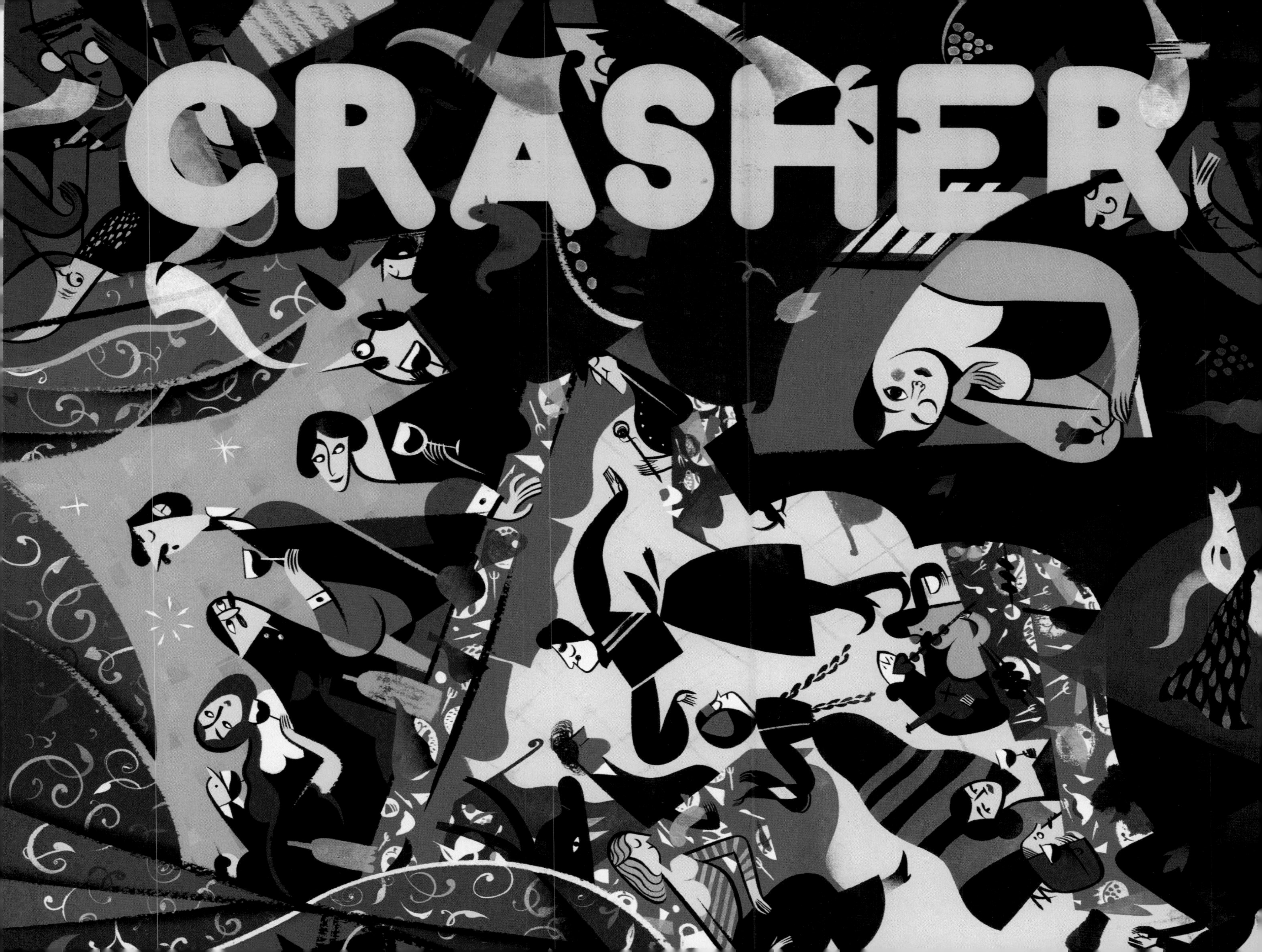
CRASHER

THERE'S A HiGH, STRATEGIC SOUTHERN RiDGE

that supervises the bend in the River Mtkvari where warm sulfur springs inspired the founding of the city of Tbilisi, the capital of the Republic of Georgia. On the easternmost edge of the ridge sprawls the battered keep of a ruined citadel, a defensive position occupied by the invading empires of the Persians, the Arabs, the Mongols, the Turks, and, most recently, the Russians. To the west is the chrome-siloed command sanctum of Georgia's secretive billionaire prime minister and his albino children. Between them stands serenely Mother Georgia.

Mother Georgia is a strong aluminum woman of some twenty meters. Her protuberant breasts swell from what looks like the outside of her plated armor. In her right hand, she holds aloft a bowl of wine. In her left hand, lowered to her long, slender, sheet-metal belly, is a sword. The guidebooks explain that she embodies the two signal virtues of this kingdom wedged between the mountains: the generosity of the host, who welcomes all comers with food and drink, and the courage of the warrior, who has defended herself, valiantly and without reasonable hope, against the clockwork onslaughts of imperial whimsy. The other interpretation is that she's brandishing the sword to make sure you finish the wine.

Her smiling enforcement of excess has been taken up by Georgia's ritual toastmasters. The Georgian ritual feast is called a *supra*, which means set table, and the toastmaster

is called the *tamada*. At a wedding, a traditional tamada is expected to give the newlyweds a sense of their connection to Georgia's national saga—the incessant incursions of imperial armies and the spirited, courageous defense of the mountain strongholds—as well as practical advice and encouragement. It's an exceedingly honorable position, and the best of them are known across their home regions for their eloquence, pacing, and windy familiarity with history and legend, as well as their ability to consume eight to ten liters of wine over the course of two dozen toasts without ever seeming drunk. Georgians will throw a supra for just about anything—a funeral, a new job, the celebration of an improvised and still half-finished home-improvement project—but weddings are their favorite pretext.

I am at the age when time is largely meted out as the interim between weddings, and recently there have been several of great significance. In the span of a month last year, both my girlfriend's sister and my brother had gotten married, and my girlfriend and I had been spending a lot of time talking about the toasts we were expected to give. Even her father had gotten in on our discussions; he'd been sending me YouTube clips of what he thought were successful toasts, models of what he might achieve. I was not immune to his sense of occasion. A great deal of energy, it seemed, went into the personalization of the wedding day, the whole mosaic of details that distinguished one wedding from the next.

My own take was that the best chance of distinction lay in the toasts; nobody but the couple would remember if the drinks were served in mason jars or empty votive candle holders, but the right wedding toast could really bring a room together.

That sort of toast is one of the few times in one's life when one's invited to mark a moment, to help articulate the swarming good wishes and hopes of a community that might only be assembled in this particular configuration one time, and it was something I took very seriously. While deadlines for other work sailed past almost unnoticed, I felt mounting pressure to put together a toast that would properly celebrate and send off my brother and his fiancée—a few minutes that would help elaborate the foundational legend of their life together—which meant that I, like my girlfriend's father, was spending a lot of time trawling the Internet for inspiration. This is how I discovered that the Georgians advertised themselves as the world's most profligate tributary drinkers. The Georgian emphasis on the importance of the wedding toast was something that I, as a person of some literary aspiration and commensurate self-importance, could get behind; I was curious about the formal elevation of public drunken garrulousness to the status of ritual. I wanted to observe a supra. I wanted to see, furthermore, if they'd in fact come up with a foolproof way to make an observant into a participant; for this was what it meant to instantiate the right fleeting community.

About ten minutes after my plane landed in Tbilisi, I had three weddings to go to. There was Wi-Fi in the airport, and as I stood in line at passport control I paged through two e-mails delivering the excited news that village weddings had been discovered, and that, in accordance with the old Georgian saying "A guest is a gift from God," I was to be an honored visitor at each. Some of the Georgians I had reached out to before the trip had mentioned that

it was actually sort of hard to go to Georgia and *not* find yourself invited to one wedding or another. They also said that most Georgians never plan anything in advance, especially weddings. All of this appealed to me; what it communicated was that Georgia was not a place where a wedding had to be a special, fragile flower, but was something with a traditional form so robust it could be assembled both hastily and with great confidence. It was a ritual with conviction.

One would take place the following day, a Saturday, in a village near the Black Sea, on the opposite side of this fortunately small country. It was about a six-hour drive, and I was advised that I'd have to take the first *marshrutka*, or cramped minibus, in the morning to make it there in time. The second wedding would take place on Sunday, also near the Black Sea, but in the far northwest, within a twenty-minute drive of the border with the Russian-sponsored breakaway republic of Abkhazia. The third I arranged while waiting in line at passport control, and it conflicted with the first.

As I approached an immigration official, a woman in the neighboring line loudly and irrelevantly told her own immigration official, in slightly accented American English, that she had flown in from Kansas City for the wedding of her stepson. I took advantage of what I hoped would be our shared air-travel disorientation to approach her as we walked toward baggage claim. I told her I was a writer interested in the cheers of the Georgian supra, and I couldn't help overhearing that she was in town for a wedding.

She did not look at me oddly. "Yes, I am. Thirteen months ago, my stepson came here with my husband to visit a former exchange student of ours here. It was my stepson's college graduation trip." He had fallen in love with a Georgian, stayed behind, and the two were to be wed the next day in a suburban village on a hillside outside of the capital. She didn't so much invite me formally as tell me that if I accompanied her to the curb I might get the church's address from her husband, who'd already been in the country for a week to help his son prepare.

I hadn't even left the airport and already I was going to have to turn down an invitation for at least one wedding, an invitation that had taken considerable effort to obtain, and the refusal of which was sure to cause some offense.

In the meantime, I had also secured a non-wedding supra to attend, conveniently located two doors down from the Airbnb apartment where I was staying. At the last minute, I had written my host and asked if he knew of a supra I might attend.

"You are in luck," he responded immediately. "We have a supra at my home on Friday." I'd been warned in advance about the deracinated supras of Georgia's urban elite. These people, I'd been told, were squandering the tradition by breaking all of the rules. They talked during the toasts, for one, and, perhaps even more gravely, they allowed themselves to sip desultorily from their wineglasses. At a classic supra, one sips water or soda to slake one's thirst; it's only when the tamada finishes each toast that one may, which is to say one must, rise and drain one's glass. The urban young people, I heard more than once, were no longer interested in the texture and pace of the ritual as it had long been practiced, but only wanted to get drunk as quickly as possible. This seemed a peculiar way to lament the contemporary decline of an institution that had for a thousand years been dedicated to

getting everyone drunk as quickly as possible. I'd long ago grown bored with authenticity questions, but it did seem a live issue to Georgians and their admirers. One of the dozens of people trying to help me find a wedding supra to crash mentioned not offhandedly in an e-mail that the supras of the Tbilisi gentry were rather like the bullshit Passover seders enjoyed by fallen New York Jews. One of the things I'd find, though, after a home supra, a wealthy urban supra, a poorer village supra, and finally a staged tourist supra, was that the supra is designed to be a self-consuming artifact. After the first few toasts, a supra could be conducted on the moon and everybody would still rise to the expectations of the occasion.

W ithin an hour of touching down I was seated in Tbilisi's Old Town, in the long shadow of Mother Georgia with her wine and her sword, at my depraved urban Airbnb supra. I'd been slightly worried that the whole thing was being staged for my benefit. I was fortunate in that there was another pretext: two sponsored food bloggers from France. Our hosts were an artist called Tamaz, along with his wife and teenage daughter. Tamaz filled our wineglasses, explaining that he had made the wine himself, below the kitchen, from the grapevines hanging over the dangerously tilted circular staircase in the rear courtyard. Tbilisi is a city of stairways long departed from their traditional axes and precipitous, slapdash wooden balconies with unmoored balustrades. Over all of them are draped the long strands of minor home vineyards. I suppose Tamaz's wine was what one would call white, but it was really something closer to a plummy amber, with the cloudy cast of unfiltered cider, or desert urine.

The toasts of a supra are structured, and the first one is always to God. Tamaz stood at the small, crowded table, and spoke for about five minutes. I loved listening to the language. It's one of the mellower of the *kh*-intensive languages, like a lullaby sung to a wolf brood. It's a little craggy but there are meadows, too. Only on rare occasion does it feature strings of more than five consecutive consonants. Georgians take great pride in the fact that their alphabet has thirty-three letters. They seem well aware that this is some 25 percent more than English has. Presumably some of them are vowels.

When Tamaz was finished, his daughter translated. "He says we have to thank God for having been born, and for giving us all we have, and that without God we would not have our health or our happiness. *Gaumarjos!" Gaumarjos* is Georgian for "cheers," though it literally means "Be victorious!" We drained our glasses and sat down and the first thing everybody reached for was *khachapuri*, the staple Georgian starch, to quell the cold bloom of vinegar sloshing in our guts. Where some cultures have rice and others have pita, Georgians accompany every meal with cheese bread. There are some regional variations, which occupy the narrow eggy carbohydrate gamut that runs from thick white pizza to bricks of lasagna. There were other dishes on the table—in fact, there was nothing but dishes on the table—and one of them was grimly recognizable as a vegetable, but the engine of Georgian consumption, and thus the engine of Georgian culture, is khatchapuri. In a cunningly circular generative device, the tang of the acidic homemade wine necessitates the sop of the dough, and then the gluey parcel of sop won't budge until it's cut with more wine. The other participant in this dynamic is Georgian water. The spring water is famous throughout the Soviet Union for its salt and mineral content. It tastes like a distant sea run through an old metal Brita filter.

Everything—the astringent wine and the caustic water; the torn, coarse bread and the wedges of smoked cheese—tastes of ore and fat and tears, and the only recourse is more salty water and more tart wine. This whole process is helped along by the rhythm of the toasts. The first five or six toasts are customarily given in rapid succession. This is mostly so that whatever resistance may have existed to the prospect of the second five or six toasts is dealt with early and decisively, such that the third set of five or six toasts faces no hesitation whatsoever.

Tamaz rose (and we rose with him) to offer another toast, this one to love. He spoke slowly, took long pauses, shifted registers, changed clip. His wife laughed. At the end of maybe four minutes, his daughter raised her glass. "He says that love is very important in our lives, and that love is the thing that brings us together." We held our glasses aloft, waiting for her to elaborate, but she was finished. We shrugged and drained our glasses.

The Frenchman turned to me. "Something here, I think, is being lost in the translation." This seemed accurate, but the mood at the table was so easy and full of goodwill that it was easy to forgive the lapses.

Then the blogger, inspired by the two glasses of rapid-succession wine, stood to offer his own toast, but Tamaz waved him down. His daughter explained that, if you wanted to toast, you had to wait for the tamada's invitation. We sat a moment in embarrassed silence before Tamaz saved face all around by asking the Frenchman to toast. He stood and praised friendship between the nations, and—*Gaumarjos!*—we drank. We followed the wine with a khatchapuri chaser, and then it was my turn. I delivered a long and impassioned encomium to my first encounter with Georgian hospitality, that wonderful, vicious cycle of forcible conviviality. The teenaged translator cut me off to

reissue my toast in Georgian right when she thought it was time for my encomium to end. She seemed to make a real effort to translate the whole thing; as she spoke, Tamaz looked at me and nodded thoughtfully. *Gaumarjos!*

By our eighth or ninth glass of wine and our seven thousandth calorie of khatchapuri, Tamaz seemed to recognize that things had gone perhaps a little far for seven p.m. He went to get his guitar.

"These Georgians," the Frenchwoman said with a winsome slur, "they can't stop singing." They needed, it seemed, some remissive structure, something designed to give everybody present an elegant way to opt out, for a moment, of the relentless alternation of liquor and khatchapuri. Tamaz began strumming the chord progression of "Hey Jude." We all began together: "Hey Jude..." I continued, perhaps innocently, with the text of the actual song, but Tamaz raised his voice to sing down my lyrical fidelity, loudly braying, "Dah dah dah dah dah, di di di di, du du du du du du du." He aggressively scatted the Beatles, brooking no actual English words, as the Frenchwoman shook a recently materialized maraca to an internal rhythm of her own. I was more than delighted to sing dah da di with my arms around the French couple. When we all finished singing, we clapped for each other and for ourselves, and I felt so proud of our collective dah da di, and correspondingly ashamed that I'd ever been disappointed by the daughter's perfunctory translations. All she'd been communicating, it was clear to me, was that there was just no possible way to convey the grace and dexterity of her father's words in a language as blockheaded as English, and she hadn't even tried. Tamaz's wife brought in some very strong Turkish coffee, to make sure we wouldn't be too tired to get more drunk later on.

Two drinks later Tamaz was on his feet again, though by then nobody was paying him much heed. I'd lost track of a few toasts, and at some point we'd left the table and were sitting around on the couches. We'd switched to *chacha*, the local variant of grappa. The Frenchman put his arm around me again. We were sharing the fruits of this death march toward good fellowship. He gouged his index finger, plump from food blogging, into my cheek. He said, "In France, when someone gives a toast, we are never serious. We try to be witty and entertaining and to make the guests… chuckle. But we never say anything serious. The Georgians, they are serious, and they use the supra as an occasion to say serious things." He stopped for a moment, and it was clear he felt he had to say something commensurate with the serious occasion he was seriously describing. It was as though our goodwill had been extended on credit, and now it was time for that small but important debt to be paid. "My girlfriend and I," he said, "we are traveling as sponsored food bloggers for the next one year and sixth months." He looked over at her. She was staring out the window and shaking her maraca. "If it all goes like it has gone so far, at the end, in Madagascar, I will ask her to be my wife."

"Yes! Yes, me, too! I mean, not sponsored food blogging, my girlfriend would never do that in a million years, but asking her to be my wife!" I was poking him in the chest, and waving the carafe of chacha. I hadn't talked to anybody else about this. I'm not sure I'd even really articulated it to myself. What a wonderful thing this had been, this supra, this Tamaz and his wisdom, these sponsored French food bloggers, this dastardly chacha. "Let's do it, both of us. *Gaumarjos!*"

Vika extended to me, in her left hand, a plate helpless beneath heavily iced brown cake; in her left hand, she held a cell phone. She looked like Mother Georgia. It was something like seven o'clock in the morning, and she was bellowing.

"GEEEEDEEEEOOOON!" she bellowed. Tamaz's family was running a complicated Airbnb racket distributed across the neighborhood, and Vika was my hostess—a stout, wonderful woman in her fifties, with red hair and bangs that arched in sprouting confusion. She put down the cake and the cell phone and defiantly tugged at the tight collar of her pink bathrobe, as if her clothes were preventing her from realizing generosity's full potential. "GEEE-DEEOON, please take your cake and please take your cell phone."

"Thank you, Vika. *Madlobt.*"

"Don't mention it, don't mention it! Is that right—'Don't mention it'?"

"That's right, Vika. You can say, 'Don't mention it.'"

"Don't mention it."

It was already too late to make it across the country for the village wedding, so it looked like I was going to the American-Georgian one in the nearby suburb. I could barely recall what had happened after the Frenchman and I had discovered our profound kinship, though I dimly remembered having gotten into a loud squabble in German on a rooftop with Tbilisi's foremost literary blogger. I felt I couldn't let one supra prevent the next one, though, so I pulled myself together.

On the way to the wedding Vika only called me twice, to make sure I was going to the place with the right *kh* sound, not the pleasant high-throated Hebrewish one, but the one that issues forth from the place where terrible beauties are born. She insisted on talking to the person next to me on the bus to make sure I was going to Tsqneti. At Tsqneti I arrived in time to witness a wedding hitch. The church had overbooked itself, so the priest asked the groom through an interpreter, his future sister-in-law, if it would be okay for them to hold a double wedding with another couple. The groom felt that that would be less special to him than a single wedding. Just like an American, I thought, wanting his wedding to be a kid-glove affair. The Georgians couldn't tell why he was making a fuss about the "specialness," but I knew where he was coming from. In any event, the bride was an hour and a half late, so the point quickly became moot. Pensioners of the forested mountain suburb lined the park benches to watch each hour's wedding.

Inside the whitewashed candle-lit church I retreated to the cool clay shadows of the transept recess and watched the bride and groom accept their ornamented wedding crowns, jewels hanging forth like the lures of crystalline anglerfish. They leaned down to kiss the golden-haloed icons, then promenaded in a series of small circles trailed by witnesses as the priest chanted the orthodox mass. Their promenade complete, the bride sipped from the ceremonial chalice. The groom began to sip but his witness tipped the chalice from below. "More!" the witness whispered in English, and even the priest laughed. The groom bled the chalice dry.

The guests filed in at dusk and took up their posts at long, rectangular tables radiating outward from a wide dance floor like the jumbled spokes of a wheel disintegrating under a tremendous load. On the far side of the room, on a raised dais underneath sepia considerations of pre-Soviet Tbilisi and the ubiquitously reproduced warm-banquet scene of Niko Pirosmani, Georgia's Chagall, a smaller table awaited the newlyweds and their witnesses. The tablecloths were mostly invisible under the tiling of plates, though here and there a little window of linen shone forth through the nearly uniform layer of porcelain. Clusters of drink formed the centerpieces: the sickeningly sweet national sodas in chartreuse and juniper, the crystal flagons of loamy white wine. There was a boastful amount of food. Stockpiled on plates were: rolled baby eggplants congested with walnut paste and studded with the vitreous sparkle of pomegranate seeds; fanned wedges of *sulguni*, a brackish cheese, some smoked and some fresh; sliced patchworks of cold fried chicken and glazed ingots of cold roast piglet; lascivious tongues of stuffed red pepper; and greenish-brown brushes of what looked like tide-pool bracken. There were baskets of the coarse, torn flat bread, and no one sat more than a foot or two away from a pile of khatchapuri. The minute the guests entered, they set to the food without formality.

The bride's sister, Ia, organized the whole thing. She spoke better than functional English—and was thus the translator for the few Americans in attendance (though the groom's father, a military man, could get by with his Russian)—and told me that it was customary for the bride and groom to enter only after the third toasts. It's an exceptional concession, extended to young people only on their wedding night, that they're allowed to remain three drinks behind everyone else. I asked

Ia if she could take special care to translate the toasts exactly, because I was interested in the precise thing being delivered; she said she'd do her best, but that I should really try to focus on the spirit with which the toasts were given, the gestures made, and the tone taken, rather than the actual words. "It's a little like a prayer," she said. "You say the same words over and over, but what's important is you say them with special feeling."

With that in mind, Ia introduced me to the tamada, Shao, a trim man

in his early forties with a calculating look. He's the second cousin of the bride's late father, and he was chosen because of his deep familiarity with the long, illustrious, tragic history of the bride's family. The groom's party in full counts the father, the stepmother I'd approached at immigration, the mother, and a well-kept German named Amos who'd also been an exchange student with the family in Kansas City. The groom's family was happy to have another American present, if only for confused solidarity. Several members of the bride's family told me, via Ia, that guests are

always welcome in Georgia, and that they hoped I'd get enough to drink. By the end of the toasts, they said, we'll all be family, I'll see.

Two-thirds of the seats were full—perhaps eighty guests—and Ia seemed a little anxious about the absences, but Shao decided he wasn't going to indulge the delinquent invitees. He gave the first toast not to God but to peace, and spoke fluently, with the domineering bounce of a talk-show host, for five or six minutes. For the first half, the guests remained silent, but by the end of the toast conversation had resumed. Ia was a little too preoccupied with the missing-guest situation to translate as the tamada went along, but as everyone lifted his or her glass to drink she rushed through a quick interpretation. "So, he toasted to peace, for the Georgian nation to finally have peace after so many years of war and invasion and being a part of other empires, so that Georgia may live among the nations in peace and friendship, with an end to war."

Ia turned to John, the groom's father. "Tamada says you must toast now."

"To what?" John asked.

"To peace," Ia said.

"To peace what?" John's a retired military man proud of his stiff bearing, but before the reception had assumed the chatty, patronizing diplomacy of an assistant dean of students. Now he was once again alive to the chain of command.

"You need to fill your glass," Ia continued. I was seated next to him, and poured. I was alive to the chain of command, too. "Yes, that's right. Now stand up, raise your glass, and say you want to take this special opportunity to toast to the everlasting peace of the Georgian people, after all the wars they've been through."

John proceeded as instructed. He'd clearly done some preparing for this possibility, and he mentioned not just war in general but the recent war with Russia, still fresh in everybody's mind. I thought he did an honorable job, and I raised my glass to him. Ia waited until he was finished, then spoke in Georgian, at much greater length. Her translation met periodic cheers. When she finished, glasses swung high, and all the men downed the brown wine. Three musicians near the dais picked up their long-necked, three-stringed Georgian mandolins and plucked out a medley of patriotic nationalist hymns, occasionally breaking into foreign songs gaily faked with nonce syllables. While the glasses were refilled, each person in the service of his or her neighbor, servers continually delivered hot dishes as though on conveyor belts, balancing each new addition on the rims of the plates below it: saucers of phyllo-wrapped chicken egg rolls, like Turkish stuffed cigars; polished bronze tureens of something sheepishly described to me as liver but was clearly scraps of spicy rosemary offal, like a *kokoretsi*; and clabbering puddles of gelatinous hominy grits, which the groom's family was pleased to recognize as grits, then condemn as tasteless. The layer of cold starters was quickly plated over, though guests continued to draw portions from each stratum. At least half the dishes were decorated with pomegranate seeds, whose role as bright, ubiquitous garnish seems to underline its symbolic presence vis-à-vis Hades and everything. This country was known to the Greeks, and must know its myths, and is self-aware enough about its draconian hospitality that it's no surprise they'd adorn each table with insistent reminders that there are always consequences to the acceptance of the most trivial-seeming gifts.

The bride and groom strode in to great fanfare; everybody stood, glass in hand. They were a toast or two early but nobody seemed to be standing on ceremony. They entered onto a short red carpet

strewn with rose petals and framed by a series of plastic white columns that come to the groom's shoulders. They stopped at the head of the carpet, where the bride showed the groom that they were supposed to smash to smithereens a porcelain plate. (I almost yelled, "Mazel tov!") The tamada toasted the newlyweds, hoping and predicting that they would be happy and healthy and enjoy many children.

Mere glasses of wine were apparently from then on incommensurate with the occasion, so they brought out the *khantsi*, or drinking horns. There's a dual theoretical basis to the horn-drinking practice, which dates to at least the seventh century. The first is the obvious fact that, while a standard glass cannot hold a liter of wine at one time, a standard horn can. The second is that horns culminate in sharp ulterior points rather than accommodatingly flat bottoms; while wine remains it can't be set down. The horn was brought to John and filled. Ia shrugged. "You hold up the horn, you make a toast to the families of bride and groom, you have no choice but to drink all wine in horn or you will not honor the union of these two families. When you are finished, you hold out the horn upside and shake it over the table, to show tamada that no wine remains."

John, a man of both duty and restraint who now faced the irreconcilability of those two virtues, offered a few words about the families, Ia expanded them considerably in translation, and then John tipped back his head. Rivulets of wine poured down his collar and over his American-flag lapel pin. He lifted his head and flipped his horn with great satisfaction, inadvertently spraying his son's mother, with whom he'd been distant but cordial, with the remaining drops of wine. The guests assembled lost it with pleasure, and many of the men came over to clap him on the back and propose that they now celebrate his first successful horn with a second, commemorative horn. Here and there men stood to interlace shirt-sleeved arms and gulp glasses over one another's shoulders. The whole thing from toast number five onward got a little loosey-goosey, and the first ad hoc toasts—challenges to the tamada's authority—rang forth from the room's periphery.

Before the horn's devastation could spread further, the drinking was once again suspended as the overheads were dimmed and servers trotted out bearing adorable fires on bronze trays; they set down plates of pork and lamb and veal shashlik cuddled close to burning embers, along with bowls of veal ribs in *adjika* sauce and something that looked suspiciously like brains. There was no longer even a pretense of order at the table: plates were placed into precarious balance atop piles of dishes now in threes and fours, food cooling like mortar in the gaps. Slices of khatchapuri from the kitchen were simply strewn and draped atop it all. I hated to be so distant and ungenerous in my acceptance of what was on offer, but I had a hangover of outlandish Georgian proportion. I tried repeatedly to explain that my first supra had simply been so successful that I was unable to rise to this consecutive occasion. People nodded with faux understanding, but there was little I could do. I could only reconcile myself to the fact that I'd be letting everybody down. But I was quickly forgiven—this was the evening's greatest point of sentimentality, when guests were drunk enough to feel moved but not so drunk they couldn't articulate it—and it was all forgotten as a troupe of folk dancers skipped in from the kitchen, the women in floor-length peasant dresses and the men in traditional black tunics with stenciled white outlines of antiquated bandoliers strung across their chests, outlines of daggers in groin scabbards.

After the dance, Ia jumped up and pushed back from the table to greet some new arrivals, whom she quickly described to me as the event's "most appreciated guests." The guests apparently knew to arrive in order of importance, and these three—two very well-manicured and -accessorized young women and a little girl—had taken their delayed influx to the extreme. The latecomers, their slender Byzantine fingers ornamented with glittering metal, sat across from me and pulled out their iPhones. Phones and cameras, until that moment, hadn't been present.

With the next toast, the now-boisterous assembly, some of whom had begun to take to the dance floor themselves, became still. This was the tribute to the fathers and grandfathers, and Ia took her time translating this one. "This is for the men who have died defending Georgia in war, for those who have died so we can have our freedom. Tamada says he would like to honor the grandfather of the groom, who fought in the Second World War and in Korea; and the father of the groom, who fought in Vietnam; and then the father of the bride, my father." Ia paused.

"My father"—and now it was no longer clear if she was translating or making her own toast—"was a partisan general in the region now known as South Ossetia, which we Georgians have always called by the name Tshkhinvali, some sixty kilometers to the north of here, which is where our family comes from." South Ossetia is occupied by the Russians, who claim to support the independence of the South Ossetian people. "My father was a partisan general for the Georgians there, and the Russians put a price on his head. He was assassinated in the lead-up to the war with Russia in 2008, betrayed by a member of his own unit, and our whole family was threatened. We fled with only our clothing to Tbilisi, and we cannot go back." If they crossed the border, they would be killed immediately.

The toast was seconded by many others, and for a few moments the mood turned solemn, but then the tamada said something to the musicians, and the mandolin trio struck up a kind of Georgian mazurka. Glasses were emptied, horns flipped, and all was again merry.

After some group dancing, for which the tamada pulled me with considerable force onto the dance floor to join a kind of spiral hora, I found myself shuffled around into a seat by the most appreciated guests, who had thus far done little but idly scan through Instagram on their phones. They'd eaten practically nothing, and their bright, unsmudged plates stared upward from the troughs of smeared dishes with haughty reproof. One of the women had lived in New York for a decade and she explained, in excellent English with little prompting, why she was so completely bored by the surrounding saturnalia.

"None of us in our generation wants to sit and listen to the tamada, especially a boring tamada like this one. We just want to be able to drink when and how we please, and to dance at a wedding, not to have to sit here and listen to this guy go on and on and on. Like, okay, right now?" The tamada was on his feet again, though nobody was paying him much heed. "He's toasting to the uncles and cousins. I'll translate for you exactly. Okay, he says he thanks this one uncle, Gyorgy, who is a great man and can quote poetry and is a wonderful person to drink with." She paused. "Now he thanks another uncle, Shota, who is a terrific guy, and he knows this well because they once got drunk together. Now he's toasting another uncle, and he's remembering all the times they shared shots of the chacha they made in their courtyard." She waited again. "His little cousin is a good boy, and he remembers the first time he saw him finish a horn. This is what the whole thing is like, and everybody is talking and nobody is listening because he's not being smart and he's not being funny and he's not quoting poetry and this is why the tradition of the supra is dying. Nobody cares to listen to this." She looked over at the phone of her sister-in-law, who was Instagramming the image of her clean plate amid the mess.

"I have a recommendation to make. As you can see, this is about to get really sloppy." She pointed to John, who was interlaced with the older men of the family in a circle, each draining a horn, and then to the groom himself, who stood in a receiving line of chacha bearers. The tamada and his deputy yelled at each other from across the room. "Leave now, with us in our car, because you've seen everything good, and this is only going to go downhill from here. At the village wedding you're going to tomorrow it will be poor people from the countryside, more authentic than this anyway."

It was clearly indefensible that I'd been at least partially persuaded by their wealth and their English and their ennui, but they were also giv-

ing me, in my hungover state, permission to take leave of the festivities. I went over to the groom's family, now clustered around the dais, to wish them well. John thanked me for being such a great guest, a really wonderful, terrific, thoughtful guy, and said he hoped I would have all the health and happiness in the world. He started to raise the horn that I might join him in one for the road, but when he caught my eye he let the horn fall to his side. He was a better man than I, and we both knew it. "Good luck," he said.

Vika's husband insisted on rising early to deposit me at the proper cross-country marshrutka for my trip to Zugdidi, the last stop before Abkhazia. Before we left, Vika offered me "tea." I warily accepted. When I came back from the bedroom with my bags, she'd set the table with a pannier of torn bread, a silver tray stacked with slabs of sulguni cheese, six large tomatoes, four cucumbers, and half of a large brown cake. On the side was a small glass of black tea. "Your tea," she said. It was enough provisions for an overland caravan to Uzbekistan.

When my marshrutka hit the westbound highway, a while later, a Nokia chimed.

"Hi, Vika!" I answered.

"GEEEDEEEOOON! How did you know it is me, Vika?"

"Because you're the only person who has this number. I don't even know this number. It's your phone."

"Yes, yes, don't mention it! Listen, how are you?"

"I'm good, Vika. Thanks. I'm fine. How are you?"

"Oh, good, don't mention it. My husband, he drop you off at marshrutka station? Yes, okay good. You go to Zugdidi, yes? Okay, good. You call me when you get Zugdidi, tell me you are there."

"Okay, Vika. Thanks. I will."

It made somewhat more sense, now, that everybody in this country seemed to be on their phones all the time. The entire population of Georgia is continuously haranguing their guests with increasingly demanding largesse. It was perhaps the world's most exhausting place to be a guest. You had to be extremely sound of mind and body to meet the hosts here on their own terms. I gave some thought to turning off my phone to get some sleep, but I was afraid Vika would be angry at me if she couldn't reach me to ask if I needed anything.

In Zugdidi I met up with Marika, who'd found this second wedding for me. She's a bottle blonde in a spandex sheath and she runs a hostel that mostly caters to Russian adventure tourists she dislikes for their fussiness and national condescension. The only delays en route to my bed were quick samples of her homemade spicy-plum marmalade and their regionally famous pepper-tomato spread and of course the celebrated Mingrelian mint-stuffed cheese.

It is the Japanese habit to apologize when giving a gift. They feel as though they have to acknowledge what a burden it can be to receive one. But in Japan the culture of generosity seems predicated on national isolation: one trapped insider's gift to another trapped insider invites an infinite compensatory regress of thoughtful gestures. In Georgia, the commitment to extremes of charity seems to have arisen in the context of almost a thousand years of near-constant invasions by neighbors with imperial ambitions. But Georgians are naturally gregarious and warm, and they get tired of all the martial posturing that's fallen to them. This must be why they like guests so much, why they consider them gifts from God. A guest is the kind of foreigner who isn't out to attack you.

Still, he might change his mind. He ought to be incapacitated while the host has the chance.

Upon arriving at the social hall, Marika went about getting us invited to the wedding, which was accomplished easily enough. Then she realized she'd gotten us invited to the wrong wedding. The wedding she'd meant to crash was across the street, in a different yet identical social hall. She had to slink back and apologize for turning down the invitation she'd cadged only moments before.

The guests at the right wedding were awaiting the arrival of the newlyweds, who finally emerged from a long white limo at the head of a procession of honking Ladas. Fireworks were set off in the vacant lot between the social hall and a half-abandoned Soviet-era tower block. They proceeded down a red carpet under a series of white plastic trellises, stopping to accept a set of Chinese lanterns, which, when plump, were released directly into the balcony overhead. One of them went down like a little Hindenburg but the other was celebrated with Roman candles as it righted itself and sailed out over the Black Sea.

The food on the table was basically the same, to start with, as at the first wedding, though it was clear that we were no longer at a banquet in the distant capital. Even thinking of describing this food now, some months later, makes me feel ill, but I know Marika would be disappointed if I didn't at least mention the local specialties: the minted feta, the brown munitions of cornmeal, cold fried quails served atop their own hard-boiled eggs, garnished with pine boughs. The singer introduced the tamada, a cousin of the groom's father, who was seated on the far side of the room. As he stood up to make his introductory remarks, somebody went over to whisper something to him, and he interrupted himself with news. Marika said, "He said he heard there is an American writer and an Uruguayan photographer here, and guests are gifts from God, and perhaps the American would like to serve as assistant tamada for the evening." At Marika's urging, though I clearly knew this drill by then, I stood and raised my glass to the tamada across the room.

The assistant tamada is expected to follow up on the tamada's serial toasts with respective toasts of his own; they can be extensions, embellishments, or ripostes—playful competition for the tamada. As one person explained it to me, the idea is that the more entertaining you can be as toastmaster, the more spellbound your audience, the longer you're encouraged by collective attention to continue, and thus the better you can put off, if for only a few minutes, the chronic inevitability of each successive glass. The tamada is supposed to have a special sensitivity to the mood of the room. He should engage the distracted, distract the engaged, slow down the drunken, and speed up the sober.

"Oh," Marika continued, "and tamada says his grandson is at that table"—a sixteen-year-old with a shaved head and a toothy smile waved at us from behind some liquor bottles he'd already been lovingly fingering—"and that he's in charge of making sure your glass is always full, and then always empty. Full when it should be full, empty when it should be empty."

The first toast: to Georgia, may it be long-lived and powerful. Marika raced to keep up with the toasts. She didn't have Ia's familial duties, so she could throw herself into the translation project with abandon; she also had a particular sensitivity to the nuances of language. Georgia invented wine, seven thousand years ago. Georgians are courageous and gracious. They like to laugh and have a good time. They have always been kind and tolerant to the minorities in their midst, all of whom are children under God. He finished and Marika elbowed me. I lifted my glass and, in what felt to me like a clear, strong voice, called out across the room, "To the great and powerful and generous nation of Georgia!"

Tamada and I extended our glasses to each other across the crowded, tinseled banquet hall. "*Gaumarjos!*" I said. The grandson held my eye as we took our glasses in a single draught.

The second toast was to peace. Food I am no longer able to describe fell in sheets around us, like unsolicited manna. The restaurant singer sang a love song to the Uruguayan, in something he alleged was Italian.

"How's this tamada?" I asked Marika. She'd told me she was a traditionalist about these things. The most appreciated women in Tbilisi might've been too hard on the previous tamada, but at least they'd given me some sense of what constituted a good one—one that didn't just drone on with a laundry list of the great drinkers he'd known—and I was keen to pay more attention tonight, to allow myself to be moved to participation in a way I hadn't been the night before.

"It's a little too early to tell." The first few toasts, before the tamada and the crowd had come loose from their moorings, were pretty pro forma. "But I like him. He seems like a very old-fashioned tamada. He has a good sense of humor, and he says the things about the past that we need to know for the future." I asked what she meant, but she shushed me as the tamada started to speak.

The third toast was to the Patriarch of the Georgian church, Ilia II. The men hastened to stand. Marika began to tear up as she either translated or extemporized her own toast. "The Patriarch is the only person who hasn't betrayed us. All of our politicians, they lie to us and betray us. The Russians lie to us and

make war against us. The Armenians, with their rocky patch of unfertile country, lie to us and try to fuck us. Nobody is someone the Georgian people can rely on except the Patriarch, and when he dies I do not know how I will be consoled. He preaches such wisdom in troubled times. He helped us turn away from aggression and from violence and toward peace. He is the only person the Georgian people trust with all of our hearts."

I stood to say a few short things about the patriarch, whom until that day I hadn't heard of, and came under a brutal shoulder-thump

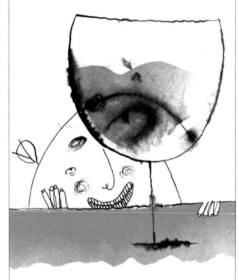

assault by a cadre of well-wishers. Marika nodded that I'd done an honorable job. The tamada's grandson looked over my way and pricked his chin; this is the universal Georgian invitation to join him for a slug of chacha. Marika considered it on my behalf. "On one hand, mixing that chacha with wine is probably not a good idea. Especially when soon you will drink from horn. On other hand, you cannot say no. He is tamada's grandson." We linked arms and threw back the shots.

The next toast was to the bride and groom—may they be happy and healthy and have a lot of

children. Before I drank I turned to Marika. "I've got a question. There's supposed to be such a big difference between various tamadas, and it's a skill that people are known far and wide for possessing. You speak excellent, evocative, poetic English, but the way you translate these toasts—with the exception of the one to the patriarch—they sound pretty generic. Is something being lost in translation?"

"It's the nuance, which maybe just can't be conveyed in English, or it's the little scraps of poetic allusions. For example, in the last toast, there was a short part of a line from Rustaveli, and it's something all Georgians know by heart." She reeled off a tripping, rhyming couplet from *The Knight in the Panther's Skin*, the national epic of Georgia's golden age.

Before she could continue, the tamada was on his feet and out of a torrent of stern Georgian I picked out something that sounded suspiciously like my own name. There was some commotion. Apparently he'd caught me raising my glass only to put it down undrained. He'd missed that I'd enjoyed a shot of chacha with his grandson instead. He was piqued that his authority had gone challenged by this supposed gift of God.

A man materialized beside me with a horn. Marika put in a vote to go easy on me, but it went pointedly ignored, and the horn-chalice was filled until wine splashed out onto the pile of plates below. I bankrupted it as required, flecking the final droplets out onto the head of the grandson who'd gotten me into trouble. The tamada stood and pronounced me redeemed. From this point forward, I would be welcomed as a true Georgian. "On one hand, nice," Marika commented. "On other hand, uh oh for you." I felt a swell of pride to know my participation had been sensed and sealed, and an attendant swell of terror.

For the next three toasts—to the witnesses, the parents, and the grandparents—I was very careful about making eye contact with the tamada, and each time I protected my newly bestowed clan membership by letting him watch the wine disappear. Even Marika's translations gained a new luster. It was true; this old man was a fount of wisdom and grace, regardless of the particular words he was using. I could feel the kindliness we felt for each other across the room. Or maybe Marika and I were just feeling toast-softened, swept up and close in the raising high of the horns amidst the reassuring tamada patter. Women weren't expected to drink at these things the way men were, but she'd been so summoned by the toast to the patriarch that she'd allowed herself more wine than was her usual custom. She told me about her young son, and what it was like to start a business there, and her memories of the war in 1992, and her fear of Russia's power, and how much she'd hated these weddings as a child but how much she loved them as an adult.

Around midnight, Marika said, "It's important to go pay our respects to the bride and groom." Neither the Uruguayan nor I had a whole lot of coherence going for us by that point, but she held us aside until we could properly pronounce the string of chipped consonants that meant "Congratulations." The bawdy atmosphere quieted as the three of us approached the dance floor before the raised dais. The newlyweds couldn't have been older than twenty, both of them rosy and taut

and, now that I could see them close up, extremely attractive. We stood before them like supplicants before prom royalty, and I may have bowed a little, and the Uruguayan and I pronounced the unpronounceable Georgian words, and they smiled and thanked us and, before we walked away, they told Marika to tell us that it had truly been a special honor to have us there with them, in Zugdidi, to celebrate this wedding day that they would always remember, and that I should provide my own

brother a chance to give a wedding toast—because, as they reminded me, I wasn't so young. Marika looked a little teary as she ushered us out. "I know," she said to me, "that you didn't say much for those toasts, but you said them with just the right drunken enthusiasm, and I can tell you that that meant a lot to those people."

The story goes that the supra developed as a religious tradition at a monastic academy in Telavi in the mountains north of Tbilisi. Telavi was known throughout the

Byzantine world as a philosophical center, and the toasts were expected to resemble the progression of toasts in the Symposium. At a winery in Sighnaghi, on a hill above the vineyards of eastern Georgia, a tourist guide named David explained to me and a few friends that the supra is both a tradition of enjoying time and a way to make drinking pleasant: "We say that chacha is the shortcut to happiness."

Sighnaghi was rebricked and retiled and whitewashed in 2007, as part of a World Bank initiative to develop tourism in Georgia's wine country. The effort was made in large part in response to Russia's 2006 ban on imported Georgian wines, a retaliation for a network of natural-gas and light-crude pipelines that circumvented Russia. The Russian ban cost the young industry, one of Georgia's only promising sectors, something like $20 million a year. There were those who said that flashy initiatives like the rehabilitation of Sighnaghi were nothing but cheap vanity projects. But David didn't agree. Things were looking up, he said, and now there were guests like us; he could run a business explaining the customs of his country to curious visitors.

He drove us along the restored ramparts of the town wall to his one-for-one last supra, something he does for tourists. I was a little supra'd out at that point—there'd actually been another one, high up in the remote valley of Svaneti with a large table of adventure-sports Russians, where I'm pretty sure I ended up toasting to a Georgia peacefully reunited with the so-called breakaway regions of Abkhazia and South Ossetia—but my friends had just arrived, and they didn't want to miss out on the tradition of which I'd somehow become a connoisseur. I was glad I wouldn't have to face another authentic one, though; I was afraid it would kill me. I had managed to measure up once to the proper Georgian standard for a grateful guest, but for now I was happy to be treated like another milquetoast foreigner. Plus it wasn't going to be a wedding, so I didn't have to feel the weight of the expectations of a new life. He led us down through his living room and into a large basement, where twenty-five tourists had just fallen upon the usual elaborate spread. "Here present we have"— and he waved his hand around the room—"guests from all over the world." There was conversation in Hebrew and in French and in Polish and at least two languages I didn't immediately recognize. The tables, like all of this small, wonderful nation's long-suffering tables, wept quietly under the burden of its people's offerings.

David got up to make a toast but nobody noticed; everybody kept talking in the profusion of tongues. Someone at our table started to knife-clink a glass, as was our custom, but David asked her to stop. They don't usually call for attention so baldly. He waited and after a moment the room drew naturally quiet. "I will make the first toast tonight to the parents. The parents are how we are the here. The parents are the why we are the here. We will never get them to the back. They will make the much more, but no! Come the time maybe we have the sons and we have the daughters, we will make to our own kids, maybe they will make to our kids. So I toast to the fathers and the mothers and the kids."

There were cheers and cries of *Gaumarjos!* and all of the tourists emptied the wine in their raised glasses.

David took his seat. "I do reduced version of the tradition, maybe only three or four toasts, to give the idea to you, and I do it in English language, which is hard for me, but I try. Tourists don't know the tradition, but it is warm and nice to do this with the tourists, so I go in the going step by step."

After a few minutes he stood and once again waited for the talk to subside. It took the Israelis the longest. "Now is the time to toast

to everybody, people very nice and very good. We choose our work people, we choose our friend people, but this toast is to the peoples we are not choose, we are not choose in our hearts and minds, people we don't and can't choose. To our brothers and sisters, better than our friends and our neighbors. We are in the same blood. From here are in the coming, if they are in the happy and if they are in the rich, then we and I are also in the happy and also in the rich. To cook for them and to help them, some

chance to give them and we will give them. *Gaumarjos!*"

There was something helplessly and hypnotically moving about David's delivery. It didn't deviate much in content from the other translated toasts I'd heard, but there was something about the simple elegance of his words and the looping cadences of his occulted English that touched us all.

Sometime later he offered his last toast, though everybody had been happily drinking and flirting in the interim. Everybody was silent the moment he stood. "This toast is to the countries and the peace. Here tonight we are Georgians, we are USA and Lithuanians, and Polish people and Israel people and Russia and Belgia. I want to toast to freedom betweens the countries and peace betweens the countries, love to the neighbors and the friends, betweens two people and betweens two countries, betweens to everybody and all the countries of the world. The people are in the like to come to Georgia, and Georgia is in the like to have the peoples. All of us to have the like to be in the touch. We are all in the like and in the touch. All of the people in the toast are in the very touch. *Gaumarjos!*"

We all felt deeply in the touch, and everybody couldn't help but smile and laugh as we brought our glasses to touch for the final time. The Nokia in my pocket started to buzz, which I took as Vika's distant communion with the spirit that held us there. I'd call her back when David was finished. My friend Maria wiped her lips and turned to David. "We are all so moved. Each toast you make only gets better and better. The words are so simple but the emotion is so strong."

David smiled. "Because," he said, "alcohol." LP

GEORGIA ON MY MIND

Recipes by
Christina Nichol

Photos by
Colin Lane

BADRIJANI

MAKES 4–6 SERVINGS

Some time in the summer, when the palm trees in the Republic of Georgia were swaying over the Black Sea in the slow motion that heat brings, I called Zviko, my boyfriend, and lied to him. I told him I had lost my keys to my apartment and therefore I'd better come over to his house. It was his brother's birthday and I knew that his mother was preparing *badrijani*, my favorite eggplant dish, and this was the only way I'd ever get the recipe.

When I'd first arrived in Georgia, one of my colleagues at the university where I was teaching showed me how to make badrijani the student way, with mayonnaise. We burnt our fingers as we slathered green cilantro-and-garlic mayonnaise over strips of freshly fried eggplant, and waited for them to cool a little. I usually hate mayonnaise, but as we ate the badrijani with pieces of *lavash*, I remember thinking it was the most divine thing I had ever tasted. (To this day, my family in the U.S. refers to it as "goddess dung.")

Later, when I told Zviko that I knew how to make badrijani and described the process, he said, "I hate mayonnaise." It was the first thing we discovered we had in common. "To make badrijani with mayonnaise is the cheap way!" he proclaimed. "It must be made with *walnuts* like my mother makes it!" But Georgia, at least at the time, was a rather conservative country regarding the relationship between the sexes, and it wasn't so easy just to say, "Can I come over to your house and watch?"

On the afternoon of his brother's birthday, Zviko picked me up in his red Lada, the one he had recently fixed up after his neighbor had been using it as a chicken coop, shaking his head and laughing a little as he dropped me off at his house. His mother wrapped the curtains from the window around her head like a scarf and yelled down to him to come eat. He waved her away and drove off to his job as an oil inspector on the ships in the harbor, his mother yelling after him not to eat the food on the ship, his brother yelling after him not to get AIDS, his other brother yelling, reminding him to drink a lot of milk to help with the gas fumes. It was like that—everyone yelling but also humanely happy. Jubilant yelling seemed to be a key ingredient of Georgian life.

His mother was a heavy woman with dirty, sturdy feet, who walked with the walk of someone who trusts the ground and who isn't afraid of garlic. Her hands were dirty from digging potatoes, and when she came in from her garden she wiped her hands off on the pages of English grammar books, complaining that Zviko had a good job now, so why hadn't he bought any napkins? From her cupboard she pulled big jars of eggplants swimming like swollen eels in salt water. I wanted to ask her if it was really necessary to salt the eggplant in order to sweat out the bitter brown juice, but it seemed she didn't want to speak Russian anymore, and so we communicated instead in grunts, pounds, and squeezes.

I sat on a stool and watched her pound the cloves from two heads of garlic with coarse salt in a mortar, using a stone she had obviously found on the beach. When the garlic had turned into paste, she scooped it out into a bowl with her finger and started pounding handfuls of coriander, the stems included.

Meanwhile, the eggplants were frying. She wouldn't let me near the stove, afraid the grease would pop into my American eyes, and stood tending the strips with a fork until they were puffy and golden like loaves, which she then set aside on the remaining pages of English grammar to cool. She added the smashed coriander to the garlic and set in on the walnuts. When she had

Illustrations by Roman Muradov

smashed those up, she added them to everything else she had already smashed, and then reached her hands in and squeezed it together. She added the *khmeli suneli* (whenever I've asked which spices make up khmeli suneli, I've been met with a shrug and told, "They are Georgian housewife spices." My recipe for it follows). On top of that mixture, she added a splash of old white wine that had turned to vinegar. She tasted it, grunted, added more salt, and then held out her wrist for me to taste it too. She then added a handful of cayenne pepper until the mixture turned a fiercer orange than any badrijani I'd ever seen and had more oomph than any badrijani I'd ever tasted. It was exaggerated, like her *khachapuri*, which she now set to work on, kneading handfuls of margarine into the cheese, the dough already prepared. Her khachapuri was thicker and lumpier than anyone else's. She had a thick family.

1 **Fry the eggplants** until cooked through and lightly browned, and season to taste with salt.

2 **Smash the remaining ingredients** (except the pomegranate seeds) with a mortar and pestle. Squeeze it together with your hands.

3 **Coat the fried-eggplant strips with the paste.** Roll up the eggplant. Top with pomegranate seeds, if you wish.

INGREDIENTS

3	eggplants, peeled, sliced lengthwise into ½" strips, salted, and squeezed
+	salt
+	oil for frying
1	onion, chopped and sautéed
5 cloves (or more!)	garlic
1 to 2 C	walnuts
2 bunches	fresh coriander (cilantro)
a splash	white wine vinegar
2 T	**KHMELI-SUNELI SPICE** (see page 95)
+	cayenne (optional)
+	pomegranate seeds (optional)

KHMELI-SUNELI SPICE

1 **Blend all ingredients** in a coffee grinder. Supposedly, a tea made from an infusion of this mix was used to restore an exhausted army in the twelfth century.

INGREDIENTS

2 T	dried marjoram	2 T	dried ground marigold petals
2 T	dried dill	1 T	black pepper
2 T	dried summer savory	2 T	fenugreek seeds
2 T	dried mint	2	bay leaves, crushed
2 T	dried parsley	a pinch	saffron
2 T	coriander seeds	1 t	dried basil
1 T	dried fenugreek leaves	1 t	thyme

Zviko came home late, after we had already started celebrating. All the brothers were still yelling. He was working too hard these days, and though he was big, I couldn't understand how he stayed that way because when he was under stress he only seemed to eat bread—the end pieces. He sat there eating the end pieces.

Birthday parties are very important in Georgia. Often they will have three birthday cakes— usually one made by a downstairs neighbor—and invite the whole apartment complex. A couple of years ago, Zviko wrote me an email to wish me a happy birthday. He wrote, "Happy Birthday from all your Georgian friends!" I hadn't heard from him in four years and wondered why he was writing now. It was two o'clock in the afternoon in Florida but after midnight in the republic of Georgia. I imagined he must be home, feasting and drinking with his friends, and, on a whim, decided to send me a message. I imagined them singing that song that goes, "I'd rather kiss the lips of a wine jug than the lips of a woman." The image made me happy. I wrote back, "Thanks Georgian Friends!!" adding a second explanation point

in order to speak that "We die for friends!" language. "Georgia is always on my mind!" I added. I wanted to keep it light. Our break-up had been difficult.

He wrote back to say that actually he wasn't in Georgia but on a ship off the coast of Africa, near Togo. "I'm in Africa now," he BlackBerried. "Working on storage vessel. Have no news from Georgia, but I'm sure all is fine there. I hope you are well."

"I am well," I wrote back. "I am living in Florida." Then, because he always used to say that America was a boring heaven but Georgia was an exciting hell—and what I had just written seemed to confirm that—I added, "But it's dangerous here too. Many alligators."

He wrote back. "True saying, 'Better to fight alligators than Nigerian pirates.' Being on vessel is not much fun, just a lot of work. Now on vessel we have Ukrainian crew and they are on vessel already 7–8 months and not seen shore during this time, so you can imagine how crazy they are :-). When we were in Cotonou every evening we were having attacks from pirates, but now we moved to Lome and here is a bit quiet for now. We carry gas oil, 75,000 metric tonnes. We

must fight pirates with fire fight water with high pressure, but so far, thanks to God, had no incident on my vessel. We keep 24hrs watch on deck and radar and if we see boats approaching, immediately inform Navy, and prepare crew with fire fight hoses on deck, but if we see they are armed, then we all go down to engine room, lock the doors, and switch off all electrical supply and engines."

I wrote back something I had always wanted to tell him: "In the novel that I wrote about Georgia, in the end, the character that I based on you, moves back to the village, helps his aunt make *tkemali*, and has a happy life."

He wrote back, "Life is not a novel, so happy ending is a bit far off. We have no bread on the ship. We have to eat our borscht with cookies."

He wasn't at home in Georgia, where he should be, with his friends and his family. Instead, he was keeping watch on an oil ship fighting pirates, having to eat borscht with cookies. It put my life into a little perspective. I think that is why I had wanted to marry him. I wanted to marry "putting my life into perspective"—to be permanently soldered to it.

AMERIKELI KHACHAPURI

In the middle of one cold, electricity-less night, when I was still living in Georgia, Zviko knocked on my door. I opened the door holding a candle and he said, "You shouldn't open the door without asking who is there first." He stood there holding a white mass of something in his hands. "I know you wanted to learn how to make khachapuri so I went to my friend's bakery and asked him for some dough. He thought I was on drugs, but he gave me this anyway. Here." And he transferred the sticky mass into my hands.

The electricity was out but my oven ran on gas so in the candlelight we rolled out the dough with an old wine bottle. We crumbled over it the salty-sour Georgian farmer cheese called *sulguni*, sold in huge blocks in the market, mixed with the yolk of an egg and some butter. We scooped the sides up over the mixture and rolled it out again.

Each region in Georgia makes its own khachapuri. In Adjaria, where I was living, the dough is usually shaped into a boat, which holds a cargo of cheese, a half stick of butter, and a raw egg that cooks in front of you at the table. Abkhazian khachapuri (*achma*) is more like a cheese lasagna or kugel. But we were making Emeruli khachapuri, the most common household type. On fast days it can be filled with potatoes or beans, in which case it is called *lobiani*. There are so many different types of khachapuri that the Tbilisi State University allegedly developed an economic metric called the "khachapuri index" that measures inflation by the price it takes to make the national cheese bread.

As we waited for it to bake, we stared at my remaining candle as it slowly melted and started leaning leftward. Zviko, with characteristic Georgian humor, remarked, "That candle would not make a very good Viagra commercial."

When the khachapuri was done, we sat in the dark, warming our hands by it, and ate. It turned out like his mother's—rich and thick and golden brown. For once, Zviko wasn't eating only the ends of bread pieces.

It is for this reason that I never learned how to make proper khachapuri dough. The Georgians managed to evade showing me in the same way they evaded my requests to milk their cows, as if my American hands just didn't have the right skills. I tried making it in the U.S. but the flour was never right. The cheese was never right either. I finally gave up and just bought frozen puff-pastry sheets and it turned out delicious enough. Sulguni, the cheese you stuff khachapuri with, isn't readily available in America; the closest resemblance I've been able to create is a mixture of havarti, feta, muenster, and mozzarella.

1 Mix together the cheeses, egg yolk, and butter, and distribute between puff-pastry sheets. Cook according to package instructions.

INGREDIENTS

½ C	havarti, crumbled
½ C	feta, crumbled
½ C	muenster, shredded
½ C	mozzarella, shredded
1	egg yolk
3 T	butter, softened
2 sheets	puff-pastry

TKEMALi

INGREDIENTS

1 lb	underripe plums, red or green
¾ C	water
3 T	lemon juice (depending on the tartness of your plums)
1 T	olive oil
3 cloves	garlic, minced (or more to taste)
1½ t	ground coriander
½ t	salt (or more to taste)
½ t	red pepper flakes, hot, (or more to taste)
¼ C	fresh coriander (cilantro), chopped
¼ C	fresh dill, chopped

1 **Blanch the plums in boiling water** to ease skin removal. Rinse them off in cold water and pare the skins off. Using a spoon, remove the pits.

2 **Combine the peeled plums,** water, lemon juice, oil, garlic, coriander, salt, and pepper flakes in a saucepan, and boil over medium heat. Reduce the heat to low and simmer, covered, until the plums are very soft, about 5 minutes.

3 **Transfer the mixture to a food processor or blender** and process to a smooth purée (or allow to cool and just squeeze with your hands). Return the purée to the saucepan and stir in the cilantro and dill. Bring this to a boil over medium heat, then reduce the heat to medium-low and simmer until the sauce is reduced to a thick, almost jam-like consistency, about another 5 minutes.

4 **Remove from the heat and taste for seasoning,** adding more salt, pepper flakes, or lemon juice to taste. Cool to room temperature and serve over potatoes or *shashlik*.

There is a Georgian word with too few vowels that's spelled *gvprtsgvni*. It means, "I peel myself." I don't know if you would ever use this phrase unless you were trying to woo someone or speak from the perspective of an eggplant but, in any case, Georgian words taste how they sound. Wild plum sauce is called *tkemali*. It is the sound your tongue makes when it curls from the sour taste of plums. I'm not sure if I love tkemali so much because I love the taste or the taste of saying it.

Spring is the time for tkemali making. You pick the plum when the whole town smells of strawberries—the aromatic, tiny, wild kind. This is also the time when security guards—and those others who don't really identify with their work—sneak away from their jobs and go hunt for nettles and wild herbs for their wives to make *phkali* and *kingkhali*. The plums can be green or purple, though the purple ones will leave squeeze-stains on the fingers. Georgian food involves a lot of squeezing. (Maybe that's why

the women are such good Olympic shot-putters.) You pick the plums just before they are ripe. You squeeze the plums, boil them, add garlic, coriander, dill, chili pepper, salt—some add pennyroyal when that's in season too—and the khmeli-suneli spices.

After the sauce has stewed on the stove, you bottle it, and pour it over meat or potatoes. Tkemali is the Georgian equivalent of ketchup. Though whenever I get my hands on a good bottle of tkemali sauce, I sneak it straight from the bottle.

SATSIVI

Whenever I would tell anyone in Georgia how much I loved badrijani, they would say, "Yes, but have you tried *satsivi*?" with this smitten look in their eyes. Satsivi is holiday food, a sacred sort of dish, especially when made with turkey. It tastes like warm earth, if the earth were delicious. I never bothered to learn how to make it because I couldn't imagine eating it without Georgian village wine. I tried to find Georgian wine at the Russian stores on Geary in San Francisco, but for some reason those bottles had a strange aftertaste of hamburgers. You need to eat satsivi with the village wine that comes directly from the ground out of one of those old-fashioned water pumps, the kind that Helen Keller used when she first learned how to sign "water."

But recently I found a wine produced by a man named Josko Gravner. He employs a purely natural winemaking process, much like the Georgians, who insist it is why they never get hangovers. (Perhaps closer to the truth is that they eat so much butter and bread beforehand.) Gravner grows his grapes on the Slovenian/Italian border and uses the 4,000-year-old technique of storing wine in clay amphorae. He extends the maceration of the grape skins, uses open-top wood vats, and eschews added yeasts and sulphur dioxide. Perhaps most important is his philosophy that wine is a product of nature and not man.

I returned to Georgia recently, and felt that I was finally mature enough to learn how to make satsivi. First, we had to buy the right kind of walnut. At the market, we had to taste each vendor's walnut. Georgians can tell by the smell of a wine which hillside the grapes were grown on. Likewise with walnuts. They all tasted the same to me, but my friend insisted that we must find a walnut that was not too sweet, not too bitter. Finally satisfied, we returned home to cook. To make satsivi, you need a long afternoon, preferably with a sister or a woman who feels like your sister, because the texture of the walnuts must be right for it to work, and this is a boring process to accomplish.

1 **Boil the chicken (or turkey)** with a chopped onion. Reserve the broth.

2 **Pound the walnuts in a mortar,** preferably one made from the boxwood tree that grows in Abkhazia, and that's been in the family for six generations. The walnuts cannot be ground too fine and also must not have any pebble-sized pieces in them. (This is the part where you have to sit and painstakingly pick out any pieces.)

3 **Transfer the walnuts to a bowl** and add the onion, khmeli-suneli, coriander, garlic, vinegar, and a little of reserved chicken broth. Squeeze the mixture with your hands, just until the oil begins to separate. Add more broth until the sauce lightens a little in color and has the texture of watery hummus.

4 **When the chicken has cooled,** remove the meat from the bone, leaving a few pieces whole. Coat and mix with the walnut sauce, and add salt to taste.

5 **Serve at room temperature with white village wine.** Remember, in Georgia, real men only drink white wine.

INGREDIENTS

1	chicken (or small turkey)
1	onion, chopped
2 to 3 C	raw walnuts
1 small bunch	fresh coriander (cilantro)
2 T	**KHMELI-SUNELI SPICE** (see page 95)
3 or 4 cloves	garlic
splash	white wine vinegar
+	salt

Classic **AYCE** Challenge
NUMBER TWO

Eat six saltines iN UNDER A MiNUTE *without drinking anything.*

Illustration by Ian Huebert

EVERYTHING FOR EVERYBODY

by **Brette Warshaw**

It's lunchtime in Boca Raton, Florida, and a man in a foot-high toque and a white chef coat carves bright red pastrami in thick, even cuts. He takes out a roll—baked that morning—and smears one side with mayonnaise, the other with mustard. He layers on the pastrami, and guides me toward the bowls of horseradish and coleslaw. On my way back to my seat, I take note of the half dozen premade salads on offer, from egg to red quinoa, but opt instead to make my own at the salad bar: asparagus, cucumbers, avocado, almonds, and radishes. For dessert, I eat a bowl of

raspberries and cantaloupe and strawberries, and then vanilla soft serve with rainbow sprinkles.

I'm at St. Andrews Country Club, where my grandparents, forever New Yorkers, have owned a second home big enough for my twelve-member family for most of my life. We are one of 700 predominantly Jewish families (hailing largely from New York City, Long Island, and Philadelphia) with houses here.

When my family visits St. Andrews, we are greeted by name (the staff has a packet of photos they've committed to memory). We eat from endless buffets—buffets with latke stations and fajita stations and mu shu

Photographs by Justine Kang

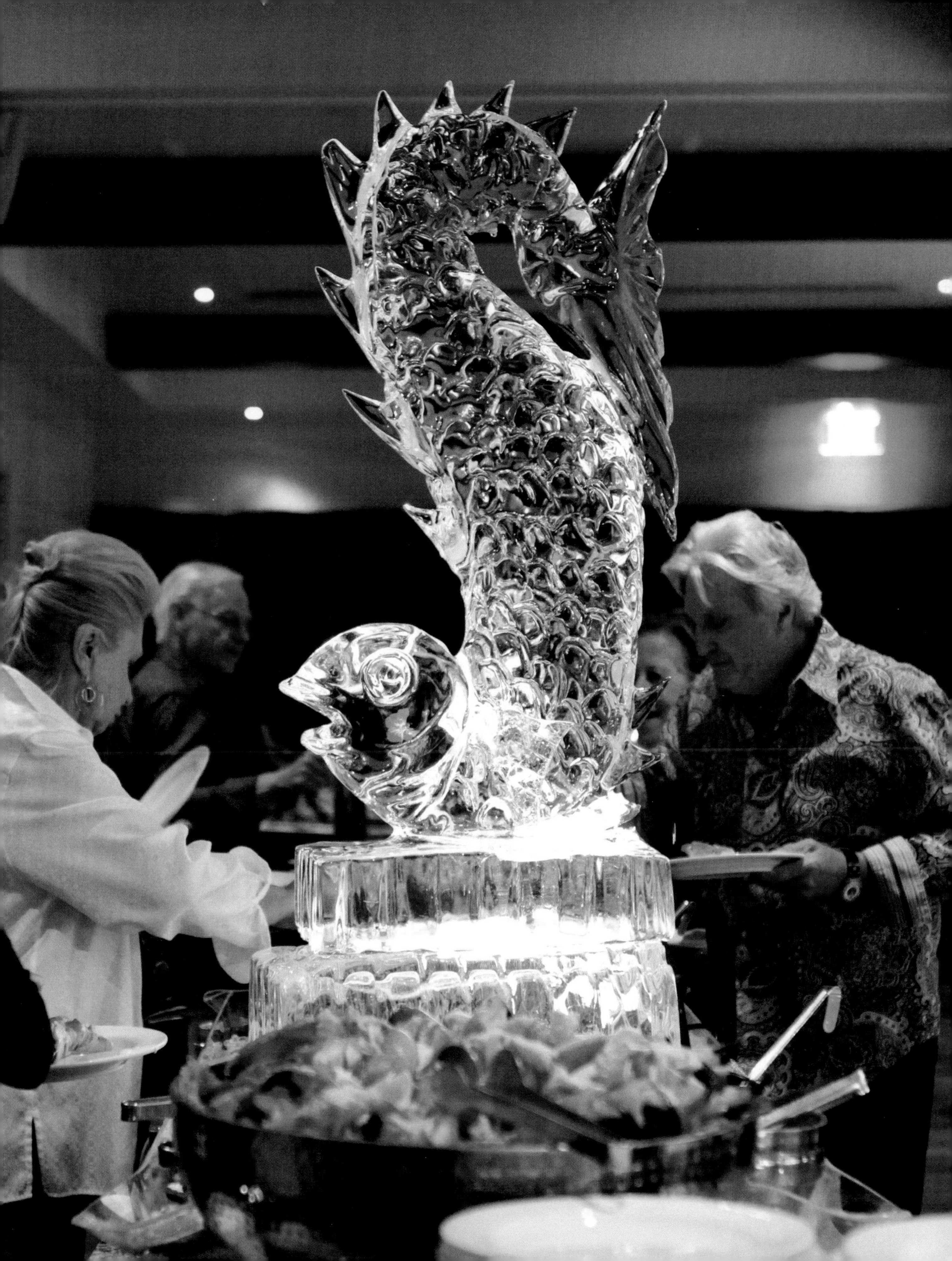

lobster stations, all in a cruise-ship-sized, glittering dining room filled with dolled-up, senior citizens with Long Island accents. The women's hair is done up (the men's, too, if they have it). They roam the dining room—navigating the built-in marble-countered carving stations, pizza oven, salad-chopping station, two omelet stations, and ice cream freezer—with children and grandchildren in tow. "Here's my grandson, Jacob—isn't he handsome?" "Jordana's bat mitzvah was last month—you should've seen her!"

I've been one of those mortified grandchildren, in an embarrassing dress that my mother saved expressly for Prime Rib Night or Seafood Night or Deli Night, smiling and nodding and being kissed relentlessly on the cheek. I wanted to slink away to eat in peace but I realized that the dresses and the accents and the cheek-kissing meant a great deal to my very wonderful, loving grandparents. And recently I started to appreciate and wonder what it was like to have to cook and serve the expanses of food that are the backdrop for all the *kvelling*.

Lunch and dinner are served daily. Lunch is always a buffet; dinners alternate between themed buffets and à la carte service. (There's a more casual dining option, too, which is in a separate building and serves the kind of stuff that the members might cook at home, if they did cook. Most don't.) During holiday season—when all the children and grandchildren come to visit—there are themed buffets every night.

At any given lunch buffet, there's pastrami, corned beef, white- and dark-meat turkey, tongue, turkey pastrami, prime rib; shrimp salad, crab salad, barley salad, wild-rice salad, white quinoa salad, red-quinoa salad, Niçoise salad, ambrosia,

Waldorf salad, chicken salad, tuna salad, potato salad, salmon salad, the regular salad bar; two omelet stations with fifteen toppings; strawberries, grapefruit, oranges, canned peaches, canned pears, watermelon, cantaloupe, honeydew, mango, figs, blueberries, raspberries, pineapple,

papaya; bran muffins, chocolate chip muffins, blueberry muffins, corn muffins, lemon-poppyseed muffins, eight kinds of ice cream, and vanilla and chocolate frozen yogurt.

"Everyone here has a lot of money; they're well traveled, and they like to go out and have a good

time," Steve Viggiano, the friendly, quick-talking executive chef tells me. After growing up in a Jewish-Italian neighborhood in Queens, he graduated from Johnson & Wales in 1979 and went to work at the Boca Raton Resort. Then came Pier Sixty-Six in Ft. Lauderdale, and then a string of Ritz-Carlton hotel gigs: Naples (Florida), Phoenix, Palm Beach. After a short stint in the meat business, he joined as the chef for St. Andrews. He's worked here for fourteen of the last sixteen years. "So you have to find that happy medium between being like an

experience dining out and being like a home, taking care of the guy who just wants to come in and get a chop steak or a piece of grilled salmon, and the other person that's brought guests on a Saturday night."

Steve uses what he calls the "Caesar salad analogy" to describe this problem. "Everybody has their own interpretation of Caesar salad. Some people like more garlic, some people like more anchovy, some people like more lemon. When I first came, there was always a complaint." It took years of tweaking to find a recipe that everyone liked. Aside from Caesar, there are eighteen salad dressings; some rotate in and out, but there's always Thousand Island, bleu cheese, balsamic vinaigrette, tomato feta, miso, honey mustard, peppercorn ranch, honey ginger, and raspberry-walnut vinaigrette. Beyond dressings, there's olive oil and red-wine vinegar, white-wine vinegar, cherry-balsamic vinegar, pomegranate-balsamic vinegar, and aged-balsamic vinegar to dress three kinds of lettuce and thirty salad items.

And then there's the phenomenon of accretion: "We'll have a case of tomatoes that are really soft," Steve explains. "So Jose [*garde manger*] will make a tomato vinaigrette, to get rid of the tomatoes. And then the next week, somebody's asking about the tomato vinaigrette. So now you have to have it *all the time*."

His customers know what they want and they're used to getting it. They will all come in at seven thirty p.m. for a Saturday night à la carte dinner, regardless of their actual reservation, because that is when they want to eat. They will order "branzino, absolutely zero butter" and "filets well done" and "lamb chops, burnt" and off-the-menu "asparagus Oscar." (Certain members of my family request egg-white omelets, well done, "like a pancake, and totally dry.") Nobody cares when asparagus or raspberries or cantaloupe grow; they want their melon in January, and they will complain until they get it.

Of the forty-two people total that work in the dining-room kitchen, all but three that I met have worked at St. Andrews for six years or more; half went to culinary school. They say it's a good gig; they're paid well and have good benefits. Each cook can work on dishes of his or her own to feature on the à la carte menus, and when holidays come up, Viggiano calls on them to help build out the menu.

The staff is used to the club's routine: the buffets, the à la carte service, the member guests, the bridge clubs, the dinners in the herb garden. Steve always decides the menu, then informs his team via a thick packet of memos they receive every week. Peggy bakes the cookies for the bridge clubs and member guests. Jamal does the salad prep for the buffets. Hansel works expo for Saturday Steakhouse Nights. Jose carves the ice sculptures and turns tomatoes into rosettes for the big,

themed banquets, a job he's done for twenty-three years. "I tell them it's a Men's Member Guest, or Italian Night, or Dinner Under the Stars, and they all know what to do."

At this point, too, they know exactly how much food will be consumed on any given night, from year to year. "I can look at this sheet here of how many covers we did last year, and I know we're going to do the same number. With the seafood buffet, I can look at how many lobsters we sold (1200 one-and-a-half-pound Maine lobsters), how many stone crabs they ate (450 pounds)—and it's always the same. It's always the same." (They also go through 60 pounds of tuna, 75 pounds of sea bass, and 200 pieces of sushi each Seafood Night.) St. Andrews spends more than two million dollars on food each year.

Food waste isn't really a problem. In addition to cooking for 3,000 diners each week, the kitchen is also responsible for feeding the club's 250 employees, so many of the leftovers from the banquets go to them. Sometimes, though, the members notice the kitchen getting creative

with their repurposing. My grandfather waxes poetic about the Italian meat salad that popped up after the Super Bowl party which, among other things, featured a gigantic hoagie. "Three days later, on the lunch buffet, there it was again!" he cracks up. "Italian meat salad! My new favorite salad!" He implores me not to tell my grandmother.

Though I've been visiting this country club all my life, I'd never met Steve before. He and his team work quietly and out of sight in the gigantic, brown-linoleum-floored kitchen, cooking 35,000 pounds of turkey a year, mixing salad dressings, carving ice sculptures. They make everything but the bread and ice cream from scratch. The only staff the members see are the ones that man the carving and salad stations at lunch: Felix, Leo, and Maria. (Felix stands on a box as he carves and wears that foot-high toque. When I met him in the kitchen, I was shocked to see that he was under five feet tall.)

One night I watched them serve 175 people in forty-five minutes, with just five guys on the line. Stray lamb chops fell to the ground and somebody started cutting tomatoes on a piece of paper and onion bits blanketed the pass. And when the night was over—and it usually ends very abruptly—they packed up and went home, and did it again the next day.

"Sometimes as a chef, we have egos, and to be a chef in a country club you can't have an ego," Steve says. "You need to take it and throw it out the door. There's no 'I'm gonna cook what I want to cook, if you don't like it then go somewhere else,' like a restaurant chef. When you're here, you can't be that way. You have to cook for like, *everyone*."

"Whatever they want," he says, "we give them." **LP**

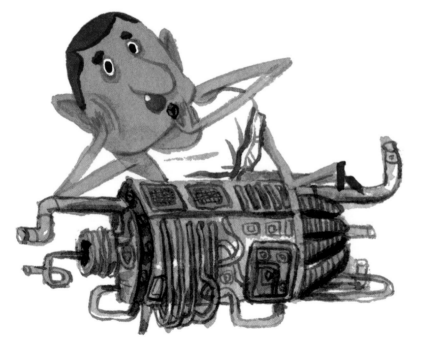

Tiger

Artist: A Yip www.ayip.hk
Street Music 2012 www.tigertranslate.com
www.tigerbeerus.com

IT'S A
MONTANA THING

by **Jed Portman**

Last huckleberry season, I woke up at four a.m. in suburban Charleston, South Carolina, and caught a flight to Chicago, Illinois, and then another to Missoula, Montana. I landed around lunchtime. It was late August, and Missoula felt like a pinewood attic: hot, dry, and musty with smoke from the forest fires in the surrounding mountains. I stopped by the Wal-Mart to buy food, a fishing license, bug spray, and a roll of bags for my little vacuum sealer. Then I drove another hour up the highway to Ovando, a small ranching community in the rolling hills on the edge of the picturesque Bob Marshall Wilderness.

I was looking for berries. And while my trip may have been longer and more expensive than most, I was hardly the only one on the hunt. During the months of June, July, and August, Montanans of all ages and occupations brave heat, bugs, and grizzly bears in pursuit of pea-sized wild huckleberries, sweet-tart asterisks of flavor with a lingering wild perfume that inspires religious devotion, in both metaphorical and literal senses.

"Our people used to collect huckleberries for ceremonies," says Earl Old Person, the eighty-five-year-old chief of the Blackfeet Nation. "There were places in the mountains where they'd go every year. And you never hear about anyone going to those places anymore. But the religious ceremonies, a lot of them took place in the summer. They'd dry the berries, so they'd have them ready when they were opening their bundles each year. They'd make soup out of them, and other things." (Blackfeet medicine bundles were—and

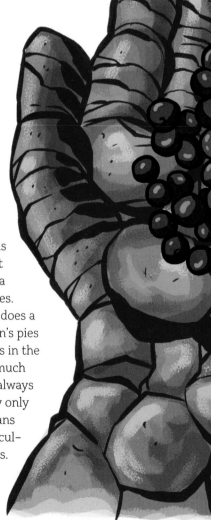

are—sacred objects kept concealed for most of the year and unwrapped at annual religious ceremonies.)

In tiny Hungry Horse, Montana, near Glacier National Park, a secular obsession has spawned a year-round business that offers a whole lot more than just dried berries. At the Huckleberry Patch, you can buy huckleberry candles, caramel corn, daiquiri mix, gummy bears, hand lotion, honey, licorice, lip balm, soap, syrup, and taffy—as well as plenty of baked goods. Last year alone, head baker Erna Fortin turned out 4,100 pies.

The Huckleberry Patch does a brisk business selling Fortin's pies online these days, as well as in the store. But no matter how much demand climbs, there will always be a catch: the huckleberry only grows in the wild. Montanans have tried without luck to cultivate it since pioneer times. "The huckleberry seems to resist it," says Marilyn

Illustrations by Brent Schoonover © 2014 Marvel

Marler, a biologist at the University of Montana. "To my knowledge, no one has ever been successful in growing it on a big scale." Even the largest operations must source their huckleberries from independent pickers, whose identities are often concealed to keep the competition from nosing in. "We have locals that bring berries in," says Fortin, whose employers spend each three-month huckleberry season freezing enough berries to last all year. "But where *exactly* we get them is a deep, dark secret. I can't tell anyone that."

The huckleberry is also a plant known for playing by its own rules. One year, local pickers will tell you, a mountain might be covered in berries. The next, the same plants will hardly bear fruit. The past few years have been particularly hard. Dry weather has caused record shortages all over the state, pushing a number of pickers out of business. Marla Hedman, who sells jams, taffies, and other huckleberry products online under the name Larchwood Farms, says that she has had to look beyond her usual circle of suppliers to stay in business. "I have five or six pages, front and back, of pickers, and I've called every one of them over the past few years," she says. "A whole lot of them have quit picking." Those who are still in the business have nearly doubled their prices: a gallon of huckleberries goes for at least $30 in most places.

Given the scarcity of wild huckleberries, and their cost, it's little surprise that some operations have resorted to cheating. The definition of the huckleberry has always been a fluid thing, a problem dating back to the European colonists who used the word as a catch-all for small, blue berries in the genus *Vaccinium*, which includes the common blueberry and more than thirty other edible berries native to North America. For years, producers all over the state have been thinning out huckleberry jams, jellies, and pies with wild blueberries from Canada and the upper Midwest—or worse. "Companies were adding grape juice, applesauce, you name it, and not telling the public," Fortin claims.

"A blueberry we call a 'blah-berry,'" Hedman says proudly. "We call our huckleberries 'Montana's purple gold.'" Nearly a decade ago, she convinced state senator Jim Elliott to sponsor a bill that finally defined the Montana huckleberry for commercial purposes. It passed, but it angered some producers by excluding members of the *Vaccinium* family that they considered fair game. "One guy down in the Bitterroot Valley got really angry with me," Elliott remembers. "He asked me, 'Why do you want to limit my business?' I said, 'I want to *protect* your business. Unless you're a liar. If you're a liar then yes, I'm screwing you.'"

But seven years later, the bill still hasn't cleaned up the huckleberry industry, says Hedman. Many of the big producers are still using blueberries. Supermarkets don't mind, and the authorities are too busy with a host of more pressing issues to investigate. But honest-to-god huckleberry flavor, Hedman maintains, stands out every time. "My husband says that I'm the most boring person in the world, because all I think about is my business and huckleberries. But they're just incredibly good. You know, I've been in this business for about twenty years, and I've only had one person tell me he didn't like huckleberries. I just stood there with my mouth hanging open. I didn't believe it."

Last night, my fiancée and I sliced into our last vacuum-sealed and frozen bag of Montana huckleberries. I picked the berries around eight months ago, and they've no doubt lost a little bit of character—not to mention context—in their journey across the United States to my South Carolina living room. But for just about any northwestern Montanan, even a mutt like myself, the taste of those frozen morsels is a Proustian trigger akin to a Texan's hunk of smoked brisket or a North Carolinian's ice-cold Cheerwine. They're worth the week that I spent trolling dirt roads and climbing brambly slopes to harvest just a couple of gallons. In fact, I'm already making plans to head back to Montana this summer, and appealing to the huckleberry gods for a good harvest. 🅛🅟

IT'S COBBLERIN' TIME!

This cobbler topping is adapted from Tartine Bakery's scone recipe. Make it as quickly and imperfectly as possible: you want craggy peaks to catch the sugar topping and get crunchy, and the part swimming in the berries to become dumpling-like. If you don't have access to the Montana wilderness, you could substitute other fruit, like blahberries.

MAKES 6 SERVINGS: A 2-QUART BAKING DISH
OR 9"×9" SQUARE OR 10" ROUND

1 Heat oven to 350°F. Make the filling: mix the sugar, cornstarch, and zest. Sprinkle over berries and toss with lemon juice. Lightly butter the pan and fill it with the berry mixture.

2 Make the topping: mix the flour, baking powder, sugar, and salt. Cut in the butter as you would for pie dough, leaving some pea-sized pieces. Quickly stir in buttermilk and zest, mixing only until the mixture begins to come together.

3 Drop the topping by the tablespoonful onto the filling to cover the top completely. Sprinkle with the sugar and

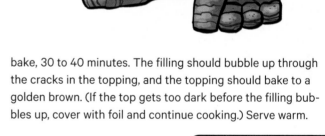

bake, 30 to 40 minutes. The filling should bubble up through the cracks in the topping, and the topping should bake to a golden brown. (If the top gets too dark before the filling bubbles up, cover with foil and continue cooking.) Serve warm.

INGREDIENTS

Recipe by
**Liz Prueitt,
Tartine Bakery**

Filling

¼	sugar (or more if berries are very tart)
1 T	cornstarch
½	lemon's worth of zest
4 to 5 C	huckleberries, depending on baking dish
1	lemon, juiced (or none if berries are very tart)
+	butter for greasing

Topping

2 C	all-purpose flour
1 T	baking powder
¼ C	sugar
½ t	sea salt
1 stick	cold butter
¾ C	buttermilk
1 t	lemon zest
2 to 3 T	demerara or other large-crystal sugar

OVER-STALKED

Recipes adapted from
Gabrielle Hamilton

THERE ARE THiNGS ONE CAN NEVER SEEM TO BUY iN APPROPRiATE QUANTiTiES AT THE GROCERY STORE.

Spices, hot dog buns, and buttermilk come immediately to mind. And celery. Always the celery. Celery's natural packaging comes in one size: more than you can eat. You need it for the mirepoix or the tuna salad, and it's cheap and it lasts forever, so you buy a whole head. But do you ever need more than a stalk or two? Maybe a cup for something really celery-ish?

And even though pickled celery is about as delicious as it gets, let's not kid ourselves. You're not pickling it. You're not making it into a jam, jelly, preserve, or marmalade; you're not curing or drying or smoking it. Maybe you'll dip a stalk into some hummus; maybe feed the kids as many ants on a log as they'll take down, but be honest: isn't there always a nearly complete head of celery heading toward middle age in the crisper?

For a long time now, whenever I've spied the wizening ends of a celery heart in my refrigerator, I've thought of Gabrielle Hamilton, the chef of Prune in New York City, who is a kind of celery whisperer.

—PETER MEEHAN

CELERY WITH MEAT SAUCE

MAKES 4 SERVINGS

I remember ordering this braised celery as a side dish during a meal at Prune that I was trying to keep light. I was anticipating something like the celery braised in beef broth that sometimes shows up at a French dinner. But instead what arrived was an ovular plate of tough, thick celery stalks braised into beefy submission, crowned by a comically oversized ice cream–scoop of Bolognese-looking sauce. My ascetic aspirations were dashed but my heart was won over.

At Prune, this is a clean-out-the-walk-in dish that takes care of any unused celery ribs along with all the pork butt and pancetta scraps the restaurant has on hand. At home, don't worry about hitting the meat quantities in the recipe below—just keep the meat-to-celery ratio intact.

1 **In a large pot or Dutch oven over medium-high heat,** sweat the meat, onions, and garlic in vegetable or olive oil.

2 **Add the wine and parsley and simmer** until the liquid is reduced by two-thirds.

3 **Add the tomatoes and celery, cover, and reduce the heat.** Cook gently (stirring occasionally) until the celery is tender.

4 **Season with salt and pepper.** Remove the cover and allow to continue simmering gently until the liquid is almost completely reduced and the sauce is just beginning to tighten up. The meat and celery will look almost sticky. Serve.

INGREDIENTS

2 lbs	meat (ideally an equal mix of ground pancetta, sweet Italian sausage without casings, ground pork, and ground beef)
+	oil
¼ C	onion, finely diced
2 cloves	garlic, finely chopped
2 C	white wine
¼ C	parsley, chopped
½ C	canned tomatoes, crushed
8 to 10 large stalks	celery, de-ribbed & cut into 3" pieces
+	salt
+	pepper

Illustrations by Helen Tseng

SHAVED CELERY, FENNEL, AND RADISH SALAD WITH BUTTERED VALDÉON TOASTS

MAKES 4 SERVINGS

When making this stalwart of the Prune menu, please note that the butter should be room temperature, almost warmer than that, and should be slathered in such away as to blanket the toast's entire face, like a layer of freshly fallen snow, and then the shards of agreeably pungent Valdéon go on top of it. The celery salad, assertive and bright, makes amends for the richness of the toast.

1 **With a sharp knife, thinly slice the celery and the fennel,** and toss together. Sliver the scallions and sugar snap peas on a bias and add to the fennel and celery. With a sharp knife or mandoline, thinly slice the radishes and add to the salad.

2 **Grate the garlic using a Microplane.** Mix together the garlic, oil, and lemon juice, and dress the salad. Season with salt and pepper to taste and toss well. Let stand.

3 **Toast the bread slices** and spread each with two tablespoons of butter. Divide the cheese among the four buttered toasts.

4 **Toss and taste the salad again before portioning,** adding salt if necessary. You want a bright, assertive, unafraid dressing on clean, crunchy, crisp, and lively vegetables: make sure your ingredients are fresh, and pay attention to the potency of the garlic as it can vary from head to head. Plate with the warm Valdéon toasts.

INGREDIENTS

1 head	celery, tough outer stalks removed, well rinsed
2 heads	fennel, medium-sized, stalks and fronds removed
2 bunches	scallions, approximately 15 pieces, root end and 1st outer layer removed
⅓ lb	sugar snap peas, stem end removed and the thread at the seam peeled
2 bunches	red radishes, tops removed and well washed
5 cloves	fresh garlic, peeled
¾ C	extra virgin olive oil
¼ C + 1 T	fresh lemon juice
+	kosher salt
+	freshly ground black pepper
½ lb	Valdéon cheese, crumbled or shaved
1 stick	sweet butter, room temperature
4 slices	fresh peasant bread, cut long and thin

Photographs by Colin Lane

If I were going to fashion a crest for Prune—and, really, when one crushes on a restaurant the way I have for as long as I have, it could come to that—pretty much every ingredient in this recipe would make the design. They're the simple, workaday building blocks that Gabrielle Hamilton has built her well-deserved reputation on (well, those and her writing in *Blood, Bones & Butter*), and they rarely shine as brightly as they do in this recipe, for which I could imagine even buying *extra* celery from the store.

1 For this recipe, you don't want the big, fibrous outer stalks of each head of celery, just the second tier of green, appetizing celery stalks. Trim the tops without losing the interior bright yellow leaves. Wash thoroughly, rinsing deep into the heads by holding directly under the faucet.

2 Place the celery in a roasting pan and cover with chicken broth. Scatter with some peppercorns and a couple of bay leaves. Don't salt, the celery itself has some salinity.

3 Cover with parchment paper and then foil and bring to a simmer on the stove top—over two burners, if necessary. Lower heat to the barest flame possible and let braise for 15 or 20 minutes until the celery is soft and tender when you pierce deep into the base with a blade or skewer.

4 Lift the cooked celery out onto a rack set over a sheet pan to fully drain and cool. If you think you'll make use of it, save the celery braising liquid—well labeled and accurately dated—to braise your next batch of celery. It will get better each time.

5 When cool enough to handle, pull off the green outer stalks to reveal the celadon, tender, beautiful hearts. Snack on the green outer stalks. Leave the hearts as natural and "as is" as possible.

6 Mix all the marinade ingredients together. Add ground black pepper for a different spark, heat, and flavor than red chili flakes. Season with salt. The flavor should be bright, assertive, and bracing. Chill the celery hearts in the marinade for at least a few hours.

7 Garnish with freshly chopped parsley as you plate, and allow to temper briefly to shake the dulling cold from the celery.

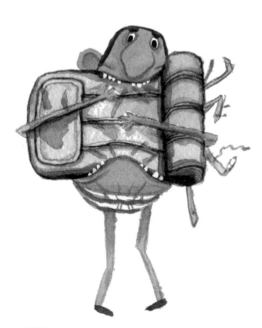

INGREDIENTS

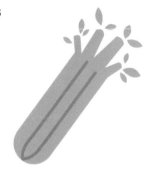

5	celery hearts
4 quarts	chicken broth
+	black peppercorns
2 to 3	bay leaves
1 recipe	MARINADE
+	parsley

MARINADE

4	oil-packed anchovies, minced
1 clove	fresh garlic, minced
big pinch	red pepper flakes, like the ones in pizza shops
¼ C	parsley, chopped
2 T	fresh lemon juice
4 T	extra virgin olive oil
+	freshly ground black pepper
+	kosher salt

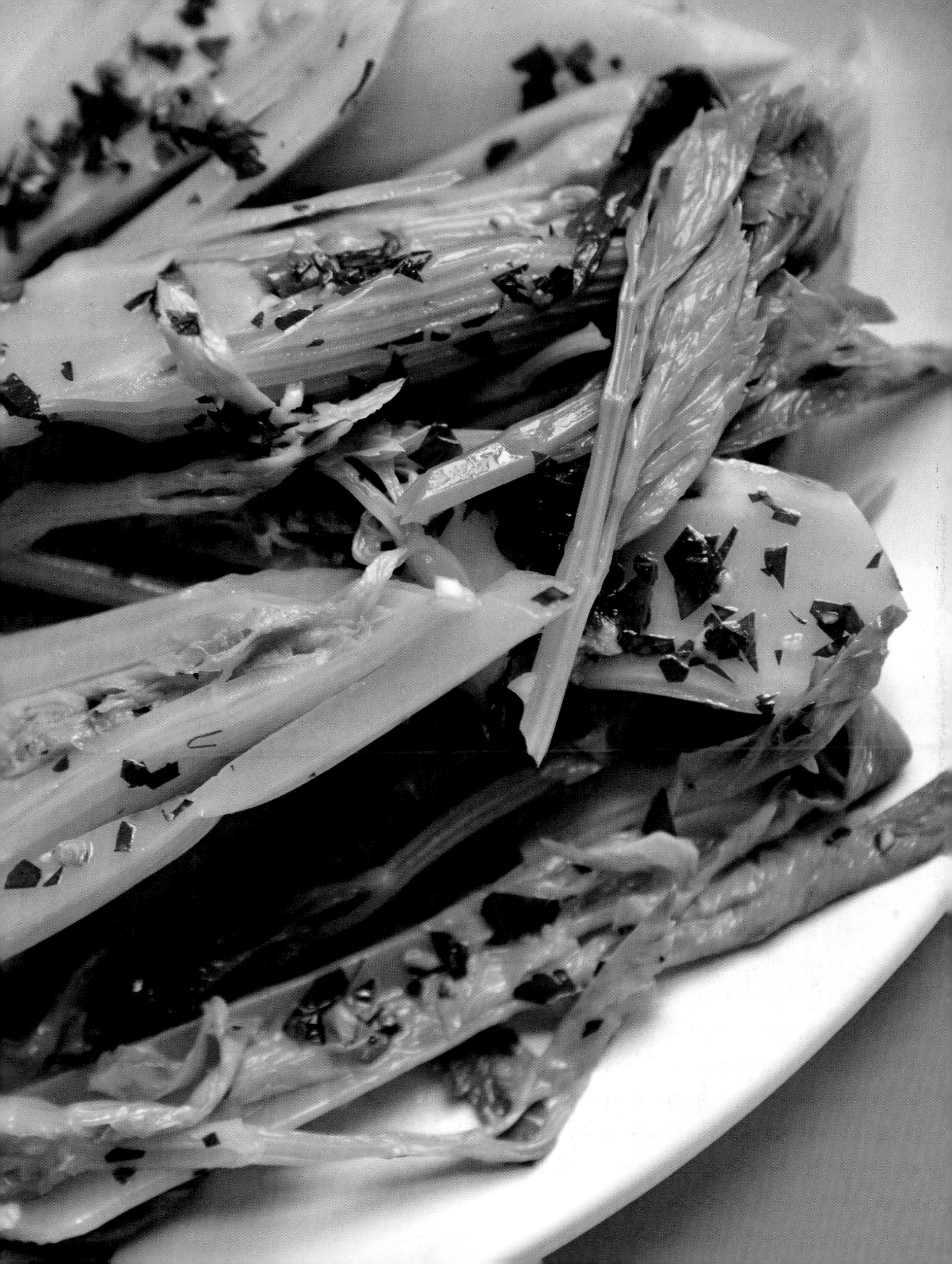

MARINATED WHITE ANCHOVIES WITH SHAVED CELERY AND WARM MARCONA ALMONDS

MAKES 2 SERVINGS

This dish has been on the bar menu at Prune since the earliest days: a pile of a celery, a pile of boquerones, and a pile of Marcona almonds shoulder-to-shoulder on the plate. I remember first encountering it more than a decade ago, whenever Prune opened, back when the latter two ingredients were still pretty goddamn novel if you'd never been to Spain, and thinking, What are these un-fishy anchovies? What are these oily, odd, amazing almonds? How do I navigate these heaps of ingredients? And, most importantly, why is the combination so amazing? The answer, I learned, is this: get in there with your fingers, a glass of something bracing in the other hand, and find out for yourself.

1 **Toss the celery** with a good drizzle of oil, a good squeeze of lemon, a few turns of pepper, and a handful of parsley. Arrange the celery next to the anchovies, and the almonds next to the fish. Serve with a lemon cheek.

INGREDIENTS	
1 C	sweet tender inner branches of celery, thinly sliced, leaves left whole
2 T	extra virgin olive oil
+	lemon juice
+	freshly ground black pepper
+	parsley leaves
about a dozen	marinated white anchovies
¼ C	Marcona almonds, warmed lightly
1	lemon cheek

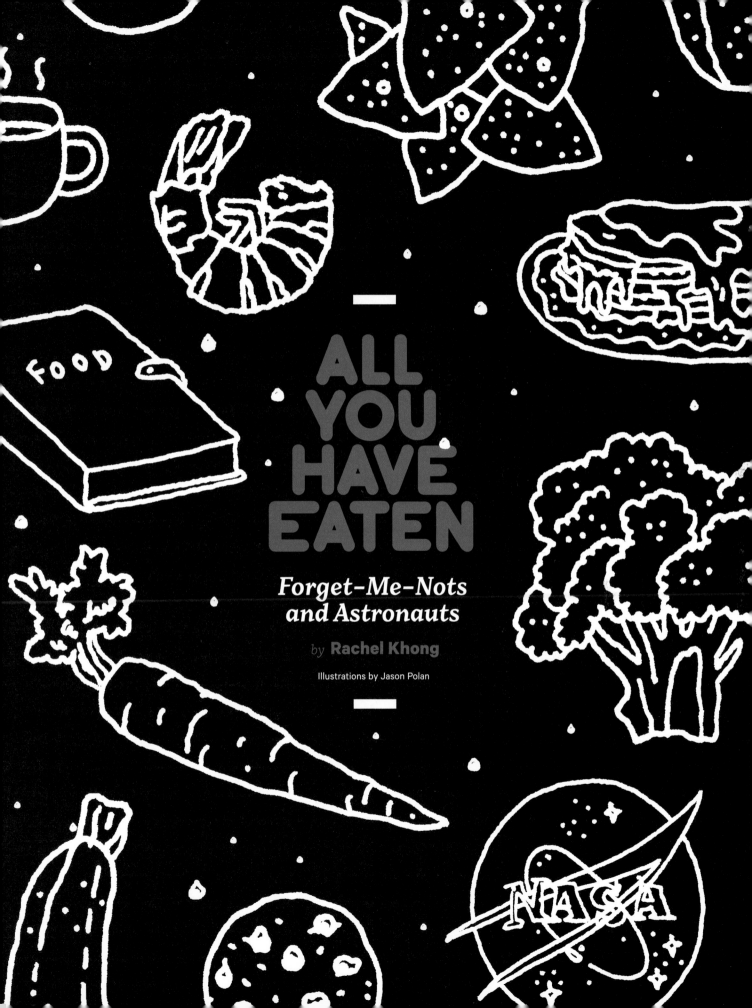

ALL YOU HAVE EATEN

Forget-Me-Nots and Astronauts

by **Rachel Khong**

Illustrations by Jason Polan

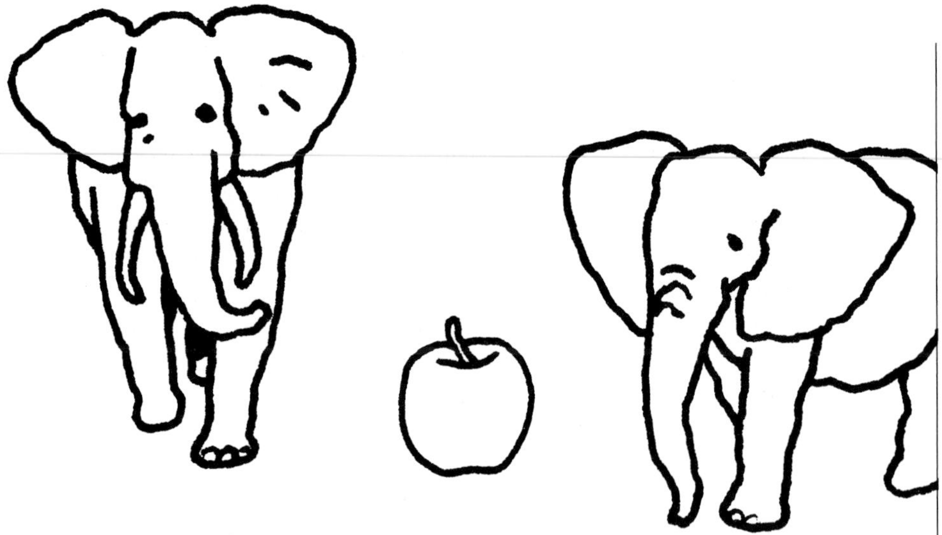

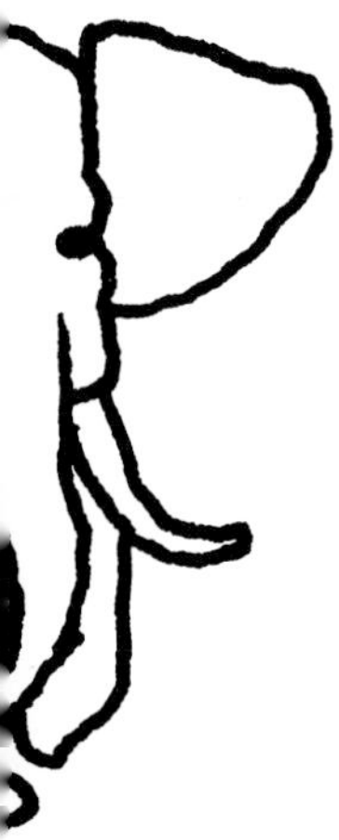

Over the course of his or her lifetime, the average person will eat 60,000 pounds of food, the weight of six elephants. The average American will drink half a million cans of soda. He will eat about 28 pigs, 2,000 chickens, 5,070 apples, and 2,340 pounds of lettuce.

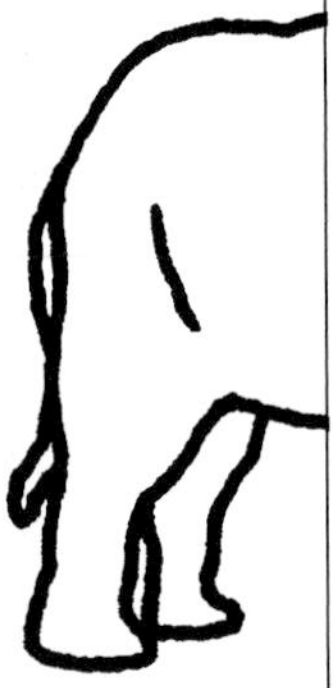

How much of that will he remember, and for how long, and how well?

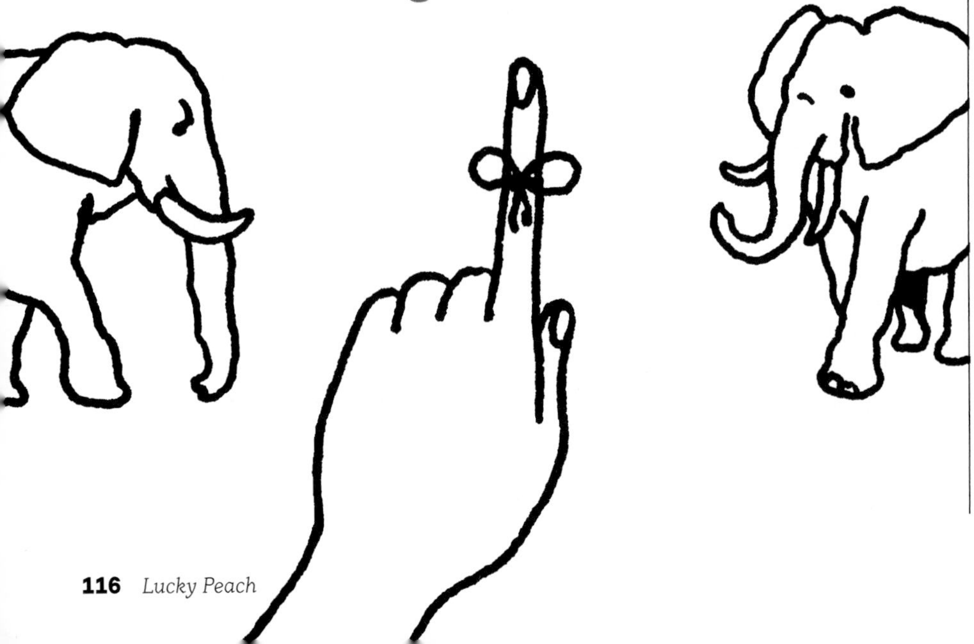

You might be able to tell me, with some certainty, what your breakfast was, but that confidence most likely diminishes when I ask about two, three, four breakfasts ago—never mind this day last year.

The human memory is famously faulty; the brain remains mostly a mystery. We know that comfort foods make the pleasure centers in our brains light up the way drugs do. We know, because of a study conducted by Northwestern University and published in the *Journal of Neuroscience*, that by recalling a moment, you're altering it slightly, like a mental game of Telephone—the more you conjure a memory, the less accurate it will be down the line. Scientists have implanted false memories in mice and grown memories in pieces of brain in test tubes. But we haven't made many noteworthy strides in the thing that seems most relevant: how *not* to forget.

Unless committed to memory or written down, what we eat vanishes as soon as it's consumed. That's the point, after all. But because the famous diarist Samuel Pepys wrote, in his first entry, "Dined at home in the garret, where my wife dressed the remains of a turkey, and in the doing of it she burned her hand," we know that Samuel Pepys, in the 1600s, ate turkey. We know that, hundreds of years ago, Samuel Pepys's wife burned her hand. We know, because she wrote it in her diary, that Anne Frank at one point ate fried potatoes for breakfast. She once ate porridge and "a hash made from kale that came out of the barrel."

For breakfast on January 2, 2008, I ate oatmeal with pumpkin seeds and brown sugar and drank a cup of green tea. I know because it's the first entry in a food log I still keep today. I began it as an experiment in food as a mnemonic device. The idea was this: I'd write something objective every day that would cue my memories into the future—they'd serve as compasses by which to remember moments.

Andy Warhol kept what he called a "smell collection," switching perfumes every three months so he could reminisce more lucidly on those months whenever he smelled that period's particular scent. Food, I figured, took this even further. It involves multiple senses, and that's why memories that surround food can come on so strong.

What I'd like to have is a perfect record of every day. I've long been obsessed with this impossibility, that every day be perfectly productive and perfectly remembered. What I remember from January 2, 2008 is that after eating the oatmeal I went to the post office, where an old woman was arguing with a postal worker about postage—she thought what she'd affixed to her envelope was enough and he didn't.

I'm terrified of forgetting. My grandmother has battled Alzheimer's for years now, and to watch someone battle Alzheimer's—we say "battle," as though there's some way of winning—is terrifying. If I'm always thinking about dementia, my unscientific logic goes, it can't happen to me (the way an earthquake comes when you don't expect it, and so the best course of action is always to expect it). "Really, one might almost live one's life over, if only one could make a sufficient effort of recollection" is a sentence I once underlined in John Banville's *The Sea* (a book that I can't remember much else about). But effort alone is not enough and isn't particularly reasonable, anyway. A man named Robert Shields kept the world's longest diary: he chronicled every five minutes of his life until a stroke in 2006

rendered him unable to. He wrote about microwaving foods, washing dishes, bathroom visits, writing itself. When he died in 2007, he left 37.5 million words behind— ninety-one boxes of paper. Reading his obituary, I wondered if Robert Shields ever managed to watch a movie straight through.

Last spring, as part of a NASA-funded study, a crew of three men and three women with "astronaut-like" characteristics spent four months in a geodesic dome in an abandoned quarry on the northern slope of Hawaii's Mauna Loa volcano. For those four months, they lived and ate as though they were on Mars, only venturing outside to the surrounding Mars-like, volcanic terrain, in simulated space suits.[1] Hawaii Space Exploration Analog and Simulation (HI-SEAS) is a four-year project: a series of missions meant to simulate and study the challenges of long-term space travel, in anticipation of mankind's eventual trip to Mars. This first mission's focus was food.

Getting to Mars will take roughly six to nine months each way, depending on trajectory; the mission itself will likely span years. So the question becomes: How do you feed astronauts for so long? On "Mars," the HI-SEAS crew alternated between two days of pre-prepared meals and two days of dome-cooked meals of shelf-stable ingredients. Researchers were interested in the answers to a number of behavioral issues: among them,

the well-documented phenomenon of menu fatigue (when International Space Station astronauts grow weary of their packeted meals, they tend to lose weight). They wanted to see what patterns would evolve over time if a crew's members were allowed dietary autonomy, and given the opportunity to cook for themselves ("an alternative approach to feeding crews of long term planetary outposts," read the open call).

Everything was hyper-documented. Everything eaten was logged in painstaking detail: weighed, filmed, and evaluated. The crew filled in surveys before and after meals: queries into how hungry they were, their first impressions, their moods, how the food smelled, what its texture was, how it tasted. They documented their time spent cooking; their water usage; the quantity of leftovers, if any. The goal was to measure the effect of what they ate on their health and morale, along with other basic questions concerning resource use. How much water will it take to cook on Mars? How much water will it take to wash dishes? How much time is required; how much energy? How will everybody feel about it all? I followed news of the mission devoutly.

It was afternoon in Belgium and early morning for me in California when Angelo Vermeulen, the crew's commander, and I spoke over Skype. He started with a disclaimer: he wasn't the crew's best cook. He's happiest eating bread and cheese (bread and chocolate sprinkles if it's breakfast); he cooks potatoes in his microwave. He told me that earlier in the day he'd had some *grobos*: rolled-up pickled herring and onion, held together by a toothpick, and "drowned in mayonnaise"—"it's *so* good," he said, looking worked up about it.

[1] At first they wore government-surplus hazmat suits—those would constrict movement and essentially do the job, was NASA's budget-minded thinking—but the crew members expressed disappointment that they weren't realer-looking space suits, and mid-way through the mission, Apollo-like suits were donated to them by the University of Maryland.

"Angelo used so much mayonnaise!" was what Kate Greene, a fellow crewmember, said when the two of us met a week later in San Francisco. But Angelo does not look like a person who eats "so much mayonnaise."

"Far superior genetics. We ran out of mayonnaise early," Kate said. "But it wasn't just him, it was all of us."

Their crew of six was selected from a pool of 700 candidates. Kate is a science writer, open-water swimmer, and volleyball player. When I asked her what "astronaut-like" meant and why she was picked she said it was some "combination of education, experience, and attitude": a science background, leadership experience, an adventurous attitude. An interest in cooking was not among the requirements. The cooking duties were divided from the get-go; in the kitchen, crew members worked in pairs. On non-creative days they'd eat just-add-water, camping-type meals: pre-prepared lasagna, which surprised Kate by being not terrible; a thing called "kung fu chicken" that Angelo described as "slimy" and less tolerable; a raspberry crumble dessert that's a favorite among backpackers ("That was really delicious," Kate said, "but still you felt weird about thinking it was *too* delicious"). The crew didn't eat much real astronaut food—astronaut ice cream, for example—because real astronaut food is expensive.

On creative cooking days, meals were left up to the cooks. "On the crew there were three people who had visions for food and three people who were like, 'It's my turn to cook? What do I do?'" said Kate. "Angelo, Simon [Engler], and I were the people who were like, Okay, I'll figure something out. Sian [Proctor], Yajaira [Sierra-Sastre], and Oleg [Abramov] were the people who really had it going on. Oleg would make all these traditional Russian dishes, Yajaira would make tapas and flatbread pizzas, Sian could make a soup out of anything. I do not cook well. One time in grad school I was like, 'I'm having vanilla Slimfast and oatmeal. This is the greatest meal a human being can eat!'"

The choices were of course limited on Mars, but the HI-SEAS pantry was impressively ample: grains, nuts, shelf-stable bacon, Nutella, freeze-dried and dehydrated vegetables, fruit, and meat. There was powdered milk and powdered butter ("Which you'd think would be disgusting," Kate said, "but we were slathering it on bread"). Angelo and Kate, separately and without any prompting, got very animated talking about "egg crystals" that look like "yellow sugar" and, when rehydrated, are just like beaten

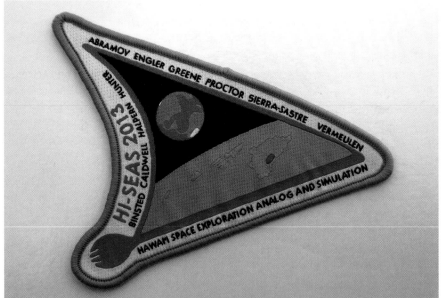

Photographs by Angelo Vermeulen

eggs. "Historically, powdered eggs have been gnarly," Kate said, "but egg crystals made *delicious* eggs." It costs $10,000 to put a pound of food in space, which makes freeze-dried and dehydrated foods especially valuable. In the absence of fresh vegetables the freeze-dried versions were, for the crew members, "almost indistinguishable from fresh stuff," Angelo said. You add water, and there's "a little bit of a sizzle when it absorbs the water."

"Freeze-dried broccoli—we all loved it a lot. We would just dump it on our plate," Kate corroborated. "Freeze-dried things were mostly better. Freeze-dried broccoli came in chunks and it was chewy. It was really good. But dehydrated broccoli was kind of mushy once you rehydrated it."

But the vegetables never varied in size ("The carrots were always the same size, the broccoli was always the same size, and after a while the flavor didn't matter," Kate said). The crew craved salt and fat, too. "One of the issues was the meat that was freeze-dried didn't have a lot of fat in it. And so we were all really starved for fat. We used a lot of oil; we just couldn't get enough. Spam was really good because it was super salty and super fatty. I had never eaten Spam but we had Spam musubi and Spam fried rice—oh my God, it was delicious."

The main food study had a big odor identification component to it: the crew took scratch-n-sniff tests, which Kate said she felt confident about at the mission's start, and less certain about near the end. "The second-to-last test," she said, "I would smell grass and feel really wistful." Their noses were mapped with sonogram because, in space, the shape of your nose changes. And there were, on top of this, studies unrelated to food. They exercised

in anti-microbial shirts (laundry doesn't happen in space), evaluated their experiences hanging out with robot pets, and documented their sleep habits.

At the end of every day, after the innumerable surveys, each crew member filled out a questionnaire about how he or she felt about everyone else: rating interactions with the five other crew members and with the twenty members of Mission Support on a scale of −7 to 7. "That's always the question: did you guys get along? Yeah, of course, but you can't *always* get along. One of the crew members said it was like being married to five other people," Kate said, "and it was."

When I asked Angelo if he thought his mood was affected predominantly by the food he ate, he seemed skeptical. "Things that were impacting mood were crew dynamics, communication with mission support, communication with your significant other. We didn't have real-time communication—no Skyping or calling—but you could be writing to each other, and a combination of all that contributed to your mood."

"We all had relationships outside that we were trying to maintain in some way," Kate said. "Some were kind of new, some were tenuous, some were old and established, but they were all very difficult to maintain. A few things that could come off wrong in an e-mail could really bum you out for a long time."

She told me about another crew member whose boyfriend didn't email her at his usual time. This was roughly halfway through the mission. She started to get obsessed with the idea that maybe he got into a car accident. "Like seriously obsessed," Kate said. "I was like,

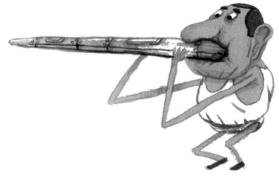

'I think your brain is telling you things that aren't actually happening. Let's just be calm about this,' and she was like, 'Okay, okay.' But she couldn't sleep that night. In the end he was just like, 'Hey, what's up?' I knew he would be fine, but I could see how she could think something serious had happened."

"My wife sent me poems every day but for a couple days she didn't," Kate said. "Something was missing from those days, and I don't think she could have realized how important they were. It was weird. Everything was bigger inside your head because you were living inside your head."

I asked Kate who the mission was harder on and she says it was harder on her wife. "When a soldier is deployed, there's a narrative that goes along with that. When an astronaut goes to space, there's a freaking narrative that goes with that. When someone leaves to pretend to go to space, there's no narrative that goes along with that. You're making it up. You're like, 'Why is this important again? Why is this something that needs to be done?' In some ways it doesn't. It's not the hero sort of role of a soldier or an astronaut. From many points of view, it's kind of ridiculous."

The mission generated a huge amount of data, which is all still being analyzed. Both Angelo and Kate were hesitant to draw any conclusions ("I'm not involved in the analysis. I just did my job," Angelo said). At some point, the results will be published in papers, and we'll have some answers about menu fatigue, about how time's passing feels in isolation, about the changing shapes of astronauts' noses.

"My personal conclusions are a little predictable, I'm afraid," Angelo told me. "Cooking is highly advantageous, for many different reasons." There were always two people in the kitchen, which was good for "crew cohesion." And he talked about cooking as being a craved-for creative outlet. It was especially gratifying for the cooks—Angelo recalled with endearing pride his *enchilagna*, a combination enchilada and lasagna he'd devised.

When I asked him about the role food played in his remembrances he sounded skeptical again: "I'm not sure how much of the event you remember because of the food," he said. "I think it works the other way around. We had monthly celebrations and the food wasn't particularly fantastic. To me it doesn't feel I remember specific instances because of the food, I remember specific instances and then the food goes along with that in my memory."

Kate: "One night Yajaira and I made tapas and it was more interesting than usual. We found some YouTube flamenco. It was pretty goofy. It had an ambience to it."

Angelo: "Certain foods got particular focus, through Sian's outreach program"—during the mission, Sian recorded a cooking show; the episodes are still available online—"so of course I remember salmon patties. I was in front of the camera and the video is on YouTube."

Angelo doesn't normally keep a journal, but kept a daily journal in "the Hab" that was submitted to a study at the mission's end. Kate opted out of that particular study but kept a personal journal for herself. She doesn't typically maintain

a journal, either: "The only one I ever kept, from when I first realized I was gay, I put it in a box of books I sent media mail to Nashville and it got lost, never to be found again. So the only journal I ever kept in my life, just the one journal from when I was sixteen—it's gone forever, and thank God. Because it's horrible! It's the worst. When I was on Mars I wrote every day about how I was feeling. I was looking back on that, and it's odd how not helpful it was."

Kate recalled the day she remotely drove a rover in Canada as one of the most exciting experiences of the mission ("I kind of got it stuck on a rock"). When she asked Jean Hunter, the head of the mission, for the record of the meal she'd eaten that morning, she was surprised at how unextraordinary it was: granola and milk and tea.

Breakfast on July 9 for subject XXXX:
Body mass **133.4 lb.**
Satiety rating before breakfast: **-2**
Satiety rating after breakfast: **1**
Foods and ratings:
ANCIENT GRAINS:
    Appearance: **8** Aroma: **8**
    Interest: **8** Acceptability: **9**
    Finished: **Y** Additional servings: **N**
EARL GREY TEA:
    Appearance: **8** Aroma: **8**
    Interest: **8** Acceptability: **not rated** Finished: **not rated**
    Additional servings: **not rated**
No condiments No comments
Granola: **84.6 g** Milk **120.6 g**

hen I look back on my meals from the past year, the food log does the job I intended more

or less effectively. I can remember, with some clarity, the particulars of given days: who I was with, how I was feeling, the subjects discussed. There was the night in October I stress-scarfed a head of romaine and peanut butter packed onto old, hard bread; the somehow not-sobering bratwurst and fries I ate on day two of a two-day hangover, while trying to keep things light with somebody to whom, the two nights before, I had aired more than I meant to. There was the night in January I cooked "rice, chicken stirfry with bell pepper and mushrooms, tomato-y Chinese broccoli, 1 bottle IPA" with my oldest, best friend, and we ate the stirfry and drank our beers slowly while commiserating about the most recent conversations we'd had with our mothers.

But reading the entries from 2008, that first year, does something else to me: it suffuses me with the same mortification as if I'd written down my most private thoughts (that reaction is what keeps me from maintaining a more conventional journal). There's nothing especially incriminating about my diet, except maybe that I ate tortilla chips with unusual frequency, but the fact that it's just food doesn't spare me from the horror and head-shaking that comes with reading old diaries. Mentions of certain meals conjure specific memories, but mostly what I'm left with are the general feelings from that year. They weren't happy ones. I was living in San Francisco at the time. A relationship was dissolving.

It seems to me that the success of a relationship depends on a shared trove of memories. Or not shared, necessarily, but not *incompatible*. That's the trouble, I think, with parents and children: parents retain memories of their children that the children themselves don't share. My father's favorite meal is breakfast and his favorite breakfast restaurant is McDonald's, and I remember—having just read Michael Pollan or watched *Super Size Me*—self-righteously not ordering my regular egg McMuffin one morning, and how that actually hurt him.

When a relationship goes south, it's hard to pinpoint just where or how—especially after a prolonged period of it heading that direction. I was at a loss with this one. Going forward, I didn't want *not* to be able to account for myself. If I could remember everything, I thought, I'd be better equipped; I'd be better able to make proper, comprehensive assessments—informed decisions. But my memory had proved itself unreliable, and I needed something better. Writing down food was a way to turn my life into facts: if I had all the facts, I could keep them straight. So the next time this happened I'd know exactly why—I'd have all the data at hand.

In the wake of that breakup there were stretches of days and weeks of identical breakfasts and identical dinners. Those days and weeks blend into one another, become indistinguishable, and who knows whether I was too sad to be imaginative or all the unimaginative food made me sadder.

hen I asked Kate why she chose to spend four months in a dome with five strangers on pretend Mars, she said she'd always wanted to be an astronaut. And even if she couldn't go to Mars herself, she wanted to help in whatever way she could; she wanted to help with the research that might help other people go to Mars.

"And I wanted to see if I *could*," she said. "I'm always really curious about who you are in a different context. Who am I completely removed from Earth—or pretending to be removed from Earth? When you're going further and further from this planet, with all its rules and everything you've ever known, what happens? Do you invent new rules? What matters to you when you don't have constructs? Do you take the constructs with you? On an individual level it was an exploration of who I am in a different context, and on a larger scale, going to another planet is an exploration about what humanity is in a different context."

In summer of 2008, I moved to Gainesville: a college town in the Florida panhandle, and as different for me as contexts get. It seemed unreal when I lived there, trying to write and dating people completely wrong for me in the wake of this busted-up thing. Even now, it seems unreal.

The temperature in Florida in August hovers consistently around 100 degrees. Despite the heat, I cooked constantly. A few days after moving to town, enticed by a beautiful photo of browned eggplant in the newspaper, I cooked it in my small, hot, Florida kitchen: linguine with fried eggplant, tomato, and basil and parsley. I remember, that same day, falling off my heavy, old bike. A stranger named Joe or Jon tossed the bike into the bed of his pick-up truck—as effortlessly as though it were a stuffed thing won at a state fair—and took me to his house out near the mall, far from where I lived, and cleaned my ankle with hydrogen peroxide and Q-tips, and tightened my handlebars.

That place and those years felt like make-believe—one fall in particular. There was a trip that friends and I took to Key Biscayne, an island south of Miami Beach inhabited mostly by wealthy retirees. I remember that drive, drinking 5-Hour Energy drinks and eating Klonopin with a couple new friends and the wrong-for-me person I was dating, whose grandparents' condo it was we were staying in. Recently I e-mailed them to see what they could remember. They remembered parts which, pieced together, matched what I wrote down:

Five hour energy drink; One or two klonopin (two)

D: caviar with cream cheese and toast; melon with prosciutto; Caesar salad; tomato and basil salad; shrimp and scallop angel hair pasta; so much wine; café cubano.

What I remember is early that evening, drinking sparkling wine and spreading cream cheese on slices of a soft baguette from the fancy Key Biscayne Publix, then spooning grocery-store caviar onto it ("Lumpfish caviar and Prosecco, definitely, on the balcony"). I remember cooking dinner unhurriedly ("You were comparing prices for the seafood and I was impatient")—the thinnest pasta I could find, shrimp and squid cooked in wine and lots of garlic—and eating it late ("You cooked something good, but I can't remember what") and then drinking a café Cubano even later ("It was so sweet it made our teeth hurt and then, for me at least, immediately precipitated a metabolic crisis") and how, afterward, we all went to the empty beach and got in the water which was, on that warm summer day, not even cold ("It was just so beautiful after the rain").

"And this wasn't the same trip," wrote that wrong-for-me then-boyfriend, "but remember when you and I walked all the way to that restaurant in Bill Baggs park, at the southern tip of the island, and we had that painfully sweet white sangria, and ceviche, and walked back and got tons of mosquito bites, but we didn't care, and then we were on the beach somehow and we looked at the red lights on top of all the buildings, and across the channel at Miami Beach, and went in the hot Miami ocean, and most importantly it was National Fish Day?"

And it's heartening to me that I *do* remember all that—had remembered without his prompting, or consulting the record (I have written down: "D: ceviche; awful sangria; fried plantains; shrimp paella." "It is National fish day," I wrote. "There was lightning all night!"). It's heartening that my memory isn't as unreliable as I worry it is. I remember it exactly as he describes: the too-sweet sangria at that restaurant on the water, how the two of us had giggled so hard over nothing and declared that day "National Fish Day," finding him in the kitchen at four in the morning, dipping a sausage into mustard—me taking that other half of the sausage, dipping it into mustard—the two of us deciding to drive the six hours back to Gainesville, right then.

"That is a really happy memory," he wrote to me. "That is my nicest memory from that year and from that whole period. I wish we could live it again, in some extra-dimensional parallel life."

Three years ago I moved back to San Francisco, which was, for me, a new-old city. I'd lived there twice before. The first time I lived there was a cold summer in 2006, during which I met that man I'd be broken up about a couple years later. And though that summer was before I started writing

down the food, and before I truly learned how to cook for myself, I can still remember flashes: a dimly lit party and drinks with limes in them and how, ill-versed in flirting, I took the limes from his drink and put them into mine. I remember a night he cooked circular ravioli he'd bought from an expensive Italian grocery store, and zucchini he'd sliced into thin coins. I remembered him splashing Colt 45—leftover from a party—into the zucchini as it was cooking, and all of that charming me: the Colt 45, the expensive ravioli, this dinner of circles.

The second time I lived in San Francisco was the time our thing fell apart. This was where my terror had originated: where I remembered the limes and the ravioli, he remembered or felt the immediacy of something else, and neither of us was right or wrong to remember what we did—all memories, of course, are valid—but still, it sucked. And now I have a record reminding me of the nights I came home drunk and sad and, with nothing else in the house, sautéed kale; blanks on the days I ran hungry to Kezar Stadium from the Lower Haight, running lap after lap after lap to turn my brain off, stopping to read short stories at the bookstore on the way home, all to turn off the inevitable thinking, and at home, of course, the inevitable thinking.

The third time in San Francisco, we met like old friends to drink gin and tonics in a dive bar not far from my new apartment (May 11, 2011: L: enchiladas; D: tom yum noodles; gin and tonics). We hadn't seen each other at all in the years that I was away—trying out life in a different context—and while we were getting along again, the way we once had, I was preemptively worrying about what might happen down the line: that I'd remember something and

he'd remember something different, and that would be the end of us. A few weeks later, on the afternoon of Memorial Day, while we were sitting on a Mission stoop, sharing an It's-It (a San Francisco thing—an oatmeal-cookie ice cream sandwich covered in chocolate), I remembered—I possessed a record of—those intervening years of feeling wronged and trying alternately to forgive and not to forgive him, and not even standing a chance now, eating that half an It's-It—forgiving him.

I'm not sure what to make of this data—what conclusions, if any, to draw. What I know is that it accumulates and disappears and accumulates again. No matter how vigilantly we keep track—even if we spend four months in a geodesic dome on a remote volcano with nothing to do *but* keep track—we experience more than we have the capacity to remember; we eat more than we can retain; we feel more than we can possibly carry with us. And maybe forgetting isn't so bad. I know there is the "small green apple" from the time we went to a moving sale and he bought bricks, and it was raining lightly, and as we were gathering the bricks we noticed an apple tree at the edge of the property with its branches overhanging into the yard, and we picked two small green apples that'd been washed by the rain, and wiped them off on our shirts. They surprised us by being sweet and tart and good. We put the cores in his car's cup holders. There was the time he brought chocolate chips and two eggs and a Tupperware of milk to my apartment, and we baked cookies. There are the times he puts candy in my jacket's small pockets—usually peppermints so ancient they've melted and re-hardened inside their wrappers—which I eat anyway, and then are gone, but not gone. **LP**

chubo

CURATOR OF THE FINEST JAPANESE KITCHENWARE

Focusing on performance, quality and precision, we've travelled throughout Japan to bring you the finest chef's knives and culinary tools.

View the collection at **chuboknives**.com

ALL EWE CAN EAT

Everything You Always Wanted to Know About Sheep Diets (But Were Afraid to Ask)

by **Lucas Peterson**

Photographs by Naomi Harris

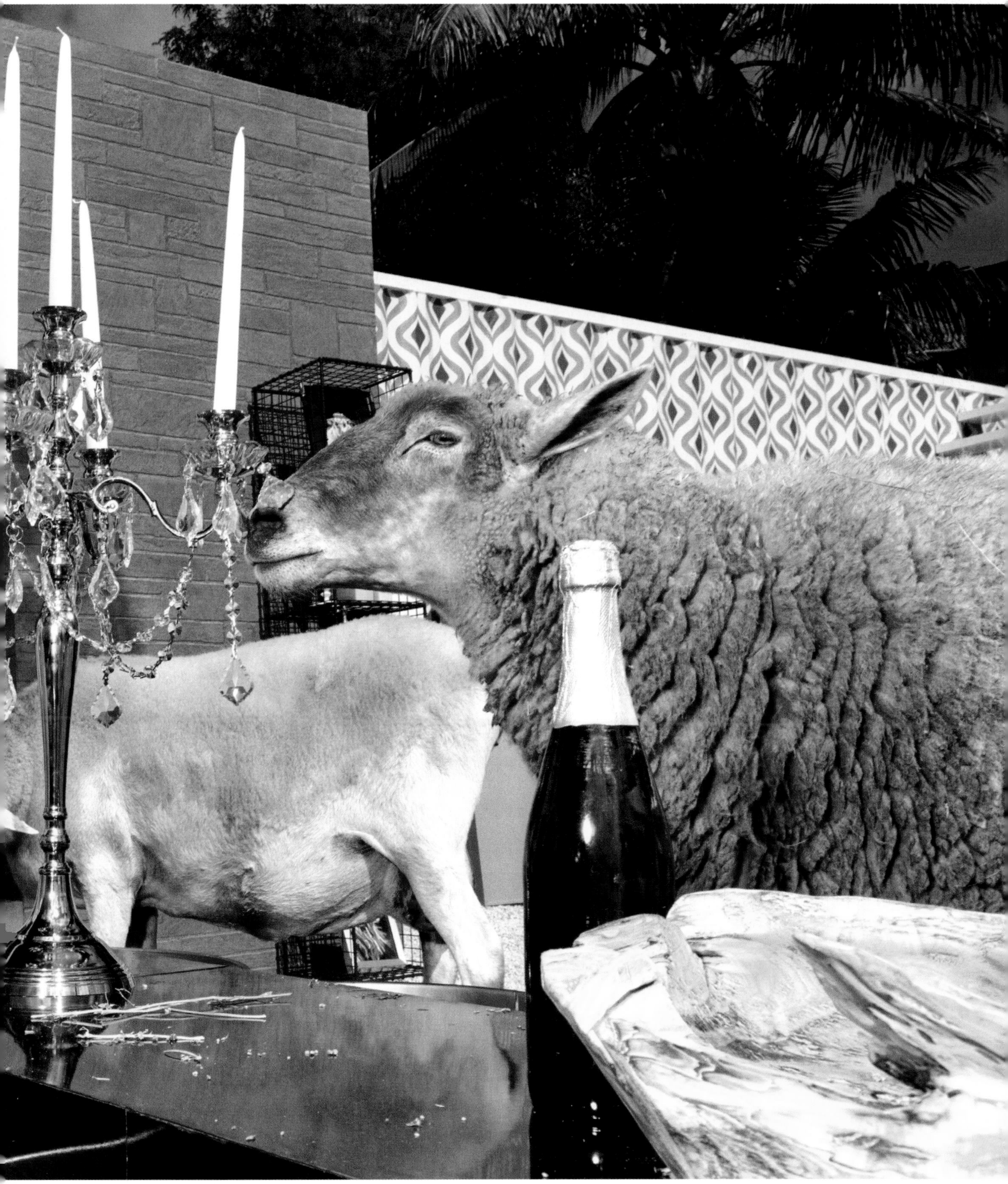

Male sheep are called *rams*; female sheep are *ewes*. Castrated males are referred to as *wethers*. Young sheep are *lambs*. Strictly speaking, meat is only lamb if it comes from an animal that is less than one year old. Meat from adult sheep is called *mutton*. In many countries, but not in the United States, there is an additional category called *hogget*, which is meat from sheep between one and two years old.

During World War II, the hogget-less United States switched the meat in many soldiers' rations from beef to mutton when beef became scarce. Some have since theorized that it was the fallout from this ration-swap that turned the Greatest Generation and their children completely away from sheep meat. (A National Research Council paper cites "A negative American G.I. experience with mutton.") Others hypothesize that the removal of wool from the Pentagon's "strategic materials" list in 1960 is responsible for the sheep's decline. The numbers are hard to ignore: sheep production peaked in the United States during the '40s and '50s at about 55 million head—today it stands at about five and a half million.

I took to the highway to learn about how those sheep we are still eating are being raised, and to see what they're eating on their way to our plates.

Dan Macon reaches out through the driver's-side window of his truck and punches a code into an intercom box, and I follow him in my own car through a sleepy gated community dotted with archetypal McMansions in their oversized, uniform luxury. Many of the plots are empty, though, and some are overrun with tall, dry ripgut brome (a grass) and filaree (an invasive weed). Macon, a stocky guy with ropy forearms, a push-broom mustache, and a straw hat, owns the Flying Mule Farm in Auburn, California, a small town about an hour outside of Sacramento, the epicenter of California's Central Valley. Today, however, like many days since the rain stopped falling, he's ferrying his animals to various locales around the county. He's here to mow the lawn, or rather, his sheep are. "We've worked for Pacific Gas and Electric, municipalities, a whole variety of customers," Macon explains. "In this case," however, "there is no money exchanging hands."

The homeowners' association of this subdivision needs their grass cut, and Macon needs to feed his animals. Because of the drought ("the worst year of three bad years in a row," says Macon) grass is practically nonexistent in the Central Valley. An average pasture this time of year could be expected to yield 500 pounds of green grass per acre. This year it's fifty. Because Macon raises grass-fed lamb, and markets it as such, he's been put in a difficult position. So he and his sheep have become contractors, and he ferries them all over the state to different landscaping jobs just to keep them fed. The sheep get to eat; the landowners get their lawns manicured. Barning the animals and giving them hay is an option, Macon says, but hay is expensive. A month of hay costs as much as nine months of pasture.

The dry grass is better than nothing, but it's not enough. "This is probably more than you ever wanted to know about ruminant physiology," Macon declaims, smiling. "But I'm concerned about the microbial flora in the gut of the sheep." Most animals are born with what is known as a "sterile gut"—a clean slate—but soon begin to acquire bacteria, protozoa, and other organisms from various things in their environment, like their mother's dung. This microbial-gut flora protects the animal from diseases and breaks down its food. When there's no balance in the diet, however (in this case no green grass), it throws off the balance of the microbes in the gut. Additionally, Macon worries that the sheep "need protein to thrive and green grass is what has the protein." No green, no protein; and protein creates muscle

mass, which creates meaty lambs and is necessary for mothers to produce milk. As it is, Macon will probably end up having to sell off some of his animals to other ranchers before they're mature, because there's just no way to feed them.

My journey to meet Macon's sheep began with a 450-mile drive up the 5 Freeway. The drive is not without certain pleasures—the mesmerizing precision of the grape vines and almond trees lining the road, Pea Soup Anderson's in Santa Nella, and trying to figure out exactly what is meant by the frequent signs that say CONGRESS CREATED DUST BOWL (more on that later). For the most part, however, it's a numbing exercise in tedium, trying to drive through hundreds of miles of flat nothingness as quickly as possible, mentally calculating how many miles over the speed limit is an acceptable level of risk, while dealing with the frequent pockets of sulfur and cattle smell that are literally breathtaking.

The 5 is the backbone of California and the Central Valley is its heart and its stomach. Historically, dry summers and mild, rainy winters have allowed for the largest concentrations of fruit and nut farms and vineyards in the country, as well as the biggest source of crops like tomatoes, asparagus, and cotton. It also is home to hundreds of thousands of head of livestock, which compete with crops for valuable water and arable land. Primarily cattle, but also sheep.

Your common domestic sheep (*Ovis aries*) is a quadrupedal herbivorous mammal from the order Artiodactyla, which are the even-toed ungulates. "Ungulate" means "hoofed," and "even-toed"

in this case means "not odd-toed." Even-toed mammals include pigs, cows, llamas, deer, and giraffes—all of whom bear their weight equally on the second and third toes of each leg. Odd-toed ungulates usually bear their weight disproportionally on one toe. (Horses, for example, actually have three toes and their hoofs are just oversized third toes.)

Most sheep produce wool. Wool is not hair, nor is it fur. Wool is different in that it is crimped, and grows in clusters. The crimps make it easier to spin into yarn. Most wool that we wear comes from Merino sheep. Some farmers have flocked toward breeds of sheep like the Dorper that produce hair instead of wool, and shed like dogs. The high labor cost of shearing and low global wool prices make it more cost-effective for many to eliminate wool from the equation entirely.

Culturally, it is difficult to overstate the importance of sheep in the pantheon of livestock animals. Domestication of sheep by humans first occurred in Mesopotamia between 11000 and 9000 BC, making them one of the world's first domesticated animals. Sheep idioms are plentiful, and biblical/mythological references reinforcing the historical importance of sheep are vast and numerous. You can probably think of five off the top of your head, but here are a few: *Agnus Dei*, Abraham and the Sacrificial Lamb, Jason and the Golden Fleece, the Lion and the Lamb.

Sheep are ruminants, like cows and goats, and are what is known as foregut fermenters. When the sheep's even-toed ungulate ancestors appeared on the Earth during the Early Eocene period fifty-four million years ago, they were marginalized by larger mammals and

had to survive on very sparse and meager food. Their complex digestive system evolved as a means of survival—foregut fermenters truly get the most out of their food. By regurgitating and re-chewing over and over, they are able to wring every last nutrient from their feed. (The word "ruminant" comes from the Latin *ruminare* which means "to chew over again.")

Sheep, like other ruminants, do not have "four stomachs," as is the folklore, but rather one large stomach with four compartments called the rumen, reticulum, omasum, and abomasum. The rumen is the largest part of the stomach, and takes up most of a sheep's abdominal cavity, with a capacity between five and ten gallons. A sheep is basically a big fermenting vat. Food—mostly grasses and clover—is consumed and passed between the rumen and the reticulum, regurgitated as a solid bolus,

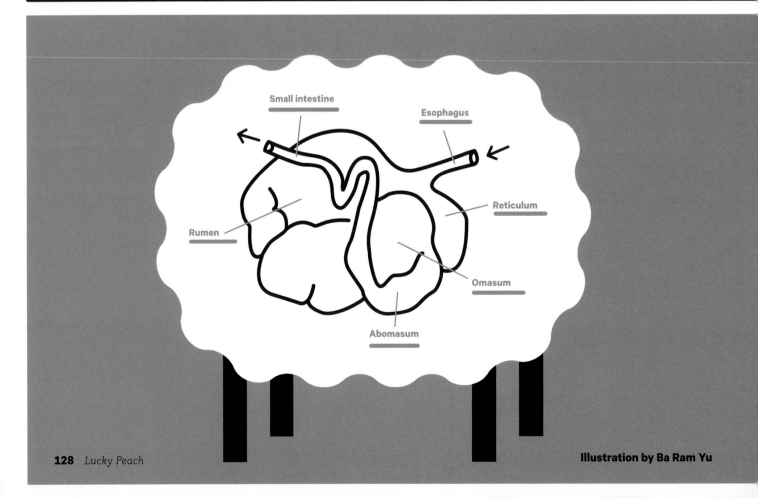

Small intestine

Esophagus

Rumen

Reticulum

Omasum

Abomasum

Illustration by Ba Ram Yu

re-chewed, and re-swallowed. This is called chewing their cud. The bolus gets broken down again and again until every last bit of plant fiber is broken into proteins and fatty acids. Then the broken-down digesta moves to the omasum, where excess water is absorbed. The final section, the abomasum, functions most like a human stomach: enzymes and acids break down what's left to allow the absorption of nutrients. This entire process creates a huge expelling of gas in the form of belching and flatulence—any interference in the process can create enormous health problems in the form of bloat, which can lead to a very unpleasant death.

But predation, not bloat, is any sheep rancher's biggest fear because sheep are more or less defenseless; there's a reason the idioms "meek/innocent/gentle as a lamb" have currency. Sheep's primary means of staying safe is in flocking together.

I visited Mel Thompson's Sierra Farms ranch outside of Oroville, CA, where he has five Maremmas—a breed of dog that originated in central Italy—that patrol his pasture at any given time. (The Maremma is a slightly more exotic breed than is typical. The most common sheepdog, according to the USDA, is the Great Pyrenees.)

"They get along with sheep, not so much with people," Thompson says, somewhat apologetically. One of the dogs has been staring me down and barking for a solid ten minutes. "Rufus! Get out of here!" He makes a motion like a baseball umpire tossing a manager from the game and sighs. "We have to go through this whenever our grandchildren come visit. Every time they come up, it takes the dogs four or five days to learn who they are." The dogs may not be people pleasers (USDA: "The guarding dog is a

working animal… It is not a pet and making this distinction at the outset is important"), but they're great with the livestock—puppies are placed with sheep as early as three or four weeks old to begin the bonding process. Human contact is minimized as the puppies learn to channel their protective instincts. Thompson says his dogs will instinctively lie with ewes that are lambing, refusing to leave the mother's side until the birthing is complete.

Still, sheep get picked off. Predation is the number one cause of sheep death, and coyotes account for 60 percent of predator losses. "You can tell a coyote kill," Thompson starts, then pauses. He wipes off his glasses on his light-blue denim shirt and continues, "because they'll grab the animal, even before it's dead, rip its stomach open, and all the rumen material, the chewed-up grass, will be lying there beside

the body in a pile. Very professionally, like a butcher. Then they go back in and grab the liver and heart and…" He pauses again, "…lungs? Whatever's nutritious." When coyotes (which Thompson pronounces "KYE-ote," two syllables) attack, they immediately go for the blood organs because there is usually a dog or rancher with a gun moving quickly toward the commotion. "You go out in the morning and find a lamb carcass that's in perfect shape, it's just missing its heart and liver. That makes it twice as bad. It wouldn't be as bad if they'd just eat everything."

"Lamb and sheep meat is finer grained and more tender than beef," according to Harold McGee's *On Food and Cooking,* "but well endowed with red myoglobin and with flavor, including a characteristic odor that becomes more pronounced with age." McGee is referring to gaminess, that distinct tangy, earthy flavor that increases as a sheep ages and the taste that offends people who don't care for lamb or mutton. It's this flavor, consumed in the form of a musty ten-year-old ewe packed into an American G.I.'s K-ration during the World War II Pacific campaign, that many people believe—Thompson included—is responsible for the fact that most American households rarely consume lamb, if ever.

The trend has been reversing slightly in recent years, especially as the organic and grass-fed movements become firmly entrenched in the eating habits of those who can afford it, but it's an uphill climb for the industry and the ranchers. Moving animals from pasture to pasture is exhausting, expensive, and time-consuming. In the middle of one of the most severe droughts California has ever seen,

questions arise: does lamb raised on grass provide any noticeable difference in taste? Or is "grass-fed" just a buzzword bandied about as an excuse to charge more for meat, or make us consumers feel less guilty by projecting an idyllic image of life before slaughter? Macon, for his part, says that he can tell when he's eating lamb that has been raised exclusively on grass: "It depends on who you talk to, but I can tell."

Most large-scale American farms choose to "finish" their animals, especially cattle, with grain—in other words, they fatten them up by feeding them corn, soy, grains, and supplements. It's a tempting solution in dry times. As far as the meat goes, this produces more marbling and, by most accounts, a mellower flavor. Providing that kind of feed is expensive, however, and for most small-scale ranchers, economically untenable. The drought will, therefore, most likely lead to leaner animals.

As new developments spring up and roads crisscross what were once rural areas, the job of the sheep rancher becomes almost impossible. And that, ultimately, is what explains why sheep are not raised in the same quantity as cattle: cows are easier, and they provide the most bang per buck. They require relatively little maintenance—you can park them in a field in December and come back in June. They're big and less susceptible to predators. Most importantly, they yield many multiples more than what a sheep could ever produce. Slaughtering an 800-pound cow creates 500 pounds of beef. Milk, though, is where cows hopped-up on artificial-growth hormones really pull ahead: a productive dairy sheep can make 600 pounds of milk a year. Top-producing cows, according to the Holstein USA website,

can produce—ready?—more than 72,000 pounds of milk per year.

Sheep dairy products are popular the world over, mostly in the form of cheese: feta and pecorino romano are the most well known. Sheep's milk is nutritious. It has roughly double the protein and calcium of cow's milk. Many people who cannot tolerate lactose find that they can handle sheep milk—the milk is fattier compared to other animals but it is naturally homogenized, meaning the milk does not separate. Molecularly, the smaller fat globules are easier for the human system to process.

Ranchers will slaughter animals themselves for personal consumption, but generally they work with an abattoir or processor in the area. The largest lamb processor in North America is Superior Farms, which happens to be located in the Central Valley. Superior will slaughter lambs one at a time if requested, but more is obviously more cost-effective—at least six per order is typical. Brought in on a Monday, the lambs will be slaughtered (or "harvested") and the meat ready for pick up by Thursday or Friday. It arrives pieced up into its different cuts, cryovaced (vacuum-sealed), and ready to sell. A 100-pound lamb can be expected to yield forty-five to fifty pounds of meat—the rest is bone, fat, and offal. Here, according to Thompson's website, is what you get if you buy a whole lamb from him at roughly $8 per pound:

8 packages shoulder chops
4 packages rib racks, Frenched
4 packages loin chops
2 packages foreshanks
2 packages hindshanks
2 packages Denver ribs
2 packages sirloin steaks
2 bone-in leg roasts
2 to 4 packages neck bones for soup

I asked Dan Macon if his daughters ever had a Fern-from-*Charlotte's Web* moment, and he chuckled. "We've always been very straightforward with our girls… but I'll tell you, last year was my youngest daughter's first year in 4-H and she took a lamb to the fair that she had raised from birth. And the last day of the fair… that was difficult." Macon went on to explain that he believes that death is not necessarily the opposite of health; that it's possible to have a healthy life as well as a healthy death, and that he wants to instill that philosophy in his daughters.

It's philosophy, ultimately, that sets sheep ranchers I spoke with apart from, for example, cattle ranchers. Both Macon and Thompson expressed the following thought, independently but identically, nearly verbatim: they don't think of themselves as raising sheep; they think of themselves as raising grass and cultivating soil. The sheep are a tool for them to work the land. That they happen to be pleasant, delicious animals is just a bonus.

Sheep are considerably better for the environment than cattle. They don't impact the soil as much, because they're lighter. Less impact

means the soil can absorb and hold water better; densely compacted soil creates runoff. Sheep spread their manure out more equally. Cow feces and urine deposits concentrate in the same places, usually where the animals sleep. And most importantly, sheep move from pasture to pasture rather than engaging in "set stocking," a common grazing practice in the cattle industry. Set stocking involves placing animals on a large tract of land—the rule of thumb is ten acres per animal—and simply leaving them there for six months. This gives cows an enormous amount of room to roam and graze, but it's awful for the grass and soil. Cows, when left to their own devices, will only eat what they like and leave everything else behind. These plants will be grazed repeatedly to the point that they cannot recover. The unfavorable plants, meanwhile, deepen their root systems and overtake the grazing area. Over time, the negative feedback renders the land useless for grazing.

Sheep ranchers, on the other hand, typically divide their land into small pastures and move their animals en masse between pastures every couple days. This gives the

sheep less of an opportunity to cherry-pick the plants they like. Manure is spread equally. And the grasses in each pasture get between forty-five and sixty days to "rest" and regrow before being grazed again. When the grasses can rest and take root, they do their jobs more effectively: preventing erosion, cleaning the air, and feeding the animals.

Remember those CONGRESS CREATED DUST BOWL signs? Well, they're not telling the whole story. The lack of rain created the current Joad-ian conditions. But Congress created a lot of things, like highways and irrigation so, sure, might as well blame them for the drought, too. There is blame to be parceled out, certainly—primarily to a seniority system in California water rights that literally hangs some people out to dry. The result is that some farmers and agribusinessmen are planting signs rather than crops along stretches of the 5 to decry the state of water politics.

The overarching problem has to do with bad soil, though: desertification is slowly creeping into the Central Valley through over-farming. When arable land is pushed too hard, salinity levels go out of whack and increasingly larger quantities of water are needed to make crops grow. This, in turn, exacerbates the effects of the drought. Here is where the sheep-philosopher comes into play: going forward, as the earth warms and cracks and begins to look more like Thunderdome, it will be necessary to make soil and grass conservation a priority. Ranchers like Macon and Thompson are already leading the way, encouraging us to turn our existing agricultural model on its head by thinking of our livestock as a tool rather than merely a product. LP

Illustration by Domitille Collardey

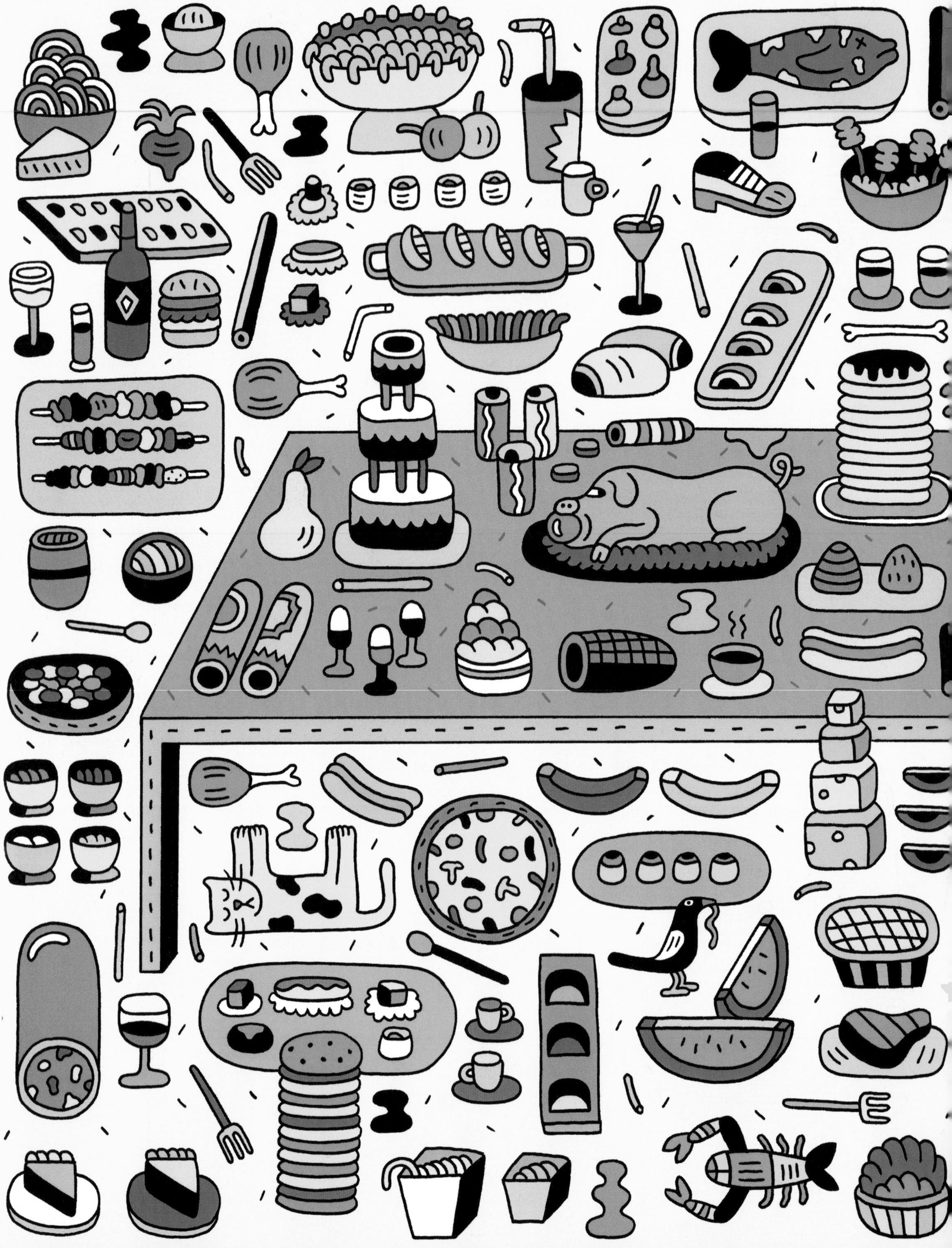

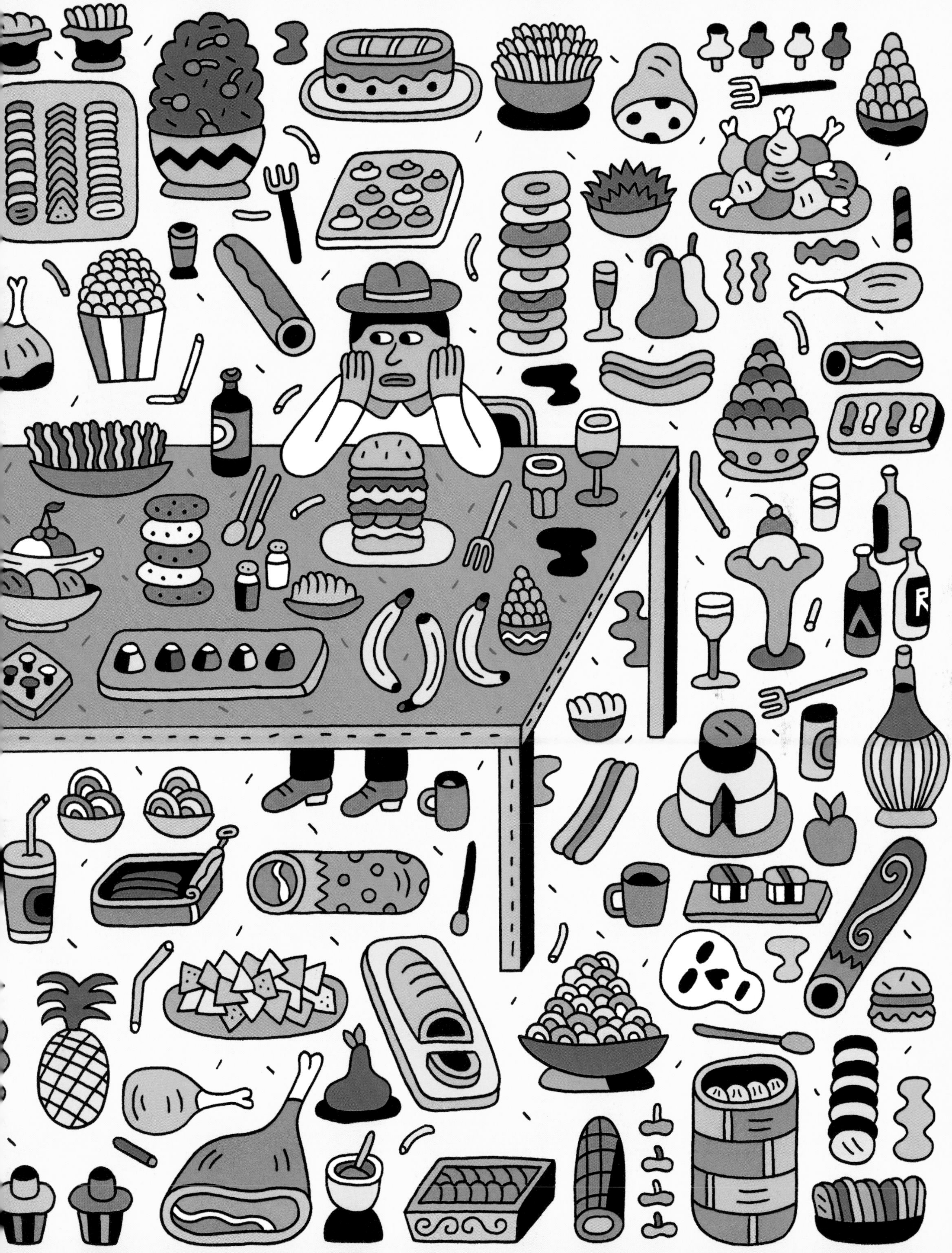

WHAT DOES HUNGER LOOK LiKE?

An interview with
RAJ PATEL
by **Rachel Khong**

Illustrations by Monica Ramos

We knew too little about hunger and wanted to fix that. Raj Patel is the guy we chose to school us: he co-teaches the Edible Education course at UC Berkeley with Michael Pollan, and his first book, *Stuffed and Starved: The Hidden Battle for the World Food System*, is an intriguing investigation into our modern conundrum: while there is more hunger in the world than ever before, there is also more obesity. He shines light onto our broken global food network, and considers what it might take to change it.

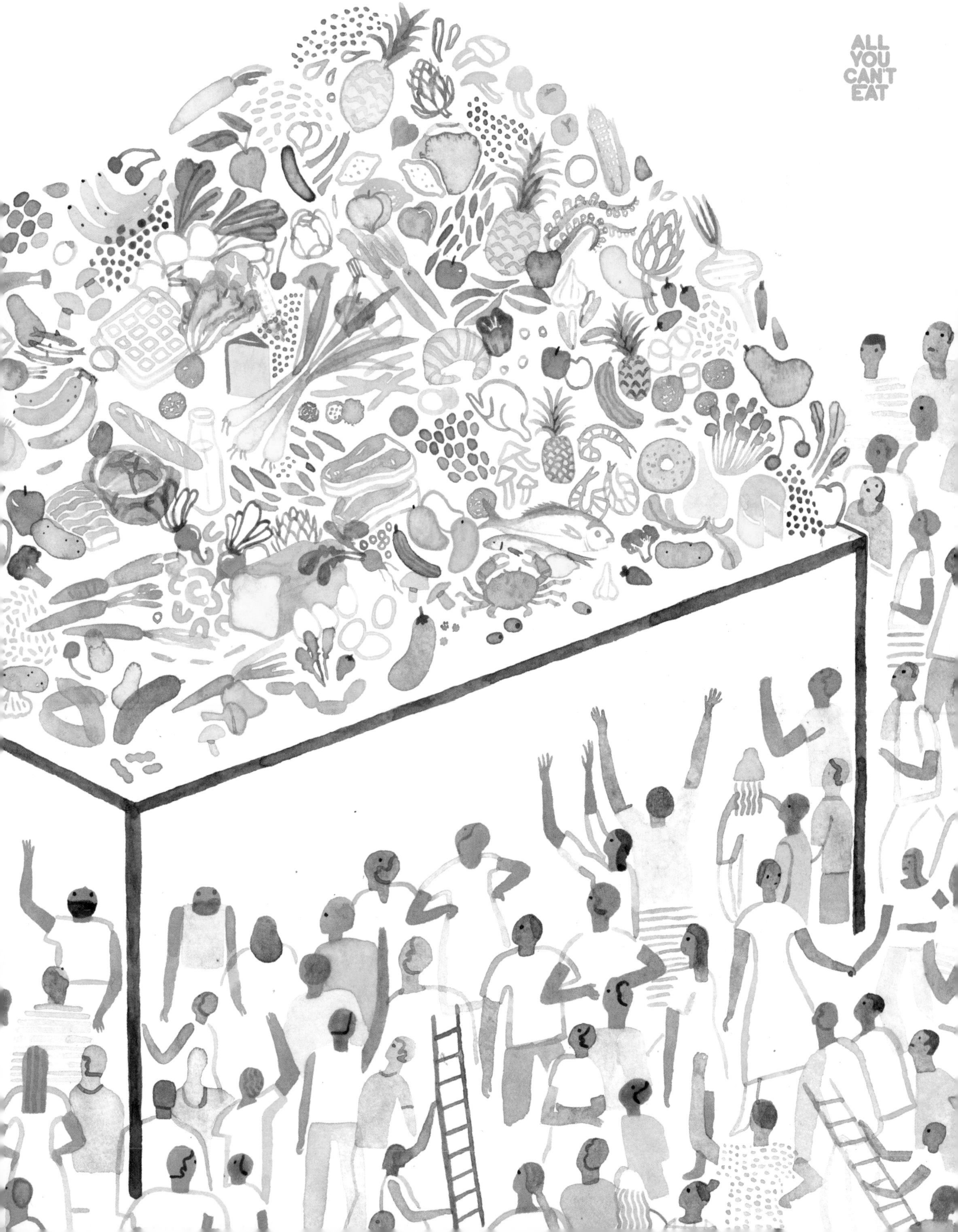
ALL
YOU
CAN'T
EAT

What does hunger look like?

The standard image of hunger that most of us carry around comes from 1980s TV and magazines, which is to say that it's an image from the nineteenth century. We think about African kids with flies in their eyes. The everyday reiteration of this image comes in the form of a line that parents take with their children on almost every continent: "Eat up, there are children starving in Africa!" Setting aside the problem of logic there—*How does eating my broccoli help starving children?*—a better question arises: What do parents in Africa tell their children?

In South Africa they say, "Eat up, there are children starving in India." They're right. There are *more* children starving in India than in all of sub-Saharan Africa. India is the country with the largest number of hungry people. It's surprising because what you usually hear of India is that it's where all the jobs have gone and where Windows and Google are setting up shop. But the people who are really struggling with hunger in any country are the people who are being paid the least, the people you *don't* usually hear about. That often means people working in the food system. Hunger looks like the hands that grow and pick and serve your food and wash up afterward.

Hunger looks gendered, and it's certainly race-related—in the United States as much as anywhere else. In America, people of color are disproportionately likely to be affected by food insecurity, and the group most likely to be affected—35 percent of them—are female-headed households. If you look at who's going hungry, it's women more than men. Sixty percent of people going hungry in the world are women or girls. When you think about who has power in the world—who has the money—this shouldn't come as a surprise.

Hunger also doesn't necessarily look like bloat or stick-thin limbs. The most profound effect of malnutrition is what *might* have been. Children who are malnourished don't follow the growth curve of children who are well fed. They look much younger, they are much shorter, their IQs tend to be impaired. And they will never reach their full potential if, during the first part of their lives, they're not given enough. Often you have malnutrition on top of other diseases, like diarrhea. When children die of diarrhea, it's the diarrhea that kills them, but it's the malnutrition that's the trigger. It makes them much more susceptible to disease, and much less able to fight it once they get it.

This sort of hunger is hard to see, because you can't see a terrible counterfactual: the theft of potential.

What's the story of hunger in the world today?

We produce more calories per person than ever before in human history. A common misperception is that the reason people go hungry is a shortage of food, but there's actually enough food in the world to feed everyone. The problem is one of distribution.

Pick up the Bible and you'll read about seven fat years and seven lean years. People understood there were natural fluctuations of good times and bad. Most civilizations have figured out ways of smoothing that out. India, before the British came, was a feudal society with landlords who had a moral responsibility to feed the hungry. If you were poor in India, it was a shitty gig and you had a landlord who was the ultimate ruler. The only silver lining on this dark cloud was that when there was a famine, when there were pests, the landlord had a responsibility to feed the peasants.

When the British came, they said, "Landlords, you don't need to be doing that. You need to have efficient markets; you need to be buying and selling labor. We will buy your wheat, Indian landlords, and we will pay you top dollar for them! It'll be amazing!" And the Indian landlords said, "No, no, no, we're fine!" And the British said, "No, no, no, we have guns!" That's an abbreviated history of colonialism, but it gets to the important bit. The British were right. Because of the shift in the economy away from the landlord-responsibility system to the free market, Indian landlords produced more grain than they ever had. India was exporting millions of tons of grain at the end of the nineteenth century. The down-

came, after more grain was being produced than ever before, there was a famine once every four years.

The Nobel laureate Amartya Sen wrote a book called *Poverty and Famines*, studying the Bengal famine of 1940s India. What he observed was that roughly four million people died, not because there was a shortage of rice, but because the people who could afford rice were hoarding it. This is a story that still matters; its mechanisms were partly behind the big food price increases a few years ago.

Here's what Sen said: Imagine you have a warehouse full of rice, and you see people outside your door hungry for rice. You could sell it to them today for a dollar a pound. Or you could hang on to it and see what they're ready to pay tomorrow. Chances are they'd be ready to pay more. By that logic, you could

they're too poor to be able to afford it.

That's the story of modern hunger. There is plenty of food around, but the way we mediate access to that food today is through the market. That's why even though we have more food than ever before, around a billion people go hungry. The story of hunger has always been the story of the desire of powerful people to be able to manage hunger, rather than sharing our abundance more fairly.

So it's not about what Thomas Malthus was worried about: too many people and not enough food?

That idea sits in the back of a lot of people's minds, and it's important to dispel. Policymakers in the United States have been thinking Malthusian thoughts. They've been concerned that there will be this horrible moment where food supply

side is that because workers were being paid very little, they couldn't afford the grain; they were being priced out of the market. You had a paradox uncovered by the great writer Mike Davis: in the 2,000 years before the British, there was a famine once every 120 years. If you saw a famine, you were unlucky; you'd have to wait more than a century to see the next famine. After the British

hoard the grain and speculate. That's what happened in the Bengal famine. There was rice in the area but hoarders hoarded, and the people who died were too poor to afford the market price. And that blew a hole in a lot of thinking about hunger and famine. What Sen said was that in every major famine since the Second World War there's been enough food in the area. The reason people starve is that

gets outstripped by population and everyone riots in the streets, driven by rage and hunger and the need to feed seething broods of children.

But the facts don't bear this out. Think, for example, of protests in 1917, when there were huge food riots throughout America. It was not because there was a shortage of food, but because the price of food had gone up and politicians weren't doing anything about it. In the front lines of these protests were women. There was no way for women to articulate their demands from the politicians—they didn't have the vote yet. The way women got the vote in the United States was food riots. They demanded lower food prices and a place at the political table.

Worldwide, recent big protests about food haven't been because poor people have been shagging and breeding and creating more hungry mouths and all of a sudden the food supply has run out. It's always been about a failure of entitlement—people not being able to get the food, and being excluded from the political system they relied on to keep hunger at bay. That's why people take to the streets. Every food protest you can think of—whether it's a protest for bread in France in the 1700s that became the French Revolution, or a protest around merchants being able to buy and sell tea in the eastern colonies of the United States that became the Boston Tea Party, or a protest over wheat prices that became the Arab Spring—all these appear, superficially, like they're about the Malthusian tipping point. But they've never been about that. Not in one case. Food was available. It's just that poor people couldn't afford it.

What does hunger look like in America?

In the United States, there are fifty million people who are food insecure: at some point in the year, they don't know where their next meal is coming from. The system that we have in America at the moment is not great. It's about getting commodity crops to the hungry, and one of the problems with that is that it just extends the domain of bad, cheap food.

Growing corn in the United States mainly for animal feed and for fuel seems to me a very bad use of some great land. We're growing food now to turn into ethanol to power our cars. There is something morally wrong about using the fruits of the soil not to eat, but to set on fire.

Ethanol is one of the main reasons we had the food-price spike in 2007 and 2008, because of this shift away from food for people to food for animals and cars. This is a structural problem with the way that capitalism works. The kind of capitalism I find problematic is not the free exchange of goods and services between people—I think that's awesome. I think markets are terrific. What I find problematic is the concentrating of market power. Think of any major agricultural commodity: there are five or six corporations that control the global market. That doesn't seem like the markets are working efficiently. That's a few companies writing manifestos about what all of us get to eat, and legislating how low our wages are going to be so that we've no real choice about what's on our plates. So what does hunger look like in America? It's profitable, widespread, and a national shame. Yet it is possible to imagine an America without hunger.

What do you picture that America looking like?

First, we need everyone to be able to afford good food. In order to make that happen, we need to end poverty. If we're going to address the issue of hunger in America, or hunger around the world, we need to raise wages for more people, so that the craft of growing, the craft of cooking and preparing, are all rewarded as they deserve to be. The way things work now, cheap food is the corollary of low wages. In America, we have a food system that's geared to produce all you can eat. But when you have a food system that's geared to produce foods that are rich in salt, fat, and sugar, and when you have very limited entitlements, you need to be rich to be able to afford to eat well in the United States.

There are now a couple of studies that show that if you're on a limited income, no matter how much free time you have to scratch-cook—and of course poor people have very little free time—you can't afford the ingredients to have a healthy, balanced diet. The food-provisioning system that we have in the United States consigns poor people to higher rates of type-2 diabetes and heart disease. These used to be called diseases of affluence, but they're now not about affluence at all—they're diseases of poverty.

We need living wages for everyone in America, and it's an easy thing to say and an easy thing to imagine. It means that we pay more taxes—in particular, rich people pay more taxes. It means we treat everyone with dignity; we treat all work with dignity. That's an important shift. Particularly low-income workers—for instance, the kind of work that happens in homes across the nations where people are looking after other people—is vital work. Society needs to recognize the value of that work so people can afford to eat.

Beyond that, there *is* a looming supply problem as well. Not enough people are dreaming about the world as it will be, particularly when it comes to climate change. This is a collective failure of the imagination. If we're thinking about how to feed the world in the twenty-first century, we need to get away from an agriculture that contributes to climate change. The kind of agriculture that depends on unlimited amounts of water and unlimited amounts of fertilizer is not okay in the twenty-first century. We don't have the water, and when catastrophe happens, there's no recovering

from it. We need agriculture that requires less water, and doesn't need fertilizers that are dependent on fossil fuels. We need agriculture that provides a portfolio of crops, guaranteeing a crop no matter how unusual or extreme the weather. There is that kind of agriculture in the world today. It doesn't produce crap; it produces nutritious food.

People have a hard time believing that small farmers can feed the world. Yet there's what's called an inverse relationship: the larger a farm is, the lower its yield per hectare. Small farms produce more on the same patch of land than bigger farms, because big farms don't bother about creating a dense, rich ecosystem of crops. Big farms only work if you've got large machines that work with a monoculture—row upon row, mile on mile of a single crop. Smaller farms can pack in a greater diversity of crops because while large farms have combines, smaller farms have farmers—skilled workers who put footprints, not tire tracks, between the crops, and tend them better. The extra care that comes from extra labor grows extra crops on the same amount of land. If you're interested in producing more food in the future, then you probably want more small farms. And if you're interested in climate-change-ready farming, then

you probably want farms growing a portfolio of crops, not a monoculture. All of this is possible, but it does mean breaking out of the chains of the imagination that we're currently in—believing the only way to farm in the Midwest is by using satellite-controlled tractors.

Solving this problem involves political organizing. You may wince, especially since politics has such a bad name these days. But everything that has been worth a damn in American history has involved political organizing. Social change is about dreaming much bigger than politicians allow, and many of us have forgotten how to do that. Not everywhere, though. It's helpful to look elsewhere around the world—the film I'm working on has found amazing stories from India to Peru to Malawi—and even to U.S. history, as a reminder that people can and have imagined eating better, systemically.

For instance, one of the reasons we have a federal school-breakfast program is because there was a terrific group in the Bay Area in the 1960s and early 1970s that decided that it was a tragedy that poor kids were going hungry, and started unilaterally to feed them because the government wasn't doing anything. At one point, this group was feeding more kids than the state of California. The group was the Black Panthers. What the Black Panthers were doing was not merely feeding people like a church—they were feeding people like they wanted to end hunger. The government felt so threatened that they were shamed into funding the federal school-breakfast program. The Panthers were smashed for their trouble, and their history revised. But no matter what you think of the Black Panthers, it's

clear that they had a vision for big, systemic change. They didn't want to add vitamins to bad food—they even warned people away from processed food, especially sugar, at a time when it seemed ludicrous to do that. They wanted good food for everyone. That's not an unreasonable dream to have.

What can we do to make that a reality today?

It's going to take both some creation and some destruction. It's hard to build a good food movement against the marketing power of large corporations. Curtailing their ability to market to kids, to fund our schools and sporting events—McDonald's at the Olympics, really?—is a reasonable way to give space to a generation of children who know and love good food. It's political, and it's a way of creating more freedom.

But more and more people are on board with the idea that in order to have more freedom for people, we need less freedom for Big Food. Food-movement politics is already beyond "vote with your fork." Of course voting with your fork is important. Ten years ago, no one thought to shop discriminately, but now people know to, and that really pleases me. Beyond that, the next thing to think about is sustainability: not just environmental sustainability, but also sustainable labor practices.

We need to think about the work of people who are cooking the food and also the work that makes it possible for some people to cook the food and other people to take care of the kids. It's more than just raising minimum wage. We need something more aggressive. When you've got obligations, ten bucks an hour is not going to cover it.

But with a little compassion and a lot of imagination, we can change a great deal. **LP**

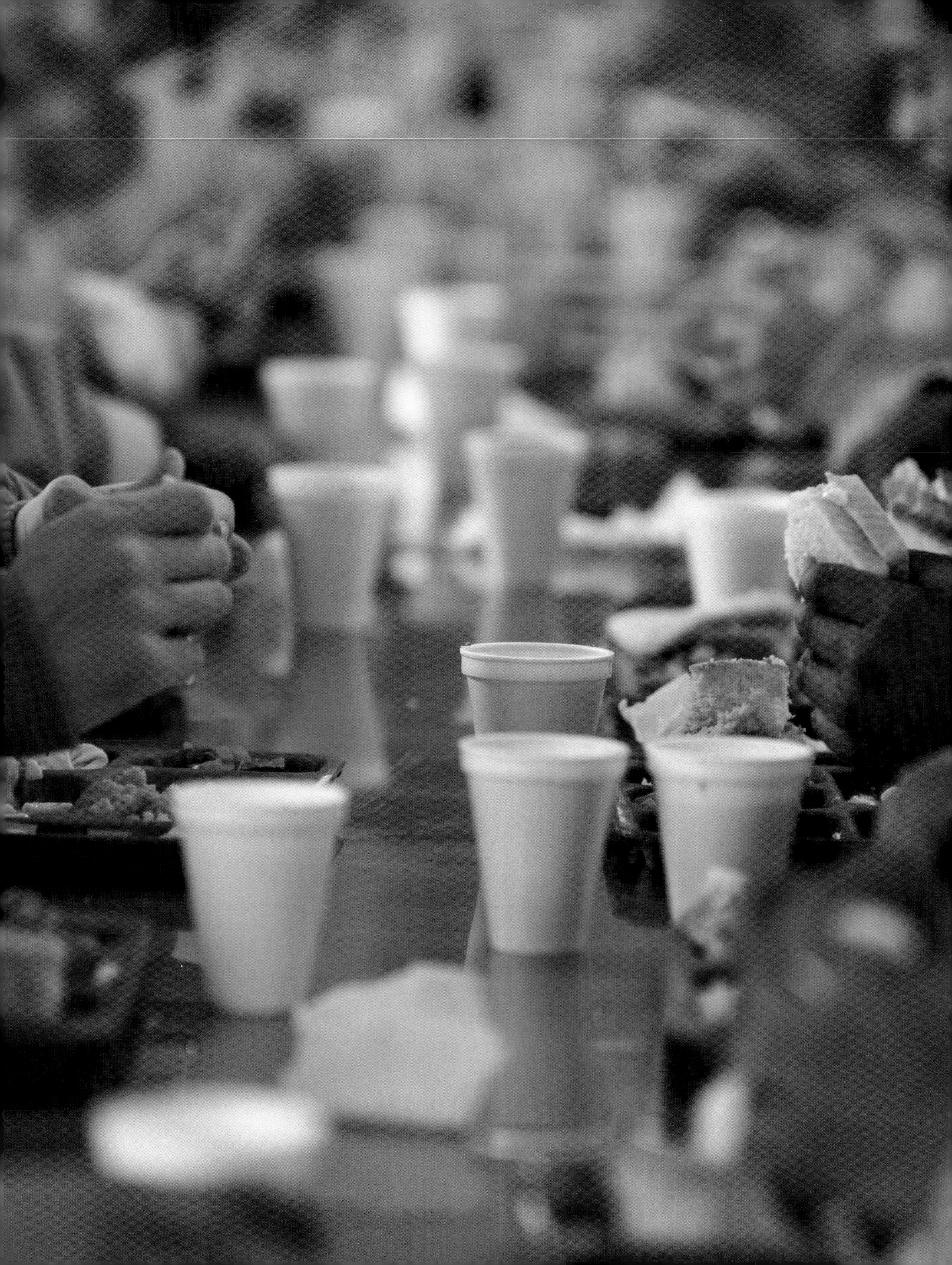

January 23rd, 2014
Fish Sandwich Day
Westville Correctional Facility

FiXED MENU

**Eating with the inmates of
Westville Correctional Facility**

by **KEViN PANG**

I type this sentence twenty minutes after eating leftover spaghetti and clams for breakfast, a Hungry Man-sized portion at nine a.m. It is an exertion of my free will to do so. It is within my civic right as a dedicated grocery shopper and keeper of leftovers, imprinted in the Charter of Man, that I am free to eat however much I want, of what I want, when I want.

In prison, that right is stripped away. Craving pizza on a Saturday night? Feel like washing it down with cold beer? It's not happening. Your right is reduced to eating portion-fixed food dictated by a warden on a set schedule. If you're hungry after dinner, you'll go to bed hungry.

The thought of losing this control sends me into a panic attack.

The town of Westville sits beneath the southern curve of Lake Michigan, an hour's drive from Chicago, past the belching steel plants of Northwest Indiana. It is every small American town that ever existed, a patchwork of green and brown rectangles on Google Map's satellite view. On the two January days I visited Westville Correctional Facility, the winter's second polar vortex was bearing down on Middle America, plunging daytime wind chills to -25 degrees Fahrenheit. Westville's position south of Lake Michigan also makes the area prone to biblical lake-effect snowstorms. And so, against the howling white-out squall, the eighty-five-acre prison—occupying about one-eighth of Westville—appeared utterly *gulag*-ish.

The first thing you notice when walking into Westville, however, is that the staff is unflinchingly Midwestern. Their jocular disposition—beginning with your pat-down officer at the security checkpoint—is unnervingly pleasant. I remember a coroner I met years ago who had the most inappropriately morbid sense of humor—he mimed the suicide victim on the gurney blowing his brains out, complete with exploding hand gestures from his temple. It was, I realized, a coping mechanism to deal with the darkness he sees daily, one that might explain why the prison staff (at least in the presence of a reporter) seemed so sunny.

Photographs by Armando L. Sanchez

To enter the prison compound proper, you step through a mechanized door into a holding cell, and wait as that door closes before a second door slowly grinds its metallic gears open. When that second door clangs shut with a sound just like in the movies, you enter a world of around 3,300 inmates, each serving an average of four years for offenses from burglary and drug possession to arson and worse.

Their favorite pastime seems to be staring at you. An Asian reporter and Hispanic photographer are curios when every day's the same day: wake up at five a.m., don your beige prison garb, work your twenty-cents-an-hour job, sit around in the dorms until lights out at eleven p.m. So the inmates are eager to talk, if just to break up the monotony. And when you mention you're here to write about food in prisons, it's like ramming a car into a fire hydrant and watching the water gush skyward.

"Why don't you grab one and eat with us, bro? And you tell us what you think," says Shaun Kimbrough, who's wheelchair-bound and serving a five-year sentence for aggravated battery. "It's gonna hurt your stomach, but we're used to it."

The Westville cafeteria, or "chow hall," is where the state of Indiana spends $1.239 to feed each prisoner each meal, three times a day. They line up single file, shuffling forward until they reach a waist-height hole in the wall. Every five seconds, a hardened plastic tray of compartmentalized food slides into view and is quickly picked up. The transaction between server and inmate is an anonymous relationship, a food glory hole.

Today is fish sandwich day at Westville, and conspiracy theories abound.

"They know y'all coming, that's why they served fish," Kimbrough says. Apparently fish is one of the better-tasting offerings the prisoners see, in the way that canker sores are the best kind of ulcers. "That's a top-notch tray right there. But that fish patty, it ain't meat. It's just breading."

The fish patty sits atop three slices of white bread—two to make a sandwich, and the extra slice presumably to meet the 2,500 to 2,800 daily calories as recommended by the American Correctional Association for adult males under fifty. There's also a corn muffin, steamed carrots and green beans, plus mac and cheese sloshing around in a puddle of bright orange water. Some trays hold elbow pasta, others have corkscrew. Beverage is a Styrofoam cup of powdered tropical punch.

The most coveted items on the tray are the salt and pepper packets. Every person I surveyed, without fail, used the word "bland" in describing chow hall food. Rather than prepare separate trays for inmates with high cholesterol or blood pressure, the kitchen serves low-sodium meals for the entire prison population. Even with the added salt, though, it tastes like a vague notion of lunch, with all the flavor and pleasure of food eaten one hour after dental surgery.

Says Thomas Powell, who's serving time for drug dealing: "You're salting something with no flavor to begin with. It's tasteless. It's horrible. It's repetitive day after day." Powell brings packets of powdered ramen soup seasoning to sprinkle over his food. He is not alone in his desire for flavor—up and down the rows of steel tabletops, inmates pull out bottles of hot sauce they bring from the dorms, dousing their breaded fish and three slices of white bread.

The next most frequently utilized food descriptor is "mush." Food texture is difficult to retain when most meals are prepared several days before service—cooked, then quickly refrigerated in an industry-standard practice called blast-chilling. Reheating it, workers in the production kitchen claim, turns everything into a one-note texture more suitable for nursing homes.

Two entrées exemplify mush: goulash and chop suey.

On days these dishes are served, many inmates will skip their meals altogether. Hearing them describe the dishes is like listening to grandpa recall war atrocities he witnessed: spoken with a heavy sigh, best left in the past.

On goulash: "Noodles in red sauce ... his tray may have meat, mine may not ... the noodles have been overcooked so much, it's compacted together so it's like mush. You try to pick up one noodle and eighteen go along for the ride."

Two inmates have a conversation explaining chop suey:

"It's a bunch of cabbage and water."

"That's it. It may have a few grains of rice."

"... And corn if you're lucky."

"See, in mine, I don't remember corn."

An inmate named James Rogers speaks more broadly about dining in incarceration: "I've been here for six years. It has never changed. You came here on a good day. If you came out when they served the other stuff, you'd be horrified. We have no choice but to eat it."

I ask Warren Christian, in Westville the last five years for robbery, how long it took him to adjust to prison food.

"Years. It took years. Some people never get accustomed to it."

What was the turning point?

"Finally accepting the situation you're in. That you're not going anywhere until they release you."

Food is also served three times daily to the inmates at Westville Control Unit, its maximum-security ward, aka "supermax." Two types of offenders get a ticket here: 1) Those whose behavior while incarcerated necessitates segregation from the general prison population, and 2) Shot-calling gang leaders and inmates who committed a heinous crime.

The prison isn't bragging when they call it supermax. To reach fresh air from lockup requires getting past nine gates of electrified or impenetrable steel doors. Regardless of the guards and a separation of bulletproof glass, supermax is a frightening place to be. The inmates know you're there. Suddenly everyone appears at their cell-door window, a dozen pairs of eyes laser-trained in your direction. They scream at you. Through the glass partitions, we hear muffled banshee wails demanding to know our business.

For the correctional officers who deal with these hardest of the already-hard, protocol is to err on the side of extreme caution. They're required to serve food in pairs while wearing body-armor vests. One officer's job is to lock and unlock the cuff door, the steel flap where food slides through, while the other delivers the tray through the slot. Even for murderers, food hygiene is imperative, so guards wear latex gloves and hairnets while serving.

Truth be told, most of the time the place is more boring than dangerous.

"Boring is good, it's just a nice easy day for everybody," says Sgt. Carrie Sipich, a ten-year veteran at Westville.

In Sipich's domain, rapists and killers are schoolchildren who get occasionally unruly, like when they throw trays or swallow razor blades. Nothing shocks her anymore. One time when an inmate inserted a plastic spork up his penis hole, her reaction was an exasperated, *Really?*

She says: "I need a vacation because I'm laughing at things that aren't funny."

Horror stories about prison food reach their unappetizing nadir in the form of one particular dish. Its official name on Aramark Correctional Services recipe card M5978 is "Disciplinary Loaf." Inmates know it as "Nutraloaf," a baked foodstuff with the express purpose of providing the required daily nutrients and calories, and nothing more. Flavor isn't an afterthought, it's discouraged.

Nutraloaf's awful reputation is built upon myth, which simultaneously serves as a deterrent for bad behavior. No one I talk to has ever been punished with Nutraloaf, but everyone knows someone who has. Nutraloaf is reserved for offenses such as taking part in a riot or assaulting prison staff. Violators get

placed in segregation and served a nineteen-ounce brick of Nutraloaf twice daily, typically for three consecutive days or until, in the words of Indiana Department of Corrections spokesman Doug Garrison, it achieves its intent of "behavior modification." Sgt. Sipich says she's only seen it served to two offenders in her tenure.

Officially, Nutraloaf is a blend of shredded cabbage, grated carrots, dry pinto beans, mechanically separated poultry, dairy blend, soy oil, scrambled-egg mix, and twenty-four slices of bread. It's shaped into a loaf and baked at 375 degrees for fifty to seventy minutes.

But Jesse Miller, serving in Westville for armed robbery, says he cooked Nutraloaf when he worked in the kitchen at another prison. He claims the recipe is more slapdash: "Say a meal was pudding, meat, green beans, potatoes. They throw that all in a blender. They'll throw Kool-Aid powder in it too. They can't say, 'I didn't get my juice.' 'Yes you did, it's in the Nutraloaf.' Then they pour it in a pan like pancake batter. It looks like vomit. I tasted it. It had no taste. It was like eating a sponge."

I didn't get to try Nutraloaf, but Jeff Ruby, dining critic at *Chicago* magazine, wrote about sampling it shortly after the Cook County Illinois Department of Corrections began implementing the Aramark recipe in June 2010. This is how he described it: "a thick orange lump of spite with the density and taste of a dumbbell … the mushy, disturbingly uniform innards recalled the thick, pulpy aftermath of something you dissected in biology class: so intrinsically disagreeable that my throat nearly closed up reflexively."

Kelly Banaszak, a spokesperson for Aramark, says its recipes are developed by registered dieticians: "While nutrition plays a big role, variety, taste, eye appeal, among

others are considered in creating healthy, satisfying meals every day."

Aramark is the largest provider of prison-food services in the country, serving one million meals a day in more than 500 correctional facilities. For governments, privatizing prison-food services is an easy cost saver. Aramark, which also provides food for schools and sporting venues, holds contracts with six state-prison systems. That includes the Indiana Department of Corrections, which saved $7 million in the first year it contracted with Aramark in 2005. This year, that cost breaks down to $3.717 per Indiana prisoner per day.

When food costs are regimented and calculated to the tenth of a cent, inmate satisfaction takes a backseat. At an Aramark-contracted Kentucky prison in 2009, dissatisfaction over food was a contributing factor to a riot in which six buildings were set on fire. At the state hearing, a correctional officer present at the riot said that food quality plays a role in prison safety: "If you're hungry, you're going to get ornery."

In the recorded history of inmates vs. prison food, inmates usually end up on the losing side. In 2009, state budget woes forced the Georgia Department of Corrections to eliminate Friday lunches. It had already cut lunch on weekends, compensating with larger portions during breakfast and dinner. In 2010, Cook County Jail in Chicago stopped delivering breakfasts to inmates at four thirty in the morning, opting instead to serve it in the chow hall. Sheriff Tom Dart said he expected inmates would choose sleep over breakfast, at a savings of $1 million a year.

I bring this up with John Schrader, Westville's public information officer. He strikes a balance of empathy with the inmates while batting down many of their conspiracy theories. One persistent rumor is that kitchen workers once discovered a food box that read: "For zoo use only." Another is that the kitchen will "stretch out" the meals by adding water. Untrue, Schrader says.

He says the reality lies somewhere in the middle. For example, once a month the prison organizes an outside-food day with a local restaurant, like the Westville Dairy Queen, where inmates can order burgers and Blizzards. (The restaurant gets a five-digit payday; Westville gets a cut of the sales.)

He agrees the food at the prison is bland and portion sizes are tight. But he also says inmates should have realistic expectations.

"Food cannot be used as a disciplinary measure. I can't say you're getting less food because you're acting out. Food is essential. It's a basic human right. But we're also not going to give you shrimp," Schrader says. "It's not the quality of what you can get out in the real world. But is it something that's bad? Absolutely not. If I really wanted to be healthy, I'd stop eating at home and start eating three meals a day here."

Charlie Smigelski, a registered dietician from Boston, disputes the notion that prison food is healthy. Smigelski briefly worked in the Suffolk County Massachusetts House of Corrections as a medical-care contractor. He seems particularly aggrieved speaking about his experience: "At my prison, vegetable is a joke. You might get seven or eight carrot coins at supper, some wimpy lettuce. No one is looking at quality. Calories are made up by sugar—heavily sugared peaches and pineapple. They're living on white rice, pasta, and four slices of bread. Commissary food is by and large abysmal as well. Prison is supposed to be about the loss of liberty, not loss of life."

This idea of prison foods—mainly, "What is good enough?"—requires a fair bit of philosophical reconciling. Constitutional scholars have argued the extent to which prisoners' rights are afforded ever since the 13th amendment was adopted: "Neither slavery nor involuntary servitude, except as a punishment for crime whereof the party shall have been duly convicted, shall exist within the United States." These terms leave a lot of leeway for interpretation when it comes to deciding what's for dinner in lockup.

One argument is the inmates broke societal law and deserve to be here, thereby forfeiting their right to complain about the mushiness of food. Another is that taxpayers foot the bill, so if they don't like the watery goulash, well, tough shit. The counterargument is that the $3.717 spent on each prisoner covers not only food costs, but labor, paper towels, and cleanup supplies, plus equipment repairs. At that price, you cannot possibly provide sustenance resembling anything a free citizen would deign to call food.

But is being fed poorly inhumane? Should criminals be deprived of any pleasure from food? Isn't that counterproductive if the purpose of imprisonment is rehabilitation?

Prisoner advocacy organizations exist in every state, in the form of religious groups and the ACLU, but getting substantive legislative reform for prisoners' rights is perhaps the steepest of uphill battles. For one, making the voting public empathize with criminals is a hard sell.

"I think prisoners are the most dehumanized people in our society by far. There's no comparison," says Jean Casella, co-director and Editor-in-Chief of Solitary Watch, an organization that studies prison conditions, specifically solitary confinement. "What the public will

tolerate in terms of how badly we treat prisoners is really bad."

In her reporting on inmates kept in segregation, Casella tells me one of the most common privileges to be revoked is access to commissary food. "I question the idea of food deprivation on top of losing your freedom. Within prisons, there's no judge or jury. It's prison officials deciding if you go to solitary and be deprived of sunlight and human contact. It's prison officials who put you on Nutraloaf. I think it's barbaric."

Jean Terranova is now director of food and health policy at Community Servings, a Massachusetts agency providing medically tailored meals to people with critical illnesses. When she was a criminal defense attorney, she remembers seeing clients go into prison and within a short period of time, start looking like a different person. "They're not getting the proper nutrition, they become lethargic. You're creating a litany of physical and behavioral health problems by being short-sighted at the beginning and not seeing the huge costs in health care later."

A 2010 report from the American Medical Association warns: "The high concentration of long-term inmates, with their corresponding increase in health-care needs as they age, has contributed to concerns about the nutritional adequacy of their diets as a means of preventing and managing chronic disease." The report projects that by 2030, more than one-third of prisoners in the U.S. will be over the age of fifty.

"Food is such an important part of the lives of people who are confined. With so many restrictions on their daily lives, meal time is one of the very few activities prisoners have to look forward to," Terranova says. "If you give them good food, it could vastly improve the psychosocial dynamic of the place."

Whether or not you believe prisoners deserve decent meals, the fact remains that prison food is terrible, full stop. So in many cases, inmates take matters into their own hands. Every two weeks, prisoners with enough money (mostly through the generosity of outside family) can order snack foods from commissary. The type of food available is stuff you'd see in the nonperishable aisle at 7-Eleven: summer sausage, precooked rice, cheese, tuna pouches. Well-off inmates will use up every dollar of their $70 limit per order. Those without outside financial support have a tougher go—prison jobs only pay around $25 a month, and most of that is spent on soap, toothpaste, socks, and other necessities.

Antonio Bishop, in Westville for arson, puts it bluntly: "If you don't have commissary food, you'll *never* make it."

Goods bought through commissary are the currency of the underground prison market, where services are rendered in exchange for food, even if prison policy prohibits the practice.

"If you want someone to draw a portrait for your family, you pay them in commissary," says Zach Adams, serving for parole violation. "Maybe you have [postage] stamps and I don't. Or, you say, 'Make me a nice birthday card for my son, I'll give you some of my food.' I mean, you're not supposed to, but yeah, it's a black market."

Others tell me cigarettes and K2, a synthetic marijuana, are also traded for commissary food. The going rate for a prison tattoo is six soups, a meat log, and a few bags of chips—about $5 worth of food. (Prison tattoo ink can be made by microwaving bottled hair grease; the

needle is fashioned from a piece of metal window screen.)

What's most remarkable to me is the culinary creativity the limited resources of prison yield. All Indiana Department of Correction offenders in dorms have access to an ice maker, hot-water dispenser, and microwave. That's enough to concoct some wildly elaborate dishes out of commissary food. At one of Westville's sister prisons, inmates

at Rockville Correctional Facility even published a fifty-three-page cookbook of commissary food recipes, from twice-baked potatoes to salmon soup.

I coaxed David Lawhorn into sharing his proprietary cookie cake recipe: "You take Oreo cookies, split them apart, and put the cream in a separate bowl. Take the cookies and crush it down. Then take Kool-Aid, not the sugar-free kind, put it with the crushed-up cookies, and add Pepsi to make a batter. Microwave it for seven minutes, and it turns out fluffy, like a cake you'd put in the window that costs $20. Take the Oreo cream and put that on top. I also sprinkle trail mix on mine."

Lazaro Valadez has earned some renown in dorm D-2 east for this dish: "Buy two bags of pork rinds, spicy Cajun mix, sweet corn, rice, and Kool-Aid tropical punch mix, not the sugar-free kind. You add the Cajun mix, corn, and pork rinds in a trash bag. Get Kool-Aid in a cup, mix it with a little bit of water until it's real thick, and pour it in the bag with the pork rinds. Mix all that up, and stick it in a microwave for six minutes. It comes out real gummy, and you layer that over rice. It's sweet and sour pork. It's not bad."

The most widely-traded commissary good is Maruchan-brand ramen noodles. Three bags cost $1. As food goes, it's a versatile product: its noodles can be used as a starch base and the soup packet as seasoning salt. I watch Kamil Shelton crush his "Texas Beef"–flavored ramen, boil the broken noodles inside its bag, squeeze out excess water, stuff with sausage, and form into a cylinder: prison burrito. "It's better than what they feed us in chow hall," he says.

There's no actual chicken in the prison chicken nugget recipe, but commissary connoisseurs still manage to recreate the dish as a placebo food. Two inmates named Jan Kosmulski and Troy Peoples explain:

Kosmulski: "Take ramen noodles, boil it down to literally mush. You ball it up, put a piece of cheese and beef summer sausage in the middle. Make sure it's tightly wound up. You cook it in the microwave for ten minutes until it's brown."

Peoples: "It's not actually a

chicken nugget. It's the idea. It's only in your mind. If you ain't had a chicken nugget in a while, and it's in the shape of a chicken nugget, it'll remind you of a chicken nugget."

It's commissary day at dorm A-3, and four inmates gather in the microwave alcove. They've pooled their resources, each buying specific ingredients, and for the last two hours they have collaborated on a food project. Ingredients are organized with precision like mise en place at a fine restaurant.

The chef de cuisine is Mike McClellan, who's earned the reputation as the Thomas Keller of cellblock A-3. McClellan, a soft-spoken forty-four-year-old man sentenced through 2017 for stalking, says Westville is the therapeutic community he needs to turn his life around. Having earned his associate's and bachelor's degrees, he's now at work on his master's. McClellan says he has two passions in life: Jesus Christ and cooking.

Pastor Mike, as he's known, spearheads two recipes today: tortellini and chicken Florentine soup. I try a sip of the latter, made from pouch chicken, garlic powder, ramen soup mix, powdered coffee creamer, and dried Thai rice noodles. It tastes as you might expect—one step above emergency-packet soup reconstituted with hot water.

I offer: "That's pretty good."

Pastor Mike corrects me: "No, that's excellent."

With tortellini, his attention to detail is even more impressive. Pastor Mike takes pizza dough from a Chef Boyardee pizza kit and simmers it in water for three minutes in a microwave. He lays out the cooked squares of pasta. Pastor Mike creates the filling by dicing pepperoni and pepper jack cheese with the

lid of a tin can. He hovers over his ingredients the way a molecular gastronomist hunches with tweezers.

He microwaves the filling with tomato pizza sauce and powdered creamer until it turns into a paste, which he encloses in dough and cooks once more in hot water. The finished product comes out as rustic crescents of dumpling, a nod to Pastor Mike's Italian heritage. For a moment the four cooks shed their prison wear and are dining at a fancy Italian restaurant. They eat like free men. Two hours toiling for a brief transportive respite from this forsaken place.

There's a secondary market for these kinds of prepared foods. Down the hall in dorm A-3, three inmates sit around a metal bench strewn with candy. Their setup is a complicated assembly line involving a microwave, plastic bowls, a container filled with ice water, popsicle sticks, and parchment paper. It looks like a home chemistry kit.

The three have spent the last few hours making lollipops at a pace of one every five minutes. They'll spend the next few hours making lollipops, until their candy stash runs out.

The head chef is John Hopkins, whose goatee and thick glasses makes him resemble Walter White circa Season 3 *Breaking Bad*. Seated next to him is Frederick Betts, Jr. who incredibly, is a dead ringer for Jesse Pinkman circa Season 4 *Breaking Bad*.

Hopkins learned the lollipop trade from a fellow inmate, and since that inmate's release, Hopkins has taken over as resident candy expert. He estimates he's cooked up six hundred-plus lollipops, and has mastered all the subtleties of the art.

He explains that different confectionaries have different

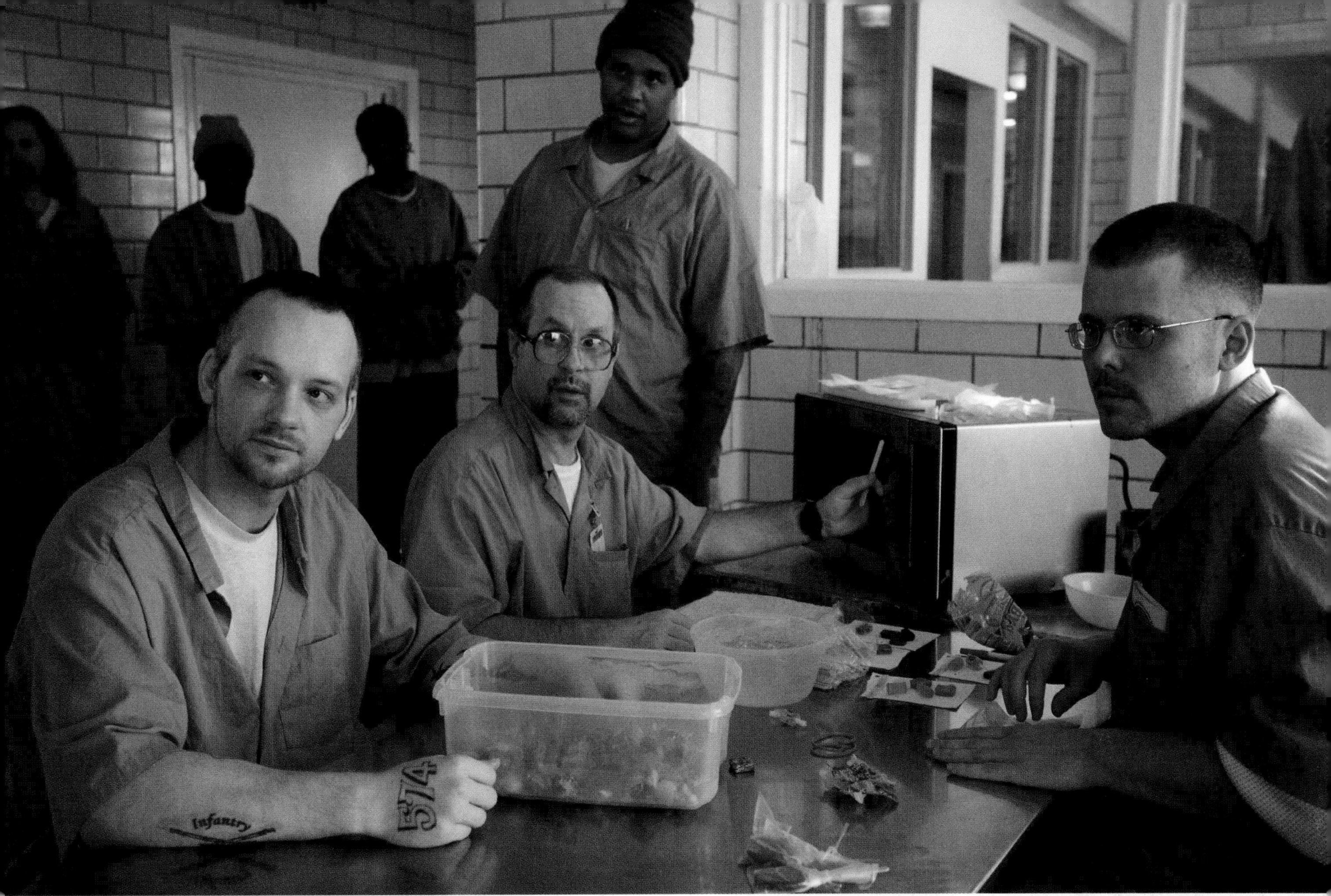
Infantry
574

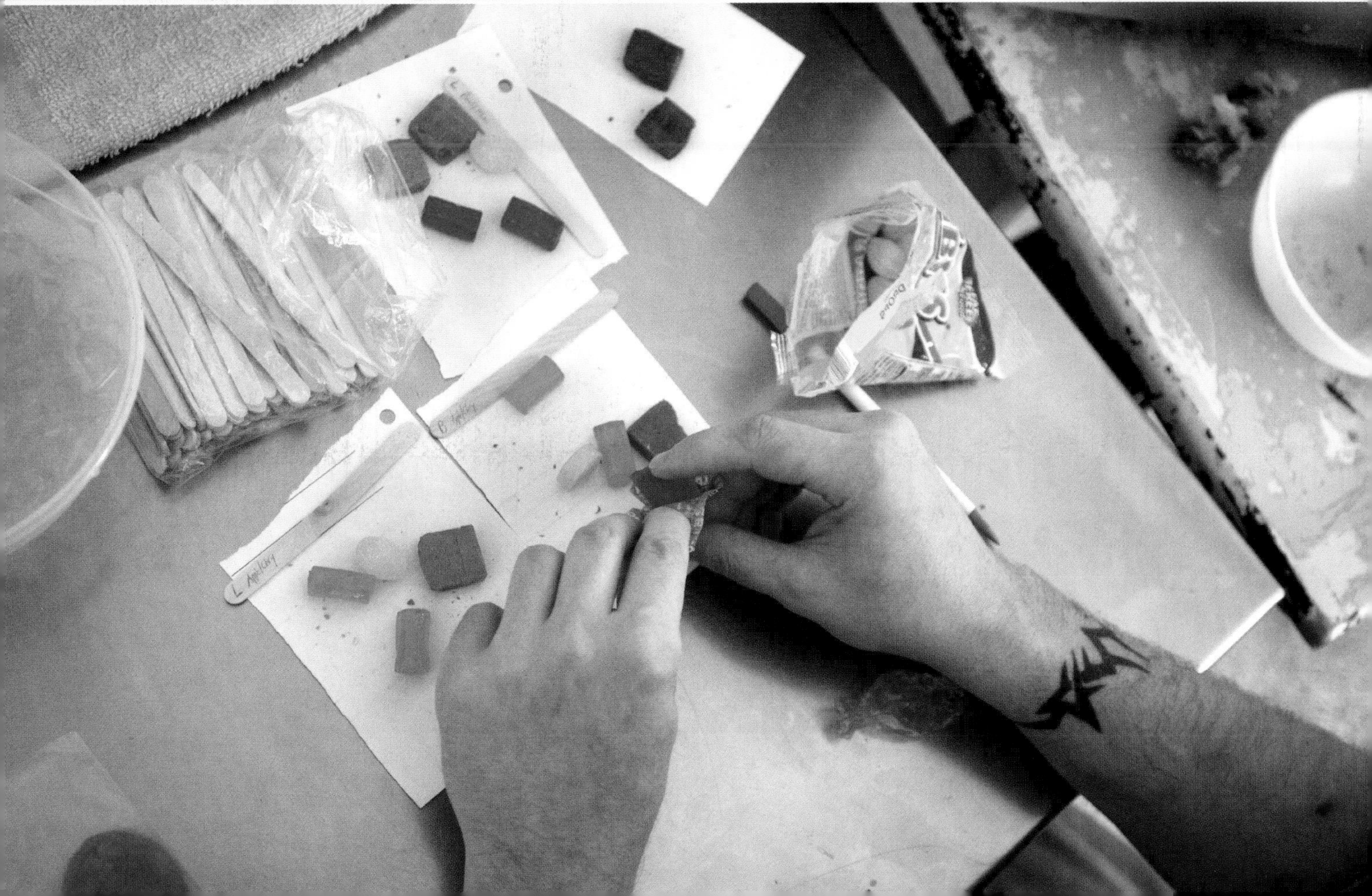

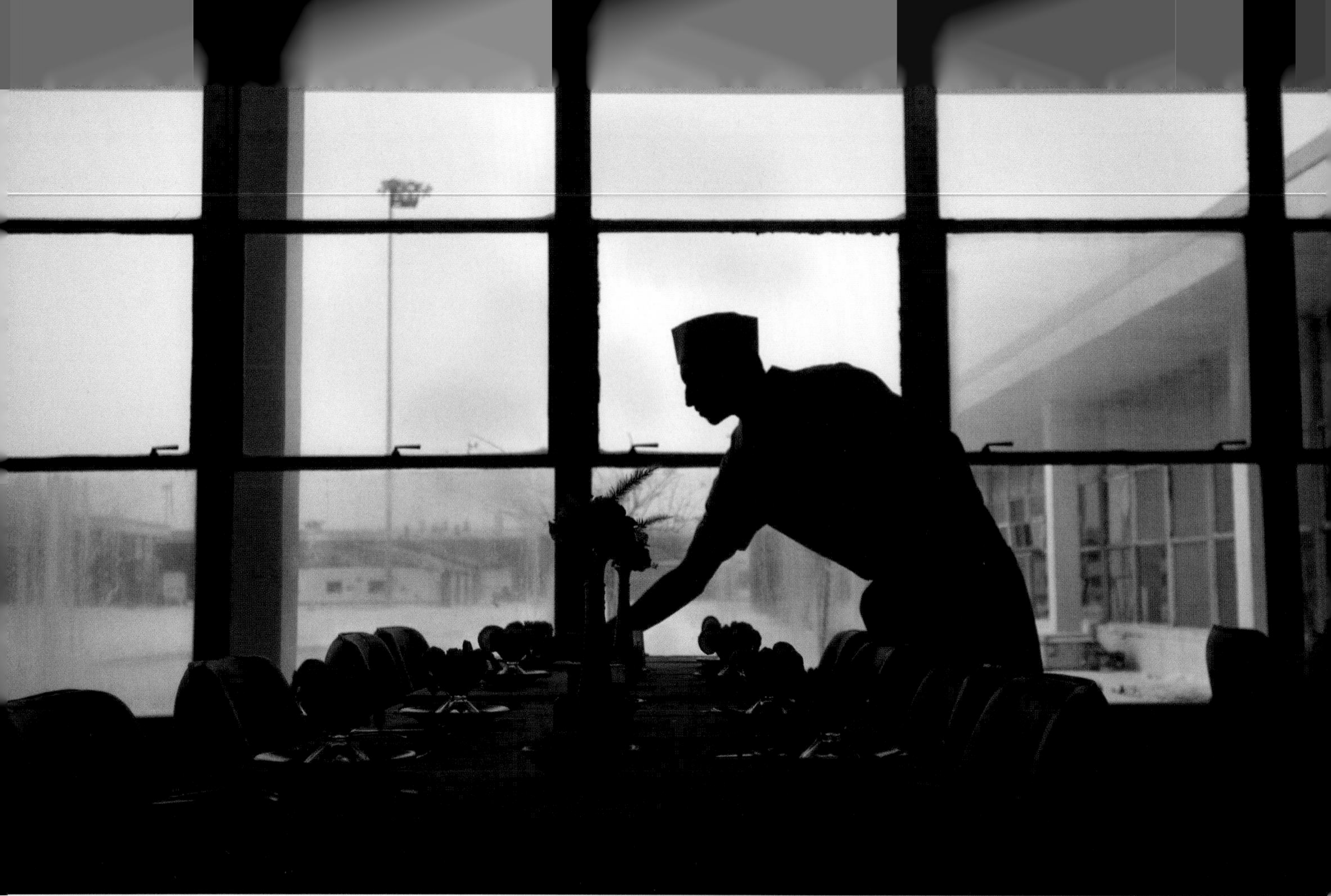

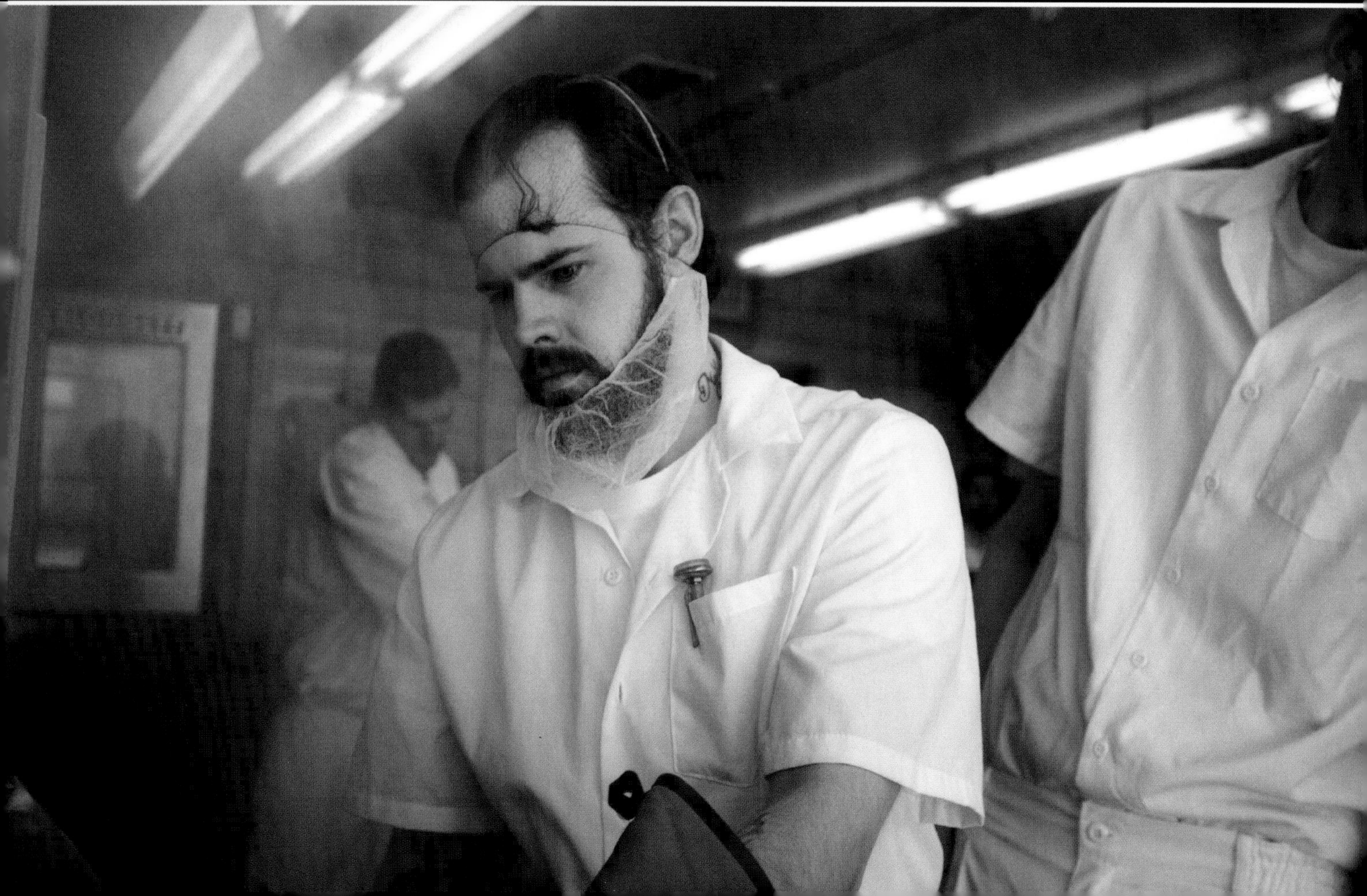

melting points, depending on whether they are made of corn syrup or sugar. So they need to be cooked on a staggered schedule, with butterscotch discs going in the microwave first, followed by Jolly Ranchers, and Now And Laters last, which only need ten seconds to soften.

The mixture comes out of the microwave bubbling, which Hopkins immediately whips with a popsicle stick. At a precise moment, he dunks the bowl into an ice bath, which releases the hardening goo from its container. He wraps this with parchment paper and molds the lollipop by hand around the popsicle stick.

"Some guys, they make it flat and round, but it don't fit in the mouth that well," Hopkins says. "We make it into an egg shape. We say, 'customer friendly.'"

The base of the popsicle stick is marked with a letter. L is lemon drop. B is butterscotch. G is grape. I can already see these in a Brooklyn boutique, labeled PENAL SUCKERS and sold for $4 a pop.

I ask John: "What are you in Westville for?"

"Manufacturing meth."

Ron Edwards, 62, has worked within every aspect of the restaurant industry, from running the front-of-house at fine-dining establishments to owning his own place. Now, he teaches culinary arts to fourteen of the luckiest inmates at Westville.

Lucky, because students taste what they cook. When the alternative is goulash, chicken parmigiana is Christmas arriving twice a week.

Those accepted into the twelve-week cooking program are screened by case managers for past behavior and future potential, which is why Edwards has never had a problem giving inmates access to sharp implements. Completing the program has major incentives, too—graduates get three months knocked off their sentences. The waiting list for this class is around half a year.

We arrive for a luncheon cooked entirely by Edwards' students. Today's guests are a mostly female-group who handle crisis management in the event a prison riot breaks out. The dining space is elegant in a way a mock restaurant at a high school home-economics program would be—adorned almost entirely in blue, decorated with portraits of inmates dressed in chef's whites.

A man with tattoos for sleeves brings out a starter course of shrimp cocktail. Shrimp cocktail! He does everything expected of a server at a white-tablecloth restaurant—walks through the dining room with erect posture, picks up silverware without a clank, and responds to your thank yous with, "You are very welcome." After the cocktail comes cream of broccoli soup and chef's salad with chopped ham. For the entrée: roast pork and gravy alongside mashed potatoes and "Hoosier beans," which are green beans with sautéed bacon and onions. Dessert is cheesecake with blackberries.

"Someone at the local newspaper recently asked for one of the inmates' recipes. It's the first time they're in the paper for something good, and not in the crime blotter," Edwards says. "The class is about teaching them the basic things about life. They don't have a lot of confidence. We try to instill that."

After the luncheon guests depart, the cooks and servers sit in the blue room to feast on their efforts. They eat their massive portions in silent preoccupation. If you remember that scene in *The Shawshank Redemption* where an exclusive group of inmates enjoy an ultra-rare treat of cold beers on the rooftop, you'll have a sense for the joy of these Westville men.

I ask them about what it means to lose the freedom to eat what they choose, and they begin to reminisce wistfully. Adam McDonald brings up his grandmother, who made him appreciate food at age ten when she taught him to cook steaks and grilled cheese sandwiches. He worked at several fast-food chains before getting sent to Westville for burglary. When he's released in six months, McDonald says he'd like to cook in a fine-dining restaurant.

"In a prison system, there are times you look around and you don't feel like anything," McDonald says. "To eat off of glass dishes and metal forks instead of plastic bowls and spoons... I've been in a better mood since I started this class."

While serving a thirteen-year sentence for cocaine possession, Jauston Huerta became a published author—writing a children's book called *Micheliana & the Monster Treats*. It's about a dragon that attacks a village, and the young princess who hatches a plan to feed the dragon to stop its rampage.

Huerta says, "Next to my family, food is a definite component that's a constant reminder my freedom has been taken. Because I have to eat something I don't want to eat. It causes you to really appreciate your freedom and what you left behind out there."

A kitchen worker walks by with a platter filled with shrimp cocktail.

Huerta's eyes follow. "That's the point. That's the point."

Says McDonald: "... to feel human again." LP

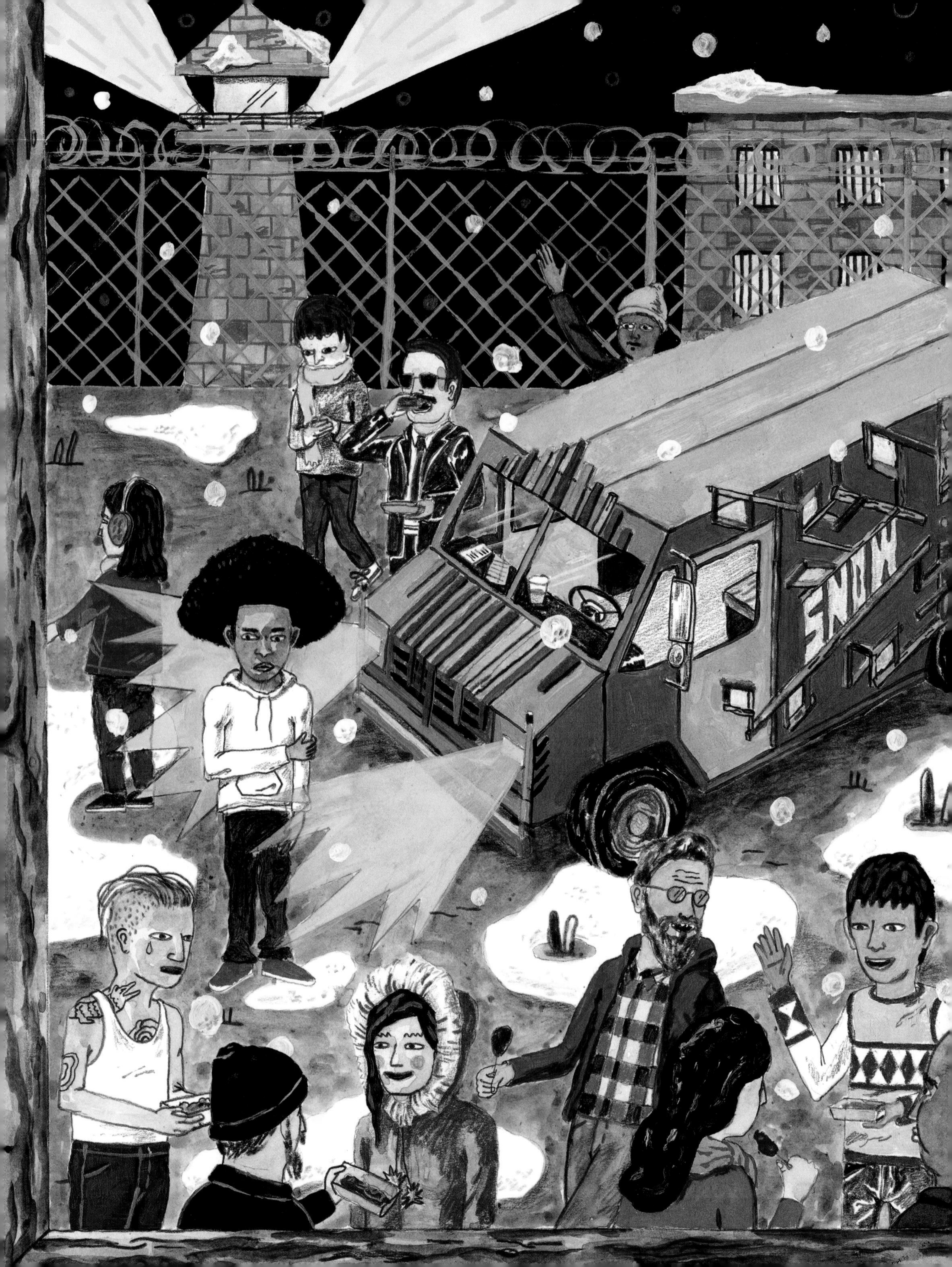
SNOW

COOKiNG FROM SCRATCH

**How a food truck is helping ex-prisoners
find their way on the outside**

by **Scott Korb**

I.

Snowday once traversed the streets of New York City in the service of the Consolidated Edison energy company. Over the past year, she's been reborn, painted silver blue, covered with a lattice-work of salvaged wood slats, and outfitted with two new griddles, a fryer, and a sink. In mid-February, she was nearly ready for her debut.

Jordyn Lexton, who conceived Snowday (and Drive Change, the nonprofit that will power the truck) took me to see her mid-makeover. Lexton is a young white woman who seems most comfortable dressed in black, and who speaks with a flat intensity and a kind of choppiness

that give the impression she's racing against something big and fast. She pointed out where the steam tables and the induction burner would go, stepping over a two-by-four and a monkey wrench in the truck's center aisle. She was especially pleased with the truck's interactive feature: along the service side of Snowday is a sliding box where cooks will create its signature dish, "sugar on snow," a taffy made by pouring hot maple syrup onto a bed of crushed ice. It's a nostalgic nod to a vacation Lexton took as a teenager to Quebec's Mont-Tremblant, where she watched huge troughs of boiled-down syrup drizzled directly into the snow. She

loved its consistency. She loved that it was both warm and cold.

What's more important, however, than bringing *tire d'érable* to the streets of New York is Drive Change's mission to reduce the state's youth recidivism rate—which now stands at about 70 percent. The truck's employees will come almost entirely from jail or prison. By first offering them training in the culinary arts, hospitality, social media, and marketing, and then providing them jobs, Drive Change is counting on keeping those young people in the free world. Gainful employment has been shown to slow the movement of prisons' revolving doors.

Illustrations by James Chong

Lexton discovered her social mission—advocacy on behalf of formerly incarcerated young people—while working as a high-school teacher at Rikers Island, New York City's main jail complex, as she pursued a master's degree at Pace University. Her earliest ideas for Drive Change were centered on advocacy, not food, and originated in a campaign in New York State to raise the age at which young people charged with crimes are prosecuted as adults. New York is one of two states that treat sixteen- and seventeen-year-olds this way. (The other is North Carolina.) Lexton recalls thinking while still teaching, "What if more people knew that this is what New York was doing to kids?"

One of her final assignments at Rikers was to have her students write letters to state officials about their experiences being treated as adults in the criminal justice system. A few of the letters, including some to a key raise-the-age advocate, New York Court of Appeals Chief Judge Jonathan Lippman, she keeps framed above her bed at home.[1] "Initially," Lexton says, "I saw the truck as totally, literally a vehicle for that voice. Kind of thinking foghorn style, having kids read out their letters, driving around"—selling sugar on snow to keep the whole thing moving.

After school, and while she was developing her ideas for Drive Change, Lexton worked for the Center for Employment Opportunities (CEO). There she learned the idea of "transitional work models"—from reentry into the community to permanent placement in a job. She says

that CEO's success has profoundly inspired Drive Change.[2] Lexton found CEO's system of paying employees every day particularly compelling, because it recognized a "clear immediacy and need" in people trying to get back on their feet after incarceration. Snowday employees, working for $11 per hour, will be paid weekly.

With employment front and center, and with the knowledge that nonprofits cannot legally lobby for any particular pieces of legislation, Drive Change's focus now is food. And beginning in March—as I'm writing this—it will offer a full menu of maple-themed dishes inspired by French-Canadian chef Martin Picard, and first created by Drive Change culinary arts director, Jared Spafford: maple pulled pork, maple bacon brussels sprouts, maple grilled cheese, and the Danish stuffed pancake known as an *æbleskiver*.

II.

Roy Waterman will admit that the bank robbery was his idea. Friends of his were in Virginia doing the same kinds of things he was doing in Queens, "selling drugs, walking with guns, using drugs, hurting people"—behaviors he now refers to as the "street package." Waterman decided to join them down South.

In late 1995, when Waterman was nineteen, one of his friends had to visit the bank, and just being there—no Plexiglas, just a counter

to hop over—planted the seed in Waterman's head. "I'm like, I'm gonna rob this place. We gonna rob this place," he recalls. "And sure on enough, we set up a time to rob it. Three of us went in there, masks on, guns out, and robbed the place."

Waterman had friends in Albany too, where there was also money to be made. In the months after the Virginia robbery, he regularly traveled from his home in Queens to the New York state capital to sell crack cocaine.

One of the other dealers in Albany, Allen Johnson, who sold heroin, enlisted Waterman and two of his friends on the evening of July 29, 1996, to help him collect $180 from Georgie Cruz. Cruz lived with Anthony Ingoldsby in a basement apartment at 51 Elberon Place. Johnson's girlfriend drove and stayed in the car as the four men approached the building.

Johnson knocked at the door, and finding Ingoldsby alone, he grabbed him by the throat, demanding to know where Cruz was. Ingoldsby fell, and the other men kicked him. Within moments, Johnson and Ingoldsby ended up together in a bedroom, door locked, and Johnson set to work on him. The noise boomed inside the bedroom, while the other men searched the rest of the apartment for the money Johnson was owed. Behind the door, Anthony Ingoldsby, who owed Johnson nothing, begged for mercy.

Finding nothing of value—although Ingoldsby was offering Johnson any money he had—one of the men rammed his shoulder into the door and found Ingoldsby bleeding from his neck and shoulders. Grabbing Johnson, the man encouraged him to stop, and then left, proceeding with Waterman and the other accomplice out of the apartment and back to the car. Johnson

---

[1] For example: "I was at the wrong place at the wrong time. But adults that's 18 and older its different because they should know more than the younger ones. I also think being on Rikers Island at 16 is mess up because it some adults going to pick on the ones thats 16…."

[2] In August 2012, Marilyn Moses, a social science analyst for the National Institute of Justice, published findings in the American Correctional Association's *Corrections Today* that challenge the basic assumption that job-placement programs reduce recidivism. Two programs, however, are singled out in this report for their effectiveness against long odds and "the overwhelming body of evidence" against success: New York's CEO and Chicago's Safer Foundation, both of which, Moses notes, "have built strong and trusted relationships with employers." Through Lexton's relationship with CEO, Drive Change is now one of these employers.

followed a minute later. While alone in the bedroom, he had stabbed Ingoldsby seventeen times and then left him for dead.

Arrested August 1, 1996, and first held in the Fishkill, New York, Downstate Correctional Facility, Waterman ended up serving time not only for his involvement in the murder of Anthony Ingoldsby, but also for the gunpoint robbery of the Virginia bank. All told, he was imprisoned for more than twelve years in both Sing Sing and the Clinton Correctional Facility, about twenty miles from the Canadian border, for the Albany crime, and at federal facilities in West Virginia, Oklahoma, and Ray Brook, New York, near Lake Placid, for the stickup job—before being released August 13, 2008, into a Brooklyn halfway house, where he lived another six months.

Waterman's parole finally ran out on February 6, 2014, just days before we first met for a Black

History Month panel I moderated about soul food and food justice at New York University, where I teach. He is now married and the owner of a Caribbean and soul-food catering company in Queens, not far from where he grew up. After meeting Jordyn Lexton last fall through a mutual friend, Yuval Sheer, deputy director of the New York Center for Juvenile Justice, Waterman joined Drive Change as a chef and mentor.

Waterman's a good talker and has lots to say about the soulfulness of soul food and the ability of a good meal to bring people together. But bromides like these are not why he has found a place with Snowday. Waterman notes, almost in passing, that the five years he's been out of prison have felt longer than the twelve years he was in. Spending some time with him, I've come to believe that it's this paradox that shapes the philosophy behind his mentoring. For Waterman—who's

a big man, though he's purposefully slimmed down since leaving prison—the lessons that matter are not about good food creating good communities. More simply, good food means good work. And though Spafford, the culinary arts director, is going to purchase quality meats and local produce and maple syrup, and train his employees to prepare delicious sandwiches and sides, in Waterman's eyes the food that comes out of Snowday will have its goodness measured by the employment of one, and then another, and then another formerly incarcerated young person. This will be hard work.

"This, out here, this is about responsibility," he tells me. "This is about working hard, paying bills, being there for people that depend on you—that's what makes this time, since I've been released, the five years, feel like it's so much longer than the twelve years, because it hasn't been easy. To me, the prison thing was an emotional, mental, not really physical thing, and out here in society, it's emotional, mental, and physical. It's taxing in so many different areas. And you get up every day and it's a routine, yes, but before you know it, days are blinking, going by, because you've got so many things to do. And before you look up, the day's over."

The grind of daily life in the free world is central to what Waterman has begun teaching the young men he's helping to prep for Snowday. Right now that's Tyrone McRae, Fredrick Coleman, and Christopher Thomas—young men recently out of prison who've found transitional work and housing at the Doe Fund. To these men, and a few others who have recently signed on to work with Drive Change, Waterman offers his own life as an example.

For the five years that he remained under correctional control after his release, "working hard [and] paying bills" meant a couple steady jobs in general building maintenance, another maintenance job in a church, and scattered employment in the field of heating, ventilation, and air-conditioning; most of 2011 he spent working part-time, collecting unemployment, and sitting for countless job interviews. His felonies, he believes, kept him out of many jobs.[3] Waterman credits his wife, whom he met in church shortly after his release from prison, for providing him stability and keeping him just on this side of debilitating depression. He applied for and was awarded seed money to found his catering company, which he opened in March 2012.

III.

Waterman will be on the truck several days per week to supervise and cook, serve food, and clean up. And behind the scenes he's participated in training sessions in the kitchen and directed team-building activities in the Drive Change offices, housed in a shared workspace in Manhattan. "My role," Waterman says, "is more mentor, leadership, guidance than it is chef." And it's a role that suits him: "I'm an assertive personality, sometimes even aggressive. I know when to address individuals. And when I start speaking people stop and they listen."

Waterman is primarily concerned about the young men he mentors because he knows they belong to a vulnerable community, even once they've gotten past the infamous question—*Have you ever been convicted of a felony?*—even after they've landed this job. Because beyond the

---

3 In most cases, refusing someone employment because of a former felony conviction is illegal.

work itself, the men on Snowday must be comfortable with being identified as formerly incarcerated.

Among people involved with Drive Change, asking about the facts of someone's crimes generally isn't done. In any case, Waterman's time in prison, not his crimes, seems to carry real weight with the men he's working with on Snowday. So does his dogged pursuit of steady work in the free world. "Who's going to talk and deal with these young people in a place where they can relate? And that's why I tell them when I first meet them, 'Look, I did almost thirteen years in prison. So, I've seen it all and done it all. And I'm not talking from an old, old man's perspective. I'm only thirty-seven.' So I let them know, 'Listen, I've been where you've been. Keep pushing. Stay focused. Pull your pants up.' You know. 'You're representative of the company. Always remember that.'"

And on the matter of race, when pressed, he'll admit that it probably matters to these men that he's black. Fredrick, Tyrone, and Christopher are, too. "Obviously. Let's face it. Jared is white, right? And, yes, he's the chef, but having Jordyn, having a white lady who grew up on the Upper East Side, and having Jared, he's a white man, says what exactly?"

Serving food to lunch crowds in New York City is grueling. And yet, more difficult for their crew, Lexton

and Waterman worry, may simply be showing up for work to face the crowds. As Lexton has said, "Disclosing, or the fact of letting someone assume, that you have had some contact with the criminal system, is crippling—implicitly."

Within the company, Lexton says, "There's no expectation from us that you're talking about your criminal history. Our message is about the future. About who you are now, and who you want to be in the future. Not about the past." But Lexton is also hopeful that, as she's found within the queer community she identifies with, more general openness—or *being out*, as it were—will help dispel public misconceptions. And so, she says, while Drive Change is "not necessarily putting that weight on the young people in our truck," she believes that the visibility of their work may help their customers continue "toward a place where we're questioning what gets people arrested or incarcerated in general."

IV.

Though he picked up a few things from his mother and grandmother, who were both from Panama and mainly prepared what he refers to as "Spanish food," Waterman learned to cook while he was incarcerated at the Clinton Correctional Facility in upstate New York. There he was part of the Merle Cooper counseling program, which served one hundred inmates and focused on community living in the Clinton Annex, isolated from the general population. The program served a group of criminals who demonstrated particular difficulty adjusting to prison life or were otherwise antisocial. (Waterman pinpoints the start of his own antisocial behavior at age six, growing up in Cambria Heights, Queens; being held back in first grade, mainly for what we might today call hyperactivity, humiliated him, he recalls. "I started gravitating more and more to outside influences," he says, "which end up being the street." By twelve he was carrying a gun. By nineteen he was in prison.)

At Merle Cooper, with counseling sessions five times per week—three in groups, twice in private—inmates were encouraged to discuss their crimes and look into their lives for the roots of criminal behavior. And though they were required to eat breakfast in the mess hall, for lunch and dinner they had access to a kitchen.

"I was cooking and baking all the time," Waterman tells me. He watched a little cooking television, and a girlfriend sent him a copy of the *Joy of Cooking*, which he'd asked her to purchase for him. "That book is phenomenal," he says. "I learned to make so much stuff from the *Joy of Cooking*. That book is excellent."

Through the Merle Cooper program, inmates could order thirty-five pounds of food per month from a farmers' market. "That's what made everything good as far as foodwise up there," Waterman says. "As far as the mess-hall food itself, it's horrible."

In Clinton, he learned to cook alongside other people. "Dominicans had *mofongo*. Puerto Ricans had their rice and beans with *sofrito*. So everyone had their signature stuff and I would watch them. They wouldn't even know I was watching them." His own favorite dish was chicken cacciatore. "I always tell guys the twelve years was bad. It was horrible. It was the worst years of my life. It was a long twelve years. A twelve-year nightmare. But I got fed, I had money in my commissary, I was able to eat good for the most part. I ate much better than a lot of people eat in the street

now when I was in Clinton. Much better than a lot of people—even when I was in Sing Sing. I ate much better in there than a lot of people I know out here."

Clinton is also where Waterman learned to cook for an audience. Sometimes other inmates would pay him to do so. They began calling him "the Chef," telling him, "You could open up a restaurant." He baked cakes and pies of all kinds—apple, sweet potato, whatever he could get. And he would sell them. He began thinking, "You know, I could go home and do this."

Last year, Clinton Correctional Facility shuttered Merle Cooper. Tom Mailey, of the New York State Department of Corrections and Community Supervision, made the point at the time that the program was not state-mandated. The local Clinton paper, the *Press-Republican*, reported the news in June, including testimonies from inmates being moved out of Merle Cooper who "explained how the program... helped them change their way of thinking, their perspective, and their feelings toward their victims." A man named Darren Davis, in prison since 1990 for murder, wrote: "It was not until I came to the Merle Cooper Program and took on this concept of how to live that I began to see my victim as a human being, a person." Jerry Perez, who was convicted on two murder charges, wrote about finally moving beyond the street package: "My personal change came from confrontational-style counseling to deconstruct my criminal beliefs and principles and to destroy those distorted beliefs I picked up in the street." Ronald Hughes had been an inmate for twenty-three years when Merle Cooper closed. "We must consider the victims and the prisoner when we make decisions to close programs that are actually

changing the lives of men who once didn't care," he said.

In prison, given a kitchen, a place to do some good work, Roy Waterman came to care about the future. This is the most important responsibility he and Lexton and Spafford and the others behind Drive Change have taken on with Snowday. Drive Change sees the young people they hire as vulnerable—this is key, and an unusual way in this country to think of a felon. Facing uncontrolled violence in the jails and without in-facility programs like Merle Cooper, they're more vulnerable still.

And so, the entire organization is intentionally designed to protect these young people—with training, a job, and good wages, a clear path with clear choices. All this, Drive Change hopes, will keep them from returning to the life that first introduced them to criminal justice and still threatens a lifetime of correctional control.

In prison, Waterman would lecture young men who had been released but later, sure enough, ended up back behind bars. Statistically, this happens 70 percent of the time. "Listen," he'd say, "I've been here all this time, and you're getting all these opportunities, and you're still coming back here. What is wrong with you? What are you thinking about?"

Then he'd return to the kitchen and maybe bake another banana–sweet potato pie. It's his specialty. "And I'm the only person who makes it," Waterman says, "even today, out here."

For now, that is. Roy Waterman's banana–sweet potato pie could be just the thing the next Drive Change truck serves, in which case he'll have to share the recipe. But first, he and the young people he's out there cooking with on Snowday must learn to do good work and, together, to make some good food. 🄻🄿

ALWAYS HUNGRY AND ALWAYS FULL

by **Sadie Stein**

"Of course reading and thinking are important but, my God, food is important too. How fortunate we are to be food–consuming animals. Every meal should be a treat and one ought to bless every day which brings with it a good digestion and the precious gift of hunger."

—IRIS MURDOCH, *The Sea, the Sea*

My grandfather fetishized his small appetite, holding it up as a model not merely of temperance but of frugality, too: "I eat like a bird" was his smug refrain, and he frequently mocked anyone who wanted more than, say, half an egg or a single chicken wing at a sitting. Great fun for his wife and kids, of course. "How much do you weigh?" he would demand first thing when we arrived to spend the summer. He always wanted to make sure he was still the lightest person around, and the one with the smallest appetite. Exactly why was never clear, but we tacitly accepted the tyranny, as one does.

My grandfather was a Faulkneresque madman and rocket scientist from Arkansas who never met a used pressure cooker or a brass animal he didn't like. He bought books by the metric ton, and covered his once–valuable Northern California property with sheds, boats, piles of salvaged rubble, and the occasional tractor-trailer. Thinking back on it as an adult, I now believe he had a very small capacity for food, and rather than see it as a limitation, he chose to make it into some kind of virtue. This is, of course, human. Maybe even a good survival tactic, in some ways.

His scavenging did not stop at the kitchen door. He added a room to the house to accommodate an immense deep-freezer. On one notorious occasion, he picked up a half-eaten sourdough-bread bowl from the beach and brought it home for his lunch the next day.

Approximately three times a week, he made the rounds for food-shopping: a produce stand that sold him old merchandise; a Navy commissary with a bargain bin; or the discount supermarket that carried only discontinued products and out-of-season Easter candies. He regarded expiration dates as academic, weevils a valuable source of protein, and mold on cheese something that suckers paid large sums for.

His tiny meals, the menus of which he dictated the night before, were brought to him on a tray. Breakfast was unvarying: a dab of shredded wheat with strawberries and half-and-half; a spoonful of scrambled eggs, hard; bacon, limp; half a piece of toast with plum jam; and a small orange juice. Lunch was subject to whim. And dinner was his chef d'oeuvre.

It wasn't that he was disinterested in eating—to the contrary. A strong, nearly fanatical, theoretical interest in food was something he

and I shared. "What are you having for dinner?" he would demand every day, and we would talk about what we craved, or loved, or remembered. And I would say, roast chicken, or mashed potatoes, or whatever I'd come across in the cookbooks I read so compulsively. In his case it was usually food from his Southern

childhood: chocolate pie, or catfish, or maybe biscuits. It often felt like he was the only person in my family whose interest, like mine, bordered on obsession. I spent my waking hours poring over recipes and put myself to sleep planning menus. My mental map was plotted with restaurants and bakeries. I could talk

Illustration by Joana Avillez

about food all day, and was usually thinking of it; it had always been like this. And we were the same way. It was not hunger; it was different. We could not get enough even if, curiously enough, neither of us had much appetite when the real thing was in front of us.

Unlike my grandfather, I didn't see this as any sort of positive. It seemed a cruel twist of fate, one designed to thwart my interests and leave me a sort of creepy window-shopper. But my grandfather's particular brand of self-justification, his eccentricity, and not incidentally, his Depression mentality (not to mention the penchant for groceries past their sell-by date) made summers with him a blessed relief from the demands of a Rabelaisian world. I always took comfort in the fact that it was a family trait, like our knobby knees and bad vision.

After my grandma died, my grandfather fell into a decline. After being foiled in a few other half-hearted attempts, he deliberately starved himself to death.

I'm on the short side, and I'm not one of those people who can gorge herself while people wonder admiringly "where you put it." It wasn't always like this: I remember being able to eat like a regular grown-up, stuffing my face after school and then eating a hearty dinner. And then one day, the way some people get tall or others grow into their faces, I woke up with a strangely undersized stomach capacity. For a while I was in denial. I refused to accept it. I would try to cram the food in before my brain realized what was going on. But it was a losing battle; a few bites in, I'd be literally stuffed, and unless I wanted to spend the rest of the day dragging myself around like

a gastrically distressed earthworm, I'd have to learn to respect my body's demands, or lack thereof.

This is not, as these things go, a dramatic problem. But it is curious because I'm such a mental glutton, a culinary voyeur. I cook all the time. I spend hours trying to get my appetite up, paging avidly through glossy cookbooks and scanning through online descriptions of food. When I travel, I make up lists of local treats to try, then walk from dawn to dusk to try to stimulate the faintest trace of appetite. Indolent by nature, I force myself to get a modicum of exercise in order to be able to do justice to meals. My heart sinks at the words "all you can eat" (not much), and the "never-ending pasta bowl" has always carried an ominous, Strega Nona–like ring.

When I was twenty-two, a friend was generous enough to invite me to dine with his family at the late Charlie Trotter's flagship. The restaurant was the crown jewel in Chicago's restaurant scene, the tasting menu an unimaginable luxury to a penniless undergrad, and the largesse of the graduation gift was not lost on me.

I made the rookie error of fasting all day to save up room for the dinner. As the alcohol in the preliminary glass of champagne took hold, I realized I'd either become immediately hammered and disgrace myself, or have to sacrifice some precious stomach space. I bolted a roll, and it was all downhill from there.

By the time the third small-plate arrived— a mackerel tartare with grapefruit—I had reached capacity. And when I was presented with a small tranche of foie gras, eating had become actually unpleasant. I stared at the parade of upcoming courses like someone counting down the songs while trapped in an amateur production of a Gilbert and Sullivan operetta. It was endless. I would have to act. I was determined to do justice to the meal, even if I had to throw up in the process.

In the end, I did. Twice. If you can avoid it, of course, it is always better not to throw up. I am not a habitual thrower-upper, so at Charlie Trotter's I managed the whole thing clumsily. By the end, my face was red and my eyes were streaming and my companions asked in concern if I was okay. But I was able to get through the rest of the meal. **LP**

Illustration by Domitille Collardey

Drink a gallon of milk
IN AN HOUR

Illustration by Ian Huebert

PROUD TRADITIONS

An interview with
Tahereh Sheerazie
by **Tejal Rao**

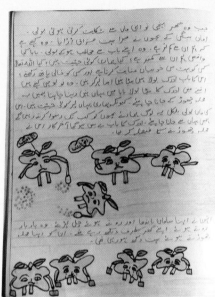

Tahereh Sheerazie is an amateur gardener living in Los Angeles, who has been working to create California-style edible schoolyards in rural Pakistan. Her students are the children of farmers in the remote Shigar Valley who dream of leaving the countryside to start new lives, unconnected to agriculture, in Pakistan's big cities. But as Sheerazie helps them slowly transform a single acre of land into a garden, she's reminding them that growing food, as their parents and grandparents once did, is a noble tradition. And that the more we care for the land, the more it will give back.

How did you find your way to the Shigar Valley?

Shigar sits at the headwaters of Pakistan's rivers, at the foothills of the Karakoram Mountains—it's very beautiful. I trekked around the area for pleasure until 2005, when the earthquake happened. That's when I started thinking: there's more to this place than pleasure. I asked the CEO of the Aga Khan Cultural Service—Pakistan (AKCS—P) which projects needed volunteers and he mentioned there was this little school with a garden waiting to be landscaped. I showed up.

It's a very rich valley soil with a lot of sustenance farming—potatoes, wheat, barley—and farmers also grow some food for themselves. Every family on this land grows its own food, which is wonderful, but typically it's not the children who are doing the farming. Usually the mothers are doing the small-scale farming for the house while the fathers tend to the bigger fields and the more commercial farmland.

What did you want to do there?

A lot of herbicides and pesticides have crept into these rural mountain communities to increase yield, create cash crops, make farmers wealthier a little faster—the same reasons it happens all over the world. But farmers are realizing that they've damaged their soil with artificial farming and the crops are not so strong anymore. In the school garden, I want to reintroduce purely organic gardening: only organic fertilizer, no pesticides or insecticides. These are things the kids' parents know about already, but have stopped doing.

With my team of interns, we developed the idea of a teaching garden together, a garden that would be connected to the curriculum.

What's a teaching garden? I mean, other than patience, what kinds of things can a garden really teach us?

A garden can teach people just about everything. My main purpose connecting gardening to the school is to connect school to the language of agriculture because that's the language most rural Pakistani children speak.

What do farmers think when they send their kids to school and—

—here I am trying to plant a garden and give them a farm-based education! I know. They wonder why I'm making them farm. They feel this is what they've done all their lives and they want a better life for their children. But I want the kids to take pride in what their parents and grandparents are doing, in farming.

What was your formal education like?

I feel I didn't get a good education in Pakistan. My father was in the army so I used to get transferred from city to city, and in every city it was a different syllabus. And because

I was the new kid, I always sat in the back. I just never knew what was going on. It was all cramming and rote memorization. But you can't memorize language. You can't memorize art. That's where the garden comes in.

In Shigar, what will nature teach its students?

One of the things we've managed to keep alive and well since the '60s is the water treaty between India and Pakistan. It's a really delicate, complicated thing. The Indus comes in and runs all the way to Karachi, where I'm from, and there is so much abundance of snowmelt and water there. These kids sit on the border of our disputed territory with India and they should know that our biggest problem with India isn't that they're Hindus and we're Muslims. No, it's water! We share the headwaters of the most important river on the subcontinent, and India has the tap. Through this business of gardening, I want the kids to understand how to use water with care. I want them to understand how major our environmental problems are.

Are these kids a mix of girls and boys?

Abruzzi was actually the first coed school of the area. Girls and boys don't mix easily. What I mean is, there's no strict segregation, but it's a conservative society so you don't sit and chat with the opposite sex unless they're your family.

How is it working out?

It's funny because in the classroom, the girls are doing their own thing and the guys are doing their own thing. But outside, in the garden, we work in mixed groups. Of course, the boys don't want to plant flowers and the girls don't want to dig rocks at first, but gardening together makes this traditional division between boys and girls a little softer. There's no romance, they're just working the land together, so it's a very nonthreatening way of bringing the sexes together.

Do you think any of these kids will go on to become students of architecture and design, of agriculture?

Many of these girls—every girl, really—want to go to school and wants to be a doctor. But in the garden, all the arts and sciences are being addressed—mathematics, physics, language—in fun ways.

I'm so convinced that every subject we study—our whole lives—everything is connected to this land. So I want school to be about more than textbooks, for kids to not be confined to the classroom. I want these kids to see possibilities other than being doctors and engineers—that's all they think that there is to be.

What have been your biggest challenges so far?

At first, the principal thought I was wasting time and money. But eventually I was able to convince him I wasn't. The other problem was that the teachers didn't see how there was a connection to the garden.

How did you make the connection for them?

That's where food came in. The fifth graders had grown tomatoes—not laterally, the way most people grow them there, but vertically—and they decided to make sandwiches and sell them to raise money. They made up their own recipe and spent about forty rupees on bread, ketchup, and mayonnaise. All of them together, boys and girls, everybody sliced, layered, decorated, and even made invitations to invite the principal and teachers. They called their sandwich the "Adda Adda Wow Wow."

The teachers saw how the students did math, measuring things as they increased the recipes, and how they learned the economics of the project by making receipts and keeping a register of income and expenses. The kids managed to raise the funds to build a boundary wall.

Why a boundary wall?

In April, all the animals—cattle, sheep, yak—go up to high pastures until October so they can graze. Then they all come back down and everybody's fields are open to every animal. It's just understood. They come and graze, so if there's any bark, any blade of grass, anything at all—they'll eat it! You have to have a boundary wall if you want to keep your garden.

You're heading back next week—what's your goal on this trip?

At the end of last year I was feeling very frustrated. This board member told me, "This is education. It takes a long time. It's not something that happens in one or two years." If you really want to improve the level of education in Shigar—anywhere, really—then you have to stay for a long time. The kids, their enthusiasm, keeps me at it. My focus is to train and show teachers that they really can connect their curriculums to gardening.

But how can you show people how to do that?

I just want to say, "Look, whatever you're studying, it's in the garden!" Instead of memorizing a chapter of the Quran in Arabic, for example, students could go outside and look for a bee. I mean that little bee must be pretty important if he has a whole chapter dedicated to him. So get out there. Find him. **LP**

To learn more about Tahereh Sheerazie's edible schoolyard project, go to *abruzzischoolgarden.com*

LOBSTERS

Fiction by
Kevin Moffett

While we waited for dinner to cool, Mom told Gavin and me a story. As with all her stories, she was the main character, trooping unsuspectingly through her day, doing a thing she always did. She liked adding tension by drawing out this part of the story. She's at Vons, shopping for the ingredients for the soup I asked for. First, she finds shredded cheese. Then ground beef. Usually she buys ground chuck but today the ground round's on sale. Then she goes in search of Ro-Tel and condensed milk, which she assumes, wrongly it turned out, were next to each other.

"Out with it, Odysseus," my brother said.

"Patience," she said, sipping her wine. "I see a group of women cradling babies near the front entrance. I thought they were on strike. They're fiddling with signs, that's what made me think that. But I need Ro-Tel so I turn the corner and don't pay much attention. I've already got the ground round, which I don't usually buy but it's on sale."

I stared at my father's empty seat across from me. He almost never came home for dinner anymore. Out doing odd jobs, he said. I stowed the extra pieces of my mother's story in his chair, let them teeter.

"As I leave," she said, "the women are blocking the exits. I realize that they're all nursing these babies. Right in the store. 'What are you doing?' I ask them. The leader, maybe she was the leader, I don't know, she had fiery dyed-red hair, she says, super irritated, *'We are feeding our bleeping babies.'* But she didn't say 'bleeping.'"

Gavin laughed through his nose. He turned to me and said, "Fucking babies." As if I didn't know what bleeping meant.

"I told her that I'm feeding my babies, too. With the groceries."

"Jesus, Mom," I said.

"Truth missile," Gavin said. He leaned in—to high-five Mom, I thought—but instead he served himself a bowl of soup. Tonight was Thursday, so I chose dinner. He got Tuesday. Mom's only rules: the recipe couldn't contain more than eight ingredients, or any weird meats like goat or rabbit. This wasn't a problem for me. The foods I liked were the ones that disguised themselves as other foods: taco casserole, crab cakes, ice cream sandwiches. The soup came from my favorite cookbook: *Can Do: America's Best Canned-Food Recipes.*

"I didn't know what else to do," Mom was saying. She sipped at the edge of her glass. The wine tasted—I knew because I'd tried it before—like chilled chemicals. "Don't mess with a woman with a baby clamped to her breast."

"Nobody ever knows what to do," Gavin said. He loved making casual declarations like this, especially when Dad wasn't around. He blew on the soup, tasted it, swallowed through a grimace, and set down his spoon. I knew what was coming. "This

Illustrations by Cari Vander Yacht

is a practical joke, right?" He scanned the pocked-white ceiling of the dining room. "Are we being filmed right now?"

"Don't be dramatic. It's onion-burger soup. Will's choice."

He poked at it with his spoon and looked at me. "Onion-burger soup," he repeated slowly, his skinny mantis face tightening in outrage. "It tastes like onion-burger dog food. Or what you'd serve in a haunted house."

"It's from a cookbook," Mom said. "Eat it or don't."

"A haunted doghouse." He swiped a napkin over his tongue. "He's not competent to choose dinner," he told Mom.

"My night, my choice," I said. "You don't hear me complain about your pukey hippie dinners. Rice and garlic and tomatoes all mashed together."

"It's called risotto, dipshit. It's an art, and Mom's getting better at it. I keep telling her, slowly add the stock, half a cup at a time, but she rushes it."

Mom ate spoonful after spoonful of soup, like bagging leaves, no joy in it at all.

I ladled a hot bowl and blew on my spoon, took a bite. I tasted it first in my nose, moist, burgery steam, then on my tongue. Salty, velveteen, humid, oily, terrible. I struggled to swallow. "Great," I said.

He reached over for my bowl and poured about half of his serving into it. "Eat mine then."

I ate another spoonful. The milk and cheese and beef grease were starting to congeal together. "It has an Italian-type flavor. Did you add oregano, Mom?"

"Probably," she said, not looking up.

I ate it all. I wasn't sure what I was doing. When I finished, Gavin dumped the rest of his bowl into mine.

"Will you *stop*?" Mom said. "You're wasting food."

Gavin asked to be excused to finish his homework. He cleared his bowl and went to his room where I could hear him loading *FIFA All-Stars*.

"Dad and I took you guys to McDonald's when you were little," Mom said to me. I knew the story. We didn't go there anymore because Gavin objected but when we did, he and I would each get a Happy Meal. Gavin only ate the bun of his Happy Meal, and I only ate the meat. They'd always have a leftover hamburger. Finally Dad insisted we order one Happy Meal for us to split, so we wouldn't waste food, and we did from then on.

"They probably thought I was starving you," she said. She always ended the story like this. As if the cashiers were closely scrutinizing how many Happy Meals some muddled-looking family bought.

I put my paper napkin over my bowl. I didn't want to look at it anymore. Slowly, a reddish amoeba mark bloomed through the white paper. Crime scene.

"He'll be hungry," she said after a while.

Did she mean Gavin or Dad? My stomach ached. I sat there thinking about the rabbit waiting for me in his vacuum-sealed bag at school. I'd opened it today and his fur was cold and smelled like acne wipes. Other kids had immediately begun guiding scalpels across their rabbits' abdomens. Peeling away muscle, guessing organs. I just stared at mine's gassed blurry eyes.

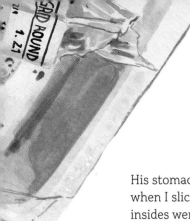

His stomach looked bloated. I knew that when I sliced into him tomorrow, his insides were going to spill out onto the tray, like one of those boil-in gravy bags.

"Another dinner down," Mom said.

Dad came in through the kitchen door while I was loading the dishwasher. His work pants were soaked from mid-thigh to his boot heels and he was carrying a white laundry bag, breathing heavy, filling the house with noise. When he saw me hand-spraying bowls he laughed and nodded. The laugh was more like a rattling smile.

A drawstring held the laundry bag secure at the top and it had illegible lettering on the side. The bottom corner, I noticed, seemed to be moving.

"Get some saltwater going in a soup pot," he said to me. "A rolling boil. Hear me?"

I hesitated and kind of peeked through the entryway into the dining room to see if Mom was still in there smoking. She wasn't.

"What're you searching for?" he said. "Permission? I'm giving you all the permission you need."

"We already ate, Dad."

"So I smell. But you didn't eat anything like this."

He reached down, opened the laundry bag, and roughly shook the contents onto the linoleum: four giant lobsters, still alive, claws locked with purple bands.

"Go ahead," he said, tossing the bag aside. "You get the first draft pick."

The lobsters looked rusted, prehistoric. They prowled across the floor in slow motion—maybe they felt heavy

after being in the water all their lives. Dad stood by the door and kicked mud from the track off his boots. During the day he worked at Santa Anita, taking care of horses, spraying stalls, combing dirt. I usually told kids he was a jockey because "groom" sounded like someone's personal barber. They'd always ask if he was short and I'd say, "He isn't that kind of jockey."

If they asked what kind of jockey he was I would've said "harness racer," the ones who rode behind horses in two-wheel carts, but no one ever asked.

"I'm pretty full," I said to him, even though I wasn't full at all. "Won't they keep until tomorrow?"

He searched the cabinets for the soup pot. I knew he wouldn't find it because I'd just covered it with tinfoil and put it and the rest of the soup in the refrigerator. "These big boys came a long way to feed us," he said.

One of the lobsters was studying my socked feet with his cockroach eyes. I backed up a little. "Are they stolen?"

"Yes," he said, slamming a cabinet door. He was holding a big enamel roasting pan I didn't recognize. "Stolen from the ocean just days ago. Snatched from the waters of Crustacea in the sad upward arc of their lives."

I knew he didn't wade into the Pacific and find them himself, but why were his pants wet? I'd seen lobsters at the supermarket with the same bands around their claws, stacked three high in a murky aquarium. I never looked long. If I pressed Dad harder, he'd cough up some story about the lobsters falling from a

flatbed truck and him trying to flag down the driver to no avail. Gavin called him a liar and a common thief but never to his face, and I saw nothing common about stealing lobsters or flowers or hundred-pound bags of rock salt or pitas from bread trays stacked in front of Vons, like, a year's worth of pitas, which were covered in green fur in a week. Or an expensive-looking bridle from the track. He threw it on top of the old beer box marked KEEP, on top of our old LEGO-builder magazines. Whenever I saw it I thought, Why steal a bridle?

He filled the roasting pan with water, salted it, and perched it on the electric burner coil. He gathered the lobsters and dropped them into the water, then quickly placed an ill-fitting lid on top of the pan. "Outstanding," he said, wiping his chin. "Know the best thing about lobster, fresh lobster?" He wasn't about to wait for me to guess. "It's like eating a peach right off the tree. Pure. You can taste the life in it still."

While the water heated up he told me everything he knew about lobsters. A lobster's brain is in its throat. It breathes and listens with its legs and tastes with its feet. Some live to be a hundred years old. He was talking loud enough for Gavin and Mom to hear, trying to lure them into the room with his voice. I tried to remember what I'd been thinking about, standing at the dishwasher before he showed up with the lobsters, but I couldn't. School? Some pair of shoes I wanted? Next Thursday's meal? Dad showing up always changed the subject to the subject of Dad showing up.

"Mom and I give you guys everything, but you settle for this." He was looking at the dry-erase board on the refrigerator, on which Gavin had written GAVIN IS A RELUCTANT GOD. I'd crossed out RELUCTANT GOD and written BLEEDING PENIS. Dad erased that with his thumb, uncapped the marker, and wrote MYSTERY. Gavin is a mystery. He said, "When you were little, I used to help steer you guys into finding something by saying 'getting warmer' or 'getting colder.' Remember?"

I nodded.

The lid on the roasting pan was rattling. I didn't know whether it was from the steam or the lobsters struggling to get out. I'd read or heard that they screamed when they were cooked, but I didn't hear anything like that.

"What else you want to know about?" Dad asked me.

"Where'd you get them?"

"Funny story," he said. He wouldn't look at me. I knew he was about to tell me a lie. "Not funny-funny, but an interesting coincidence. Well, not interesting-interesting but—"

"I'll finish up in here," Mom interrupted. I turned to see her quietly teetering in the entryway behind me. "Go finish your home-work, Will."

I stole one last look at Dad, nervously checking the lobsters, remembering what he'd said once after stealing a canoe from Sears on a trip to buy me some new school clothes, carrying the canoe proudly over his head, through the store and out to our sta-tion wagon, a blank piece of paper in his mouth folded to look like a receipt: the main thing was to look like someone who just bought a canoe. "You know what that looks like?" he asked me. When I told him no, he said, "And neither do they."

I went to Gavin's room instead of my own. I watched him play *FIFA* for a while, trying to score by making the goalie dribble all the way up the field. It was so frustrating. It never worked. I watched until Mom was done yell-ing and I heard the table being set and them eating and laughing again, until Mom came in, melted butter stains all over her shirt, and told us it was time for bed. **LP**

LUCKY PEACH RECORD CLUB

We're excited to announce the **SECOND INSTALLMENT OF THE LUCKY PEACH RECORD CLUB**: a split 7" record that pairs folk legend **MICHAEL HURLEY** (he of "Old Black Crow," of "Blue Rider," of *Armchair Boogie*, of so much greatness) with **WES BUCKLEY**, a killer folk player who Hurley handpicked to sing on the second side. The two tackle our all-you-can-eat theme by considering the effect of GMOs on what we can eat in sweet-sounding-if-pointed songs about that all-seeing eye in the sky, Monsanto.

Wait, did I miss the first record-club entry?! No, and we'd like to apologize here for the delay in releasing **BILL ORCUTT**'s unhinged take on the West Coast ice cream truck song. It turns out that a food magazine has no business putting out records, but we're trying to work our way around that. Both 7"s will be available for sale at **LKY.PH ON MAY 20!**

And, in case you're wondering, the LPRC is a Marxist hustle: you wouldn't join a club that would have you as a member, would you?

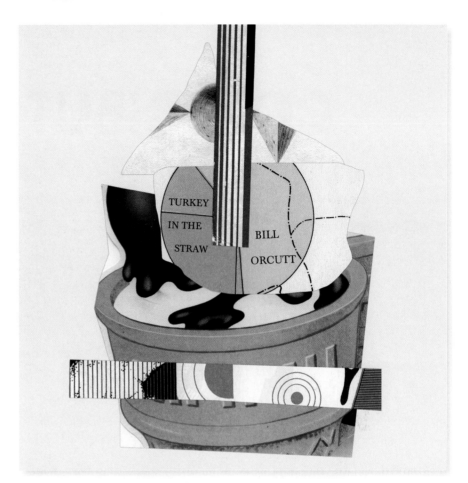

LPRC01 I Bill Orcutt I Turkey in the Straw

LPRC02 I Michael Hurley/Wes Buckley I Bad Monsanto/Mt. Santo

CONTRIBUTORS

Meiko Takechi Arquillos is a photographer living in Los Angeles. She grew up in Tokyo and loves to cook *okonomiyaki* for her good friends. More stuff on *meikophoto.com*. She also started posting her snapshots @meikophoto.

Joana Avillez is an illustrator from New York City. She is the author of *Life Dressing: The Idiosyncratic Fashionistas*, a fashionary tale of two real-life women who live to dress and dress to live. She is currently illustrating Lena Dunham's new book, the tentatively titled *Not That Kind of Girl*. More of her work can be seen at *joanaavillez.com*

James Chong is an image-maker based out of Los Angeles. He co-runs an independent publishing house called Never Press specializing in art prints and books.

Domitille Collardey is an illustrator and cartoonist from France. She grew up in Normandy on Camembert and Calvados.

Fuchsia Dunlop is a cook and food writer specializing in Chinese cuisine. She is the author of four books, most recently *Every Grain of Rice: Simple Chinese Home Cooking*, and the recipient of two James Beard awards.

Jamie Feldmar is a Brooklyn-based writer and the managing editor of Serious Eats. See more at *jamiefeldmar.com*.

Adam Leith Gollner is the author of *The Fruit Hunters* (Scribner) and *The Book of Immortality* (Scribner).

Lisa Hanawalt lives in LA and her book, *My Dirty Dumb Eyes*, was published by Drawn & Quarterly in 2013. Follow her work at *lisahanawalt.com*.

In this issue of *Lucky Peach* **Naomi Harris** managed to get the equivalent of an EGOT; shooting both the All Ewe Can Eat party in Miami and writing a story about attending a swingers buffet/party to illustrate her own artwork. To read more of her quips or see her photos follow her @mapledipped on both Twitter and Instagram.

Ian Huebert is an illustrator and printmaker. He lives in Lincoln, Nebraska.

Mark Ibold is our Southeastern Pennsylvania correspondent.

So-Min Justine Kang, raised and born in Germany, is a Miami Beach–based wedding and portrait photographer. Her portrayal work has been published in several German magazines and she has received her third annual award for best of weddings by *the Knot*.

Victor Kerlow was born, raised and educated in New York City and continues to live there, drawing full-time for a diverse range of clients including the *New Yorker*, the *New York Times*, MTV, the History Channel, and many others. In 2013, his comics and drawings were collected and published by Koyama Press in the comic *Everything Takes Forever*, and by OHWOW Gallery with Junkie Food/Bare Nuckle. Kerlow also illustrates the weekly Metropolitan Diary column in the *New York Times*.

Scott Korb is the author of several books, including *Light without Fire: The Making of America's First Muslim College* and *Life in Year One: What the World Was Like in First-Century Palestine*. His latest, *Gesturing Toward Reality: David Foster Wallace and Philosophy*, which he co-edited, is to be published in June 2014. He teaches food writing at New York University and the New School and is on the faculty of Pacific University's MFA program. He lives with his family in New York City.

Bourree Lam is the editor of *freakonomics.com*. Born in Indiana and raised in Hong Kong, she studied economics at the University of Chicago and prioritizes food wherever she goes to maximize utility.

Colin Lane is a photographer who lives in New York City with his four-year-old son Walt. He came very close to graduating from the University of Texas in Austin. He

Illustration by Domitille Collardey

can cook spaghetti and meatballs and hot dogs. Find him online at *colinlane.com*.

Hannah K. Lee was born to two immigrants from Korea in Houston, Texas. She was raised in various suburbs around LA and ended up in New York to satisfy her unhealthy thirst for glory.

Gideon Lewis-Kraus has written for various magazines and journals, and is the author of the travel memoir *A Sense of Direction*. Contact information at *gideonlk.com*.

Harold McGee writes about the science of food and cooking. He's the author of *On Food & Cooking: The Science & Lore of the Kitchen*, *Keys to Good Cooking*, and posts at *curiouscook.com*.

Kevin Moffett is the author of two short story collections and a co-author of *The Silent History*, forthcoming in June. He lives in Claremont, California.

Roman Muradov is an illustrator and cartoonist from Russia, currently living in San Francisco. His work has appeared in the *New Yorker*, *New York Times,* and other nice places. He loves tea, books, and long aimless walks.

Christina Nichol lived in the Republic of Georgia and is currently residing in Kosovo. Her novel, *Waiting for the Electricity* (Overlook), is set in Georgia and will be released in June.

Monica Padrick is a writer living in Los Angeles.

Kevin Pang is a staff writer at the *Chicago Tribune*.

Raj Patel is a writer, activist, and academic. He is currently working on a documentary about the global food system with award-winning director Steve James.

Lucas Peterson lives and works in Los Angeles. Send him self-help-book recommendations and secret driving shortcuts @lucaspeterson.

Jeannie Phan is a Toronto-based freelance illustrator, casual swimmer, and studio mate to a cool cat.

Jason Polan is an artist whose work has been exhibited all over the United States, Europe, Africa, and Asia. He is a member of The 53rd Street Biological Society and Taco Bell Drawing Club. Polan is currently drawing every person in New York.

Jed Portman is a Charleston, South Carolina–based writer and editor with a freezer full of wild rose hips, chokecherries, and bison.

Padgett Powell is a writer whose bad animal husbandry, affection for old Rubbermaid, and effort to prevent squirrel from killing his bamboo has pushed him into becoming a squirrel hunter and cook.

Monica Ramos is an illustrator, modern woman, and friend. View more work at *monramos.com*.

Tejal Rao is a London-born, Brooklyn-based writer on staff at Tasting Table. She won a James Beard Foundation Award for her restaurant criticism at the *Village Voice*.

Andy Rementer is an award-winning graphic artist from the U.S. who grew up in a Victorian beach town. He loves handmade typography, vintage colors, and fleamarket finds.

He graduated from the University of the Arts in 2004. After working and living in northern Italy, he relocated to the East Coast where he now divides his time among drawing, cartooning, painting, and animating.

Andrew Rowat finds himself in the unenviable position of being able to tell you the best seat on an aircraft just by hearing its flight number. This level of nerdiness is only attained by having no fixed address and dedicating his life to that of a camera-toting mendicant. He has been fortunate enough to find his work in *Wallpaper, Travel + Leisure, Afar, Vanity Fair,* and the *New Yorker*.

Armando L. Sanchez was born and raised in Austin, Texas, and is currently based in Chicago.

Brent Schoonover is a freelance illustrator and comic artist based in St. Paul, Minnesota.

Jordan Speer lives and works in Kentucky, where he also drinks a lot of beer and pets other people's dogs. One day he would like to drink less, and maybe get his own dog.

Sadie Stein lives in New York. She is a contributing editor at the *Paris Review*.

Cari Vander Yacht made eggs this morning and pasta for lunch. She currently lives in Brooklyn, NY.

Brette Warshaw is the managing editor of *Food52* and lives in New York City. She wants to have you over for dinner.

Lale Westvind makes animations and comics in New York City. She loves hole-in-the-wall cheap eats and motorcycles.

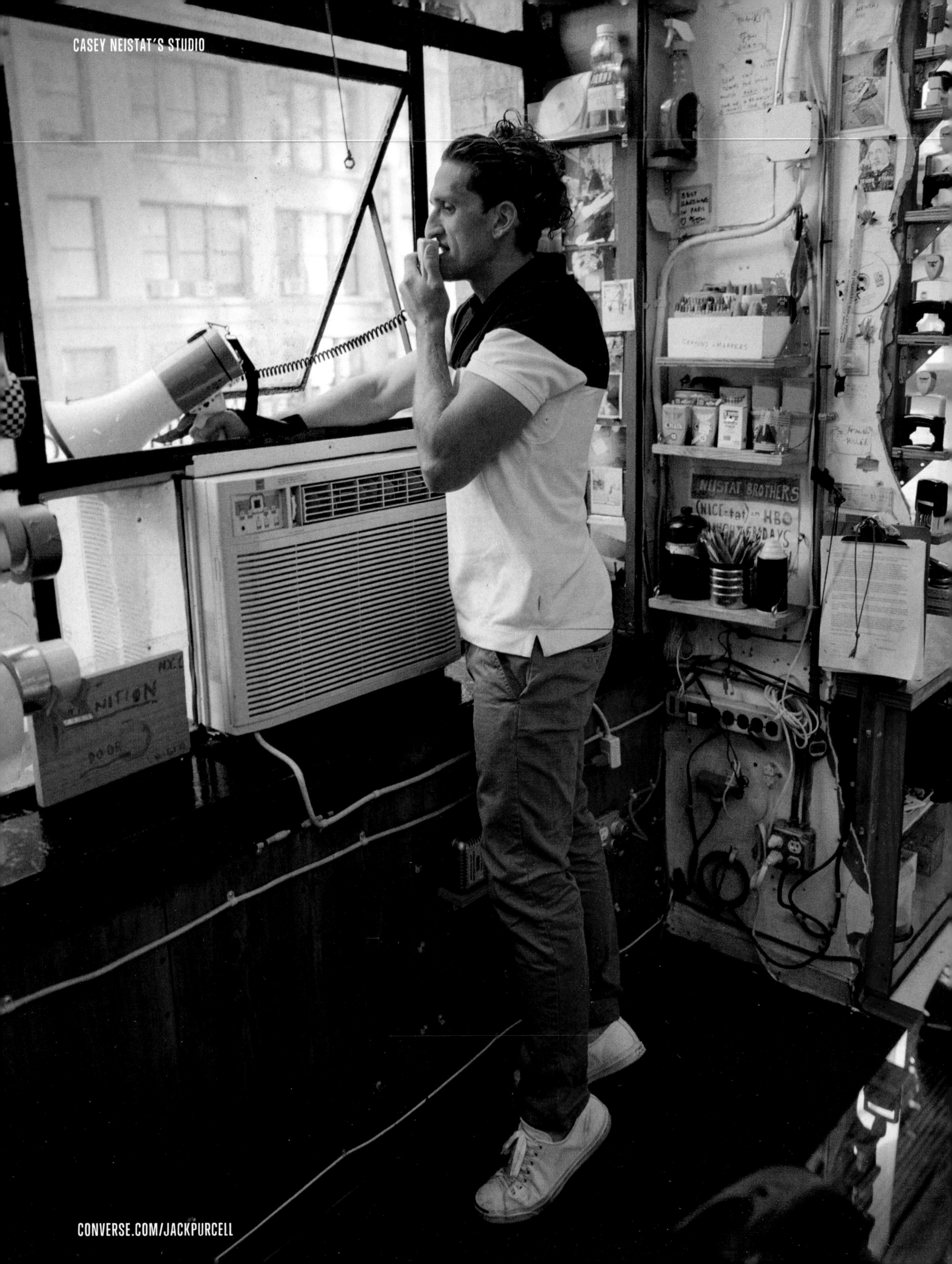

CASEY NEISTAT'S STUDIO